The Constitution Failed

Dispatches from

The History of the Future

Dr. Robert Owens

© 2010 by Robert R. Owens PhD

Reprinted here as *The Constitution Failed* by Dr. Robert Owens

ISBN-13: 978-1540337559 ISBN-10: 1540337553

All rights reserved solely by the author. No part of this book may be reproduced in any form without the permission of the author.

Unless otherwise indicated Bible quotations are taken from the New King James version of the Bible. Copyright © 1982 by Thomas Nelson, Inc.

Dedication

This book is dedicated to all the Patriots who are working to preserve the freedom and opportunity which have always been both the source and the summit of the American experiment and with great appreciation for my wife and editor, Dr. Rosalie Owens.

Table of Contents

Introduction..7

Dispatch One: Political Philosophy....................13

Dispatch Two: The Articles of Confederation...........19

Dispatch Three: The State versus the Individual..........21

Dispatch Four: A Government of Fallible Men to Rule Fallible Men..28

Dispatch Five: Checks and Balances............................32

Dispatch Six: Does Equality Mean We Are All The Same?..36

Dispatch Seven: Equality is Never Equal....................40

Dispatch Eight: Dream From Our Forefathers............45

Dispatch Nine: Since Some Don't Worry About the Constitution We Should......................................50

Dispatch Ten: Sovereignty Succession and the National Debt..55

Dispatch Eleven: The Unlimited Blessings of Limited Government..60

Dispatch Twelve: What Is Sovereignty and Who Has It?..64

Dispatch Thirteen: We Must Know Who We Are to Decide What We Will Be..69

Dispatch Fourteen: The Arrogance of Power..................74

Dispatch Fifteen: What Comes Before a Fall?............79

Dispatch Sixteen: You Say You Want a Revolution.....83

Dispatch Seventeen: Culture Kampf and the Kamikaze Congress..88

Dispatch Eighteen: Too Many Rights on the Left.........92

Dispatch Nineteen: Whose Responsibility is It?........98

Dispatch Twenty: Snatching Defeat from the Jaws of Victory Again...103

Dispatch Twenty-one: How We Got From Where We Were to Where We Are...107

Dispatch Twenty-two: The Hand Writing is on the Wall...112

Dispatch Twenty-three: The Bottleneck is Always at the Top..116

Dispatch Twenty-four: Return of the Swamp Thing.120

Dispatch Twenty-five: How True is the Truth?........125

Dispatch Twenty-six: Red Emperors Exploit Red Ink.130

Dispatch Twenty-seven: Polite Conversation............134

Dispatch Twenty-eight: Chicago on the Potomac.....139

Dispatch Twenty-nine: I Got Some Transparency for You Right Here..........143

Dispatch Thirty: If the Voters are the Mob Who Brought the Thugs?..........148

Dispatch Thirty-one: If it Wasn't so Sad it Would be Funny..........152

Dispatch Thirty-two: It's Never Too Early to be Too Late..........157

Dispatch Thirty-three: Obama's War(s)..........161

Dispatch Thirty-four: Please, Mr. Custer, We Don't Want To Go!..........165

Dispatch Thirty-five: We Can Learn What We Don't Know..........170

Dispatch Thirty-six: Pop Goes the Culture Chapter Thirty-seven..........175

Dispatch Thirty-seven: What Causes the Result?...179

Dispatch Thirty-eight: Who Changed the Change?...184

Dispatch Thirty-nine: What's a Conservative? What's a Liberal? What does it matter?..........189

Dispatch Forty: Who Are The Barbarians?..........193

Dispatch Forty-one: The Key..........196

Dispatch Forty-two: Prayers of the Downtrodden....202

Dispatch Forty-three: Why This When We Want That?..................206

Dispatch Forty-four: What To Do Now That It's Been Done..................211

Dispatch Forty-five: Is Limbaugh Really the Problem?..................215

Dispatch Forty-six: The Fix is In..................221

Dispatch Forty-seven: Without Hope You're Hopeless..................226

Dispatch Forty-eight: Payday's Coming Someday....230

Dispatch Forty-nine: Winners Write History and To The Victors Go The Spoils....................234

Dispatch Fifty: The Last Best Hope..................239

Dispatch Fifty-one: To Build a Better Mouse Trap....244

Dispatch Fifty-two: Freedom From Tyranny Is Our Goal..................250

Arguments of the Anti-federalists....................254

How Long Did the Limit Last?..................263

Conclusion: The Constitution Failed..................269

Notes..................286

Bibliography..................343

Introduction

In the following work the reader will encounter ideas and thoughts which they find at odds with the current pronouncements and efforts of the Tea Parties, Patriot Movements and other supporters of the traditional American system of limited government, freedom and opportunity. I ask the indulgence of the reader. Allow this retired house painter, retired pastor, current professor and late blooming scholar to present the observations gained through fifty years of daily study of American History and Political Science. We may agree. We may disagree. Whichever way it leads it is only by opening and holding an informed dialogue that *We the People* will find our way through this crisis created by the Progressives and their relentless drive for total power.

I believe that Preamble to the Declaration of Independence and the Constitution with the Bill of Rights included comprise the most enlightened, ennobling and beneficial documents ever penned by the hand of man. I also believe that the Constitution afforded the United States the greatest level of freedom and opportunity ever experienced by humanity. This freedom and opportunity in turn released the talents and abilities of the American people to build the greatest nation to ever exist, rising from 13 states exhausted and impoverished from years of war into a prosperous and powerful nation which by the end of the twentieth century stood upon the world stage as the uncontested sole superpower.

Simplicity is the essence of genius while over-simplification is the essence of fraud. In a picture perfect example of the truism "The victors write history" what we have been taught concerning the writing and ratification of the Constitution is actually a politically slanted version of the truth. This highly patrician account is also an example of over-simplification.

We are taught that the Articles of Confederation were an abject failure because they were too weak. Shay's Rebellion scared the venerable leaders who had led and won the Revolution. George Washington and other patriots came back from retirement to once again save the nation writing an "almost" divinely inspired document. There was only token dissent to the immediate acceptance of this tablet from the mount by some shadowy unknown people collectively called the "Anti-Federalists." However after some well-written articles by future leaders called the Federalists, *We the People* overwhelmingly voted for ratification and the Constitution immediately ushered in the blessings of liberty and opportunity for all rescuing the United States from anarchy and stagnation, Amen.

This is a thumb-nail sketch of what our thumb-nail sketch type history education once delivered as gospel in American public schools. Today, those lucky enough to live in a school district that still includes American History are instead treated to the Progressive's litany of American crimes and debauchery. However, as our constitutionally limited government exceeds all previous limits is either of these offerings good enough? Americans from all walks of life watch in stunned disbelief as the Federal Government on steroids swallows the economy, health care, the financial system, major manufacturing, the insurance industry, and anything else that doesn't move fast enough to get out of the way. Can the States themselves be far behind?

It is my belief that if we have a better understanding of where we came from and how we got here we will have a better understanding of where we are. This belief has prompted the writing of this book. It is my belief that if we understand where we are perhaps we will see the way to get back to where we wanted to go when we started, back to a limited government of the people, by the people and for the people.

No matter what we have been taught, no matter what the reality was, the reality is that the Constitution replaced the Articles of Confederation as the supreme law of the land. The announced purpose of the

Constitution's writing and adoption was to provide a limited government which respected both the rights of the States and the people. Since this was the stated and accepted purpose of the Constitution after two centuries and several decades can *We the People* deny any longer that it has failed?

Failing and failure are two different things. Everyone who has ever succeeded has failed. It is falling forward from that failure which ultimately brings success. If the Constitution has failed what do we do now? Where's the reset button. Using Dispatches from The History of the Future this book outlines the history of how we got here, it comments on where we are and it offers suggestions and recommendations for how *We the People* can once again set the limits, regain our freedom and unleash the opportunity that flow from the possession and use of our unalienable rights to life, liberty and the pursuit of happiness.

Robert R. Owens

Notes about two words or names used in this works:

The title, "Founders" is used to denote those patriots who issued the Declaration of Independence and who led this country through the Revolution to independence.

The title, "Framers" is used to denote those patriots who wrote the Constitution.

Dispatch One

Political Philosophy

Philosophy attempts to go beyond personal opinion having the goal of knowledge. Political philosophy seeks to determine the knowledge or truth which lies behind the facade of political theory which is often partisan and frequently factional.

In beginning a discourse on the birth of the United States it is necessary to build a foundation for understanding and to examine several basic assumptions which are part of the conventional wisdom. First there are two questions which should be addressed first. Is governmental natural? Are laws Natural?

The search for answers to these questions must begin with other questions. How is that which is natural known? What is human nature? Is it instinct? Comparable to how a dog knows it needs to walk in a circle before it lies down. Although it may sound strange the knowledge of nature itself is not known by nature. Humans do not come out of the womb knowing the answer. So it is not instinct in the same way dogs know how to be dogs. Just as common sense is anything you learned before you were eighteen much of human nature depends on how, where and by who a person is raised. Meaning that most of what we call human nature is more accurately attributed to nurture than to nature. Is there however, a kernel of truth eternal and universal at the base of government and behind any laws?

Is government natural? Meaning is it an intrinsic part of human nature? Or is government an artificial construct? Is it merely one choice with anarchy being the other? In answer to these questions the strongest evidence is that there is no history of humanity without some type of governance. History begins with written records so the life of man extends much further back in time than history. The study of man before history is known as anthropology and in the anthropological record there is no evidence of humanity without some evidence of governance and it is impossible to understand humanity without reference to governance. Another argument in defense of the position that government is natural is that even in the animal kingdom among social animals there is always some type of governance from the pecking order of chickens to the much more complex leadership structures of primates. Therefore it can be seen that government is natural, irrefutable by fact based knowledge.

This brings us to the next question is, are laws natural? Are there some laws which everyone would agree apply to all humans everywhere at all times? If there are then there are natural laws. Or, are laws arbitrary and merely impositions of the powerful upon the weak.

Do all humans everywhere at all times know it is wrong to kill another human? Do all humans everywhere at all times know it is wrong to steal? There may be many opinions regarding these questions but there is no doubt that there are people known as sociopaths. Sociopaths have little or no regard for the feelings of others. They often manipulate others in order to get what they want. In our politically correct era the term sociopath is no longer in fashion and is not used by psychologists and psychiatrists. Today the disorder is called antisocial personality disorder. Sociopaths have no sense of right or wrong.

If not knowing right from wrong is considered a disease among civilized people obviously having regard for others and knowing right from wrong must be considered normal. As shown by the traditional wisdom which tells us there is honor among thieves meaning they don't steal from each other meaning even thieves know stealing is wrong. A powerful influencing factor upon this type of universal law is the concept of us and them.

An example of how this works shows the power of natural law through its violation rationalized by the "us and them" factor. The name of almost all Native American tribes translates into "Human beings" or "The People" and while many tribes showed no hesitation in killing those outside their tribe, those who were not "Human Beings" they all had powerful taboo against killing anyone within the tribe. The freedom to violate what was accepted as an iron-clad law was only possible if the victim was not considered to be a human being. The same argument is being used currently to rationalize abortion.

If it is therefore concluded that there are in fact natural laws it is important to determine what they are for natural laws are always and everywhere the same as opposed to manmade laws which vary according to time and place. It is also concluded that any manmade law which contradicts a natural law is unnatural and illegitimate. Natural laws are made for humanity as they should be; man-made laws are made for humanity as they are. Natural laws speak to humanity's eternal condition and man-made law speaks to his condition limited by a finite life surrounded by other finite beings in an imperfect world.

Is the essence of government and of law eternal? Is it divine?

As a Christian I believe in salvation by grace through faith in the life, death, and resurrection of Jesus. This faith must be a born of a free choice or it is meaningless. This belief was also common among the Framers and the civilization of which they were a part. This basic Christian belief formed a foundational part of their world view. This being true it can be assumed that they believed that personal freedom and liberty of conscious had to be considered a guiding principle of any discussion of natural law. Therefore, any law of man which restricts the freedom of choice unless such restriction is for the safety or freedom of others is a violation of the natural law.

It is a result of this belief among the Founders that they chose to begin the Declaration of Independence with the words "When in the Course of human events it becomes necessary for one people to dissolve the political bands which have connected them with another and to assume among the powers of the earth, the separate and equal station to which the Laws of Nature and of Nature's God entitle them, a decent respect to the opinions of mankind requires that they should declare the causes which impel them to the separation." This direct appeal to "the Laws of Nature and of Nature's God" proves beyond dispute that the Founders stood in the Christian and Enlightenment belief in Natural Law which is why they continued, "We hold these truths to be self-evident, that all men are created equal, that they are endowed by their Creator with certain inalienable rights that among these are life, liberty and the pursuit of happiness."

Dispatch Two

The Articles of Confederation

In 1776, during the darkest days of the Revolutionary War, John Dickinson proposed Articles of Confederation and Perpetual Union. In 1777 the Continental Congress, the same one that passed the Declaration of Independence adopted the first written document creating a government for the United States. In the midst of a war against the tyrant George III the Articles reflected the understandable fear the 13 original states had of a highly centralized government and a powerful executive.

Instead of establishing an executive or judicial branch the only functioning apparatus of government was a legislative body known as Congress made up of representatives appointed by the states. This Congress was given responsibility for maintaining the army and navy, declaring war or peace, as well as conducting foreign affairs including foreign commerce. Reflecting the reluctance of the states in establishing a powerful centralized government while granting some powers the Articles denied others such as the power to regulate interstate commerce, enforce the laws it passed, coin money, levy or collect taxes. After much debate the Articles took effect as the framework upon which the government of the United States would operate from 1781 until 1788.

In reality, the Articles of Confederation did not do anything of substance to change the way the Continental Congress already operated. What they did do was institutionalize the practices Congress had previously developed. In addition, the Articles did not establish a direct link between the citizens and their government. Instead they established "a league of friendship" among the States; a league based upon and designed to protect state sovereignty as opposed to national sovereignty. The authority of the government rested on the goodwill of the States in honoring their commitments under the Articles.

As the war was won and peace returned to the land the urgency of collective action became less of need and more of an obligation. The States continued their refusal to meet their financial commitments which had been such a problem in conducting the war. As the threat of foreign interference receded further with each passing year the States also began to expand what they considered the prerogatives of sovereignty.

In February 1787 Congress issued a call for a convention to reevaluate the current national system. It was clear, however, that Congress did not want a new charter; in fact, it stated that the delegates were to meet "for the sole and express purpose of revising the Articles of Confederation."[1] Instead behind locked doors the representatives of twelve states (Rhode Island never sent a representative to the convention) wrote an entirely new document. The Articles of Confederation were the government as adopted by the unanimous vote of the thirteen states. All of them solemnly agreed to the Articles including Article 13 which stated:

> Each state must accept and agree to follow the decisions of the United States in Congress assembled. The states must follow all of the rules as stated in the Articles of Confederation. The union of states is meant to last forever. No alterations can be made to the Articles without the agreement of Congress and the confirmation by each of the state legislatures.

> Each of the delegates that sign this document has the power to commit the state that they represent to all of the Articles and their specific contents. The people of each state will agree to follow the rulings of Congress on all matters they discuss, and each of the states agrees to never violate the union. We have signed this as members of Congress, meeting in Philadelphia, Pennsylvania on July 9, 1778, the third year of American Independence.[2]

This concluding article explicitly stated that this union was meant to last forever. It also provided the manner of enforcement and established the only amendment process under the Articles of Confederation. This established amendment process was not the process followed in the ratification of the Constitution.

So how did we get from a loose perpetual union to a centralized nationalist government was it the capstone of the Revolution or was it a counter-revolution? For roughly the first 100 years the group of men who wrote the Constitution, collectively known as the Framers were spoken of and written about more as demigods than as men. They came to be confounded with a larger group who should be known as the Founders, those who led the colonies to become a free and independent nation. Both theories, was it Revolution or was it counter-revolution have been advanced and vigorously advocated by various groups since the beginning of the twentieth century. So which was it and how did we get from there to here? [3]

Dispatch 3

The State versus the Individual

In America, individualism is a kind of philosophical almost theological ideal upon which our society was founded. This foundation birthed a society of free individuals who entered into a social contract wherein they surrendered some authority and power to government to gain enough security and peace to enjoy their rights while retaining their inherent freedom and inviolable personal independence.

That man was conceived of by our founders as a created being is attested to in the Declaration of Independence when it says, "We hold these truths to be self-evident, that all men are created equal, that they are endowed by their Creator with certain unalienable Rights, that among these are Life, Liberty and the pursuit of Happiness."[1] These rights the Creator endowed us with fall into two broad categories.

The primary of these is the right to think and act as we see fit in matters which concern and affect only ourselves. Then there are civil rights. These are the rights all people possess before entering into the social contract such as, to act, to own property, to manage our own affairs in areas that might affect others all of which are not surrendered by our entrance into society, since they are inherent and endowed by our Creator. These second are the rights which no one individual can assure for themselves without the cooperation of others, hence the need for a social contract[2] and society. And although the individual is not personally capable of ensuring the enjoyment of these rights this does not give society the authority to curtail them. It's for the protection of these rights that governments are established, or as the Founders put it, "That to secure these rights, Governments are instituted among Men."[3]

All of the above refers to and elaborates upon the rights of individuals. Each individual as created and endowed is sovereign in and of their own person and should therefore enjoy the unfettered exercise of their rights which besides those already enumerated also consist of the right to equality before the law, to participate in political activity, to engage in commerce, and to express their thoughts and beliefs.

The state is nothing more than individuals bound together by the social contract which they have all either directly or indirectly agreed to. The state is not an individual. The state is not a separate entity with inherent rights of its own. This is a destructive concept which is equivalent to making the state god and is contrary to reality. For when states begin to exert their personhood, to demand their rights this always equates to the usurpation of individual rights by corrupt leaders who say by their actions, "I am the State" in the name of a vague collective that is ultimately beneficial to them.

When contemplating the forceful nature of government within the lives of men Henry David Thoreau accepted the motto, "That government is best which governs least,"[4] and he even expanded it to say, "That government is best which governs not at all"[5] making him the poster child for modern anarchists. While not embracing the extremity of Thoreau's position the reasonableness of Jefferson's is seen in his statement, "I would rather be exposed to the inconveniences of too much liberty, than those attending too small a degree of it."[6] Perhaps Thoreau had too much faith in his fellow man, but sad to say his descendants have become a people with too much faith in government. For government, once it has secured the peace and security necessary for the individual to enjoy the use of their personal rights, once it has secured the border from invasion and made provision for defense is more an encumbrance than a help.

Over the years there have been many abuses of power by the representatives of the people. The rights of the individual have been curtailed and the imagined rights of the government have been expanded at their expense. However, the American ship of state has always righted itself after the aristocratic or bureaucratic storm passed. However, today the dream weavers of collectivism are ensnaring whole generations in their cradle-to-grave web of dependency. Collectivism is not native to the human condition, and it does not spontaneously evolve from the actions or the desires of life. Everywhere it is imposed by ideologues through either the use or the threat of force. The modern manifestations of collectivism in its extreme Communism, National Socialism, and Fascism have everywhere been attended by massive dislocations of society, mass murder, war and collapse. In its milder and more immediate manifestations, socialism and corporatism leads the way to stagnation, loss of incentive and economic collapse.

In America we see the fusion of politicians, unions, interest groups and too-big-to-fail crony capitalism into a formless cross-party bloc reminiscent of the outfit which has controlled Chicago politics for generations. The principle proponents of this new conception of American society, the Progressives in the left-wings of both major political parties, have maneuvered themselves to the apex of power, and are controlling all three branches of the federal government. They have the stated goal of transforming America, and the transformation they have in mind is the collectivization of all for the benefit of the few. Washed away will be the individualism which has been our foundation and the sanctity of the rights this individualism proclaims. As an unnatural creature the collective state asserts its imagined rights at the expense of our endowed ones.

Dispatch Four

A Government of Fallible Men to Rule Fallible Men

In America today a debate rages concerning the legitimate role of government. Currently the Federal Government is controlled[1] by a group of politicians who consider themselves the ideological descendants of the Progressive Movement.[2] Beginning in the 1890's the Progressives led by Theodore Roosevelt and Woodrow Wilson championed the idea that it was time to progress past America's old ways of doing things. They felt the traditions, forms, and style of American governance and society should break-out of the mold provided by the Constitution by casting it as a "living Breathing Document"[3] that could be remolded to meet the desires of every generation.

They believed, and their descendants still believe, it is the behavior of men that defines who they are. This contrasts with our Founders who believed that it is instead the nature of men that provides this definition. Our Founders expressly stated that they believed humanity has been endowed by the Creator with rights. They felt that these rights are inalienable, meaning they are humanity's by virtue of existence. In other words, these rights have not been earned by man they have been given by God and since they have not been given by government, government cannot legitimately take them away. Instead of existing for its own right, the reason[4] for government[5] is to protect these natural rights. It is the need for the order, security and liberty for the pursuit of happiness, which justifies the establishment and continuation of government.

Thus, a government of the people, by the people and for the people should be one based upon the nature of man.[6] It is in this context that the voice of the people could almost be called the voice of God for if the Creator implanted this nature and these rights within humanity the collective expression freely arrived at and freely expressed should bring to the fore those who will respect and guard these rights.

If this is true then the will of the majority should always be the surest way to ensure the continued existence of man's natural rights. If we had a nation of perfect people this would be true; however, in establishing and maintaining government we do not deal with perfect people we deal with people as they are with all the imperfections and prejudices nurture superimposes upon nature. People who do not educate themselves enough to exercise self-leadership become the pawns of demagogues and the voice of God is perverted into the voice of the world.

Even the Founders, a grouping singular in the history of men concerning the brilliance of their intellects and the purity of their motives knew they could not trust themselves to form or maintain a government of fallible men to rule over fallible men. They knew that history is filled with examples of charismatic leaders who have proven that while you can fool all of the people only some of the time it is possible to fool enough people to take over a country. Then once you have fooled a plurality of voters to take over you can make fools of everyone doing whatever you like for as long as you like. This is why the protection of freedom is a limited government.

Power must be concentrated enough to provide order, security and liberty; however, if unrestrained power is given to a majority the opportunity exists for a faction to gain control and use it for purely partisan ends. Thus our Founders rejected direct democracy[7] in favor of the federal model of divided sovereignty and the republican principle of both direct and in-direct representation. That the source of authority emanates from the people and the constituent States is demonstrated in several ways. The Constitution itself was referred to delegates chosen by the States. In the American government as initially designed the people were represented directly by the House of Representatives and the States by the Senate. The executive was elected indirectly by the people and the states through the Electoral College. The members of the judicial branch are appointed by the executive with the advice and consent of the Senate.

This process of allowing democratic choice within a framework of restraint was designed to create a government based upon the premise of inalienable rights yet cognizant of the fallible nature of mankind. A government powerful enough to ensure the security necessary to guarantee those rights, yet retrained enough not to trample them. Many of the Progressive innovations of the last 100 years have upset this delicate balance moving us from the government envisioned by the founders to the one we have today.

The Seventeenth Amendment[8] mandates the direct election of the Senate. This left the States without any voice in the Federal Government. It also opened the door for a combination of factions acting as an unrestrained majority seeking the benefit of some at the expense of others. Often those who take the limits off government seek unlimited power for themselves. We must follow the guide of our ancestors for the good of our posterity. We must resist the temptation to seek security through government rather than security from government.

Dispatch Five

Checks and Balances

In March of 1917 as part of the swirling aftermath of the First World War starving peasants, unpaid factory workers and disillusioned soldiers overthrew the Czar, the absolute autocrat of the Russian Empire. In November of 1917 the Communist Bolsheviks overthrew the proto democrats and in July 1918 they killed the last Czar and his family ending the 300 year Romanov dynasty but that wasn't the end of czars.

Given the left's history it is interesting to see the victorious leader of our own November Revolution appointing not one but many Czars to rule over a fundamentally transformed America. This proliferation of Czars was not started by the current occupant of the White House. Ill-advised presidents before him started the process but the man from Chicago is taking it to a completely new level.

For over 150 years the Senate jealously guarded its power to confirm or reject presidential advisors. This was one of the checks and balances[1] built into our Constitution. In tune with its purpose of limiting government so that the citizens of the United States could live free without the fear of tyranny these checks and balances were cunningly devised to stop any one branch of government from becoming too powerful. Starting with FDR the presidents began to use emergencies such as recessions, wars and natural disasters to circumvent this process by appointing Czars. These Czars are presidential appointees who take and hold office completely at the president's discretion with no congressional confirmation and no congressional oversight.

At first it was the extreme nature of the situations such as WWII that led Congress to meekly accept this radical extension of executive power. The history of the English Speaking people has stood out among the histories of the world since King John signed the Magna Carta[2] in the fields of Runnymede in 1215, the first absolute monarch to admit that it was not by divine right that he ruled but by the sufferance of the people. This trend moved by fits and starts until a Prime Minister elected by the majority party in Parliament truly ruled with the advice of ministers who were likewise elected by the people. After our patriot fathers threw off the yoke of foreign control the Framers crafted the Constitution to perfect this transfer of power from one man rule to government of, by and for the people. It was for the purpose of safe guarding these hard won rights that the system of checks and balances was devised and for 150 years this helped keep the ship of state from the shoals of tyranny.

As stated earlier President Obama is not the first to make an end-run around the Constitution and congressional oversight through the use of Czars and the 111th Congress is not the first to abdicate its duty by allowing this practice to continue. However, our currently reigning Democrat president has so over-reached that he's inspired the longest serving Senator, Democrat Robert Byrd to send him a two page letter in which he expresses his concern that the constantly multiplying Czar system "Can threaten the Constitutional system of checks and balances."[3] This is unprecedented. Senator Byrd is not just the longest serving Senator he is also President Pro Tempore of the Senate and the fourth the in line of succession[4] to the presidency according to the 25th Amendment. [5]

In an administration that promised transparency Senator Byrd's words carry a sting of chastisement magnified by his years of political experience and personal historical knowledge. And the fact that he is the ranking member of the President's own party deflects the charge of partisanship which would otherwise diminish their power.

> At worst, White House staff have (sic) taken direction and control of programmatic areas that are the statutory responsibility of Senate-

confirmed officials. They have even limited access to the president by his own cabinet members. As presidential assistants and advisers, these White House staffers are not accountable for their actions to the Congress, to cabinet officials, and to virtually anyone but the president. They rarely testify before congressional committees, and often shield the information and decision-making process behind the assertion of executive privilege. In too many instances, White House staff have (sic) been allowed to inhibit openness and transparency, and reduce accountability. [6]

All the moves have been made to check-mate the other branches of government and radically alter the balance of power. Presidential Obama has unconfirmed unaccountable advisors running cabinet size programs. He has the power to issue executive orders which carry the force of law. He has the ability to interpret laws passed by Congress to mean the opposite of what Congress actually says through signing statements[7] and he has the newly discovered ability to purchase controlling shares in private companies, directing them as to firing of CEOs[8] the make-up of Boards, [9] and even the amount of advertising [10] they can run. What's next extravagant private dates that cost the taxpayer [11] huge sums of money? Restore the Constitution! Save the Republic!

Dispatch 6

Does Equality Mean We Are All The Same?

In the Declaration of Independence[1] a new thing entered the world, a country founded upon the idea of equality. The Old World consisted of societies built upon hereditary class and entrenched privilege. Beginning with words that still burn within the breast of Patriots, this great document proclaims two types of equality.

Based upon the first clause, "We hold these truths to be self-evident, that all men are created equal," the first type is equality before the law. [2] We all stand before the bar of justice on the same footing. There are not different laws for different classes. The definition of murder is the same for the homeless person, the mechanic, and the billionaire. This equality, a natural part of our creation, proclaims that neither classes nor other artificial divisions will ever be recognized in law or enshrined through legislation.

Based upon the second clause, "that they are endowed by their Creator with certain unalienable rights that among these are Life, Liberty and the pursuit of Happiness," the second type is equality of opportunity. [3] All are entitled to their life and the fruits of it. Each of us has an equal right to the liberty of action, the freedom to choose our life's path and to make our own decisions. And each of us has the right to pursue happiness. In almost all other lists such as this from the period, many of them written into state constitutions by the same people who wrote the Declaration, this is the right to own property and the happiness here is assumed to mean the right to use our own talents and the things they gain for us for our own benefit as long as we do not injure nor hinder others.

These rights and the equality they express were later protected by the Constitution. Congress shall not confer titles of nobility.[4] Congress shall not pass bills of attainder [5] convicting groups or individuals without a trial. Through the use of these and other negatives the Framers sought to secure Americans the possession of the equality proclaimed by the Declaration. The Bill of Rights [6] went even further in declaring what Congress could not do in the attempt to guarantee the continued exercise of the equality granted by our Creator. The mechanism the Framers used to keep freedom alive was limiting government for they knew governments gain power by subtracting freedom from individuals.

However, it needs to be noted that the limitations placed upon government as a means of securing the equal rights of citizens in no way states that there should be a leveling of all people or that there will not continue to be distinctions and differences among them. This was never stated and never intended. The belief in or vision of a population with standardized talents, inclinations, and goals does not match reality. There are as many different sets of these as there are people. In each individual, life should be open to choice. The only boundaries being that we do no harm nor proscribe the choice of others. This is the level playing field of creation, a pure equality of opportunity to be harvested in proportion to the Creator's gift of talents and our investment of time and effort.

As long as the role of government is limited, and as long people are free to operate within the informal social arrangements of a non-regimented, non-stratified society there's no tension between equality of opportunity and liberty. This quest for an unachievable equality of outcome has become a social goal adopted as a reason for destroying our society as it is, in the name of a new society as a small cadre of radicals thinks it should be. In the aftermath of economic or societal collapse, revolutionaries, or in the case of the American Progressives "Evolutionaries," will seek to erect in the place of popular government a bureaucratic tyranny devoted to leveling all to the lowest common denominator. Except for the levelers themselves who rise by deciding who gets what, and it's the deciders who always seem to get the most. For, some perceive that equality of all is not the same as the equality of some, or as the ruling pigs in George Orwell's novel, *Animal Farm* declare, "All animals are equal, but some animals are more equal than others."[7] This reflects the subversion of equality of opportunity into equality of outcome or as it's termed by Progressives: equal opportunity.

To build this monument to mediocrity the philosophers of progressivism subtly change the meaning of equality. Instead of the opportunity for all to succeed it becomes the certainty of everyone getting a trophy for showing up, a diploma for attendance, or a check for not working. Built upon the premise that if all are created equal all should end up equal, thus denying the goal of equality the chance to go as far and as fast as talent and hard work can lead.

Dispatch Seven

Equality is Never Equal

Equality is a sacred word in the modern American lexicon. It is the politically correct positive to the negative of discrimination. There is a philosophy known as Egalitarianism[1] based upon a belief in human equality in all social, political, and economic affairs. This philosophy advocates the removal of all inequalities among people. Egalitarianism is one of the foundational principles of the Progressives[2] currently controlling the government of the United States.

There is one major flaw with this philosophy. It does not reflect reality. No matter what anyone wants to believe, hopes to encourage, or pretends to see people are not equal. There are the physical differences of size, shape, appearance, intelligence, and temperament. There are also differences in family environment, economic situation, education, and location. There is no natural way to eradicate these inherent differences. This is where the progressive philosophy kings seek to insert the coercive actions of government to level the playing field [3] creating what they believe is a perfect environment for human activity. However, perfect equality is impossible to create, for in the artificial hothouse of government enforced equality there are still those who decide what equal is, and as the privileged commissars of the USSR taught us everyone is equal but some are more equal than others.

Founded in the fires of revolution against the tyranny of hereditary monarchs and privilege, the people of the United States sought to establish a nation unique in the world where everyone could work their way to the highest positions in a free society. Today the richest people in the country, the most celebrated in media, and the most powerful in politics, bare witness that this system works. Many of them began with nothing and today have much. However, beginning at the end of the nineteenth century when the Progressives began their Long March to power the understanding of this began to change. The Progressives present as evolution from the staid ideas of the Framers the idea that government intervention should be used to create the unattainable reality of an equality of outcome. The Progressives do not understand, or choose to ignore, that the withdrawal of government control is necessary to create the equality of opportunity which has always been the key to America's greatness.

To gain control, the Progressives changed the definition of equality from the opportunity to achieve to the absence of failure advocating governmental action to create a safety net. Unfortunately, while their plan is not based on the reality of human nature it must deal with the results of human nature. Many people, when they are given a safety net turn it into a hammock and decide life is not a challenge it is a vacation with the bill sent to someone else.

The first step the progressives identified as necessary to impose an unreal vision upon reality was education. The goal: expel God and positive views of American History to turn a nation founded upon inalienable rights endowed by a Creator into a secular Humanist commonwealth where government is the arbiter of all, and change our iron-clad Constitution into a Living Document. The press came next growing into a media monster ridiculing traditional values and extolling deviance as the new normal. To protect people from the predatory practices of rapacious capitalism government regulation became the Progressives' tool of choice.

The federal regulators led step-by-step to massive government distortion of the marketplace. Federally-funded Fannie and Freddie inflated a housing bubble. Casino capitalism run by government cronies invented bazaar financial instruments convincing people that buying funds backed by bad loans made sense. Central planners were picking winners and losers instead of the self-directed interests of consumers, thus making this economic shell game unsustainable. The Progressive's answer was more government intervention, which successfully transformed a recession into the Great Recession.

After serial bail-outs, which have not bailed out anyone except politically-connected interest groups, we have career politician Sen. Christopher Dodd's [4] going away present. Another magical mystery bill: crisis-driven financial reform, which even he admits, "No one will know until this is actually in place how it works."[5] One more multi-thousand-page document[6] redrawing how our society works all in the name of promoting equality, fairness, and security by extending government control instead of freedom.

Political and social philosophy cannot change human nature, and no matter how people wish for another reality, all we have is the real one. It is time people admit that once government acts to equalize the lives of all it must act unequally towards some. Equality of opportunity is based upon the idea of treating everyone the same. Equality of outcome is based upon the idea of redistribution. To prevent economic inequality take from those who produce and give to those who do not. To prevent racial inequality make judgments based on race using racial quotas. In this drive to create an unreal reality the Progressives have manufactured an endless supply of special classes of people, giving some extra rights and privileges while encumbering others with added burdens and barriers. The goal of perfect equality always ends in rearranged inequality. Perfection is not attainable in this life. The utopian dream that humanity can create a government funded heaven on earth has led to more carnage and human suffering than any other delusion known to man.

Dispatch Eight

Dream From Our Forefathers

What is the American Dream? When asked this question most people today are programmed to say "To own your own home." That may be Freddie and Fannie's dream. That may be the bubble inflating vote buying politician's choice for our dream, but that isn't the American Dream. Owning your own home isn't the dream people sailed in tiny leaking over-crowded wooden ships across oceans to find. Owning your own home isn't the dream people fought the Revolution to win and other wars to preserve. We the descendants of the pioneers have been sold a bill of goods. We have embraced a culture of hedonism and self-indulgence financed with a borrowed credit card.

The American Dream is and always has been freedom and opportunity.

This is the Holy Grail for which people have been willing to sacrifice. This is the singularity which made America great. This is the difference which allowed a people who were no people to become a people. Ordinary people from everywhere, members of every race, religion, ethnicity, and culture assimilated and forged into one extraordinary nationality: the American. Freedom and opportunity unleashed the ingenuity and energy of humanity. Rising above the squalid shabbiness of the statists enforced conformity as the citizen began to control and at last benefit from the fruits of their own labor.

By forsaking the dream of our forefathers we have embraced the nightmare of their oppressors forging again the very chains our revolutionary ancestors shattered. From the beginning of time statists of one variety or another have kept their iron heel upon the throat of the general population. Whether they called themselves; chiefs, or kings, emperors or gods those who believe they have a right to command the service of others have always survived as parasites leaching the produce of whomever they were strong enough to compel. Calling them tithes, contributions, donations, or taxes it has always been the same thing, "What's mine is mine. What's yours is negotiable."

Following the chiefdoms of the Neolithic villages Priest-kings combined shamanism and dynastic power to create a world wherein the possessions of all became the possessions of the ruler. In Western Civilization there was a brief anomaly when the people of Greece experimented with a new concept, democracy, power to the people. And although this was always a proscribed definition of who constituted "the people." None-the-less inventiveness, culture and scientific inquiry exploded into a Golden Age. Soon however, wars and corruption brought the brief respite of freedom crashing into the military dictatorship of the Roman Imperium and the statists once again asserted their right to divine privilege and power.

The corruption, taxes, and inflation which always define a statist government brought about the fall of Rome. Replaced in the East by a successor empire so strangled by bureaucracy and state control its very name, "Byzantine" has come to mean the triumph of red tape over individual freedom. In the West the edifice of Caesar devolved into petty kingdoms and barbarian chiefdoms where life was short, brutish, and enslaved. The common laborer became little more than chattel tied to the land and exchanged between their betters as a mere piece of property. These kleptocracies were eventually consolidated into nation-states by whoever clawed their way to the top of the food chain as the strongest or most ruthless oppressor of all. After a few generations they discovered the theory of divine-right, and by using damnation in the after-life as a whip they did their best to turn this life into a living hell.

An eruption of exploration, colonization, and conquest vaulted Western Civilization to the top of the heap translating a recent and fleeting preeminence in technology and organization into a centuries-long reign as the political and cultural hegemonic power of the world. The representatives of the divine rights of European Kings penetrated into every corner of the world where they set-up forts and bought the place for beads. Even the few who escaped actual conquest such as Ethiopia and Japan had homegrown statists asserting their right to deny rights to others. By the end of the seventeenth century the regimented sameness which flows from a lack of individual freedom gripped every portion of what was called the civilized world.

Into this world the American Revolution blazed like a comet illuminating the realms of possibility by the light of a national experiment declaring, "that all men are created equal, that they are endowed by their Creator with certain unalienable Rights, that among these are Life, Liberty and the pursuit of Happiness."[1] After fighting and winning a long war against impossible odds the United States, the land of the free and the home of the brave, unfurled its banner proclaiming for the first time in human history that here is a place where divine rights do not belong to kings they belong to all.

For over 100 years the Progressives have sought to supplant our Revolution with their evolution. These radical Evolutionaries have methodically moved America one entitlement at a time from self-reliance and personal responsibility towards the cradle-to-grave conformity which is the hallmark of modern statists. As we face the coming debates, as we prepare for the electoral and legislative battles let us remember that the American dream has always been freedom and opportunity as we reject the materialistic bribes of the Progressive nanny-state. Reject the smothering comforter promised through government programs which will enslave our children and grandchildren and drink once again the heady wine of freedom.

Dispatch Nine

Since Some Don't Worry About the Constitution We Should

One of the greatest challenges in teaching History is to convey the uniqueness in its conception of something that through the passage of time has become an accepted part of everyday life. When something has been around longer than we have it's hard to realize that it wasn't always there. It takes a conscious effort to understand that yesterday was not today only earlier, and tomorrow will not be today only later. The permanence of the now is an illusion, which helps us walk as if the shifting sands of our lives are really the solid shore of the sea of time.

When Americans organize anything of importance they immediately write a construction. In most cases American organizations include a president, vice-president, and a legislative type board. From the classroom to the boardroom from Main Street to Wall Street this is just the way we do things. The idea that there needs to be a written constitution is assumed. And looking at our history this only makes sense. For hundreds of years and for generation after generation we have lived lives of peace, prosperity, and power under the shade of the most remarkable secular document to have ever come from the hand of man: the Constitution of the United States.

The birth of our Constitution shines as an almost miraculous event in the story of mankind. From the beginning of time might has always made right. One strong arm after another elbowed their way to center stage. Once there, eventually their descendants grown fat on the plunder of the helpless became in turn plunder for the next strong arm. Those who managed through the passage of time to become fixtures in their culture reigned as monarchs saying God gave them a divine right to continue plundering those under their sway conveniently forgetting it was the strong arm of their less noble ancestors that slaughtered their way to the top. They may have arrived in chariots, but they were chariots of steel not fire.

A few centuries before the founding of the English colonies in America the people of England began to put limits on their king. They used violence and economics to wrest the guarantees of some basic individual rights, the recognition that the king was not absolute, and that there were some checks upon his power. The Magna Charta, [1] the Petition of Rights, [2] and the Bill of Rights[3] were snatched from the king's chain-mailed fist. Through the passage of time they became the accepted rights of all Englishmen. When our ancestors founded Virginia, the first English colony the charter[4] granted by the king stated that those who came to the New World were granted all liberties, franchises and immunities as if they were abiding and born within England. The colonists believed this and acted accordingly. With loyalty to the King and Parliament they set about organizing the land. Local assemblies, republican in nature were democratically elected. And it was only when George III and his ministers acted as if the colonists did not have these rights that Americans took up arms to secure those rights.

After the Revolution, when it came time to create a government the Framers turned to a written constitution.[5] In the birth of nations this was something new. England does not have a written constitution. Ours was the first: a unique attempt to limit government in order to preserve liberty. Most constitutions in the world today model themselves after ours. And if their authors did not consciously model their written document after ours the very concept of a written constitution is of American origin.

This earth-shaking event has become mundane. This ground-breaking experience now seems so common it's glossed over with the boring presentation of a high school history class, memorize some names and a few dates, regurgitate it for a test, and forget it. For the first time a people had founded a government of the people, by the people and for the people. And to ensure the tranquility and safety of the people they limited that government through the separation of power into three branches and the maintenance of a unique federal system of sovereign states united as one. This is the source and the summit of American greatness: the Constitution which established and maintained a limited government providing for life, liberty and the pursuit of happiness.

Using the ideals and moral standards of the present to interpret the past is known as Presentism.[6] Using Presentism as a lens, many citizens today believe the Constitution is a living document[7] meant to be reinterpreted with each passing generation. Others echo the former U.S. Attorney General Alberto Gonzales' point of view, "The Constitution is what the Supreme Court says it is."[7] Instead of changing the document through the established amendment process they believe they can change the document through court decisions, precedent, and legislation.

Twenty-first century America has been called post-Christian,[8] post-capitalist,[9] and post-racial.[10] I would suggest that if we continue on the path we have chosen the future may refer to twenty-first century America as post-constitutional. For if the leaders of the present can impose unconstitutional laws then we've ceased to have a government of laws and have instead a government of men. One Congressman summed up the arrogance of our leaders perfectly.

When asked where in the Constitution he finds the authority to impose the burden of purchasing health care on the American people he answered, "I don't worry about the Constitution."[11] Since he doesn't we should.

Dispatch Ten

Sovereignty, Succession and the National Debt

The tenth Amendment says, "The powers not delegated to the United States by the Constitution, nor prohibited by it to the States, are reserved to the States respectively, or to the people."[1] How do we interpret that to mean that the National Government can do whatever it wants? How does anyone interpret that to mean that this clause reserving power is trumped by the so-called elastic clause, the last paragraph of Article I, Section 8 which states, "To make all laws which shall be necessary and proper for carrying into execution the foregoing powers, and all other powers vested by this Constitution in the government of the United States, or in any Department or officer thereof"[2]? How does a rapacious Supreme Court find the temerity to grasp power beyond question reading rights that are not delegated or enumerated into the Constitution and reading ones that are expressly stated out?

Why doesn't Congress use the power given through the Constitution in Article 3, Section 2, and Clause 2? This is known as the Exceptions and

Regulations Clause which states, "In all the other Cases before mentioned, the Supreme Court shall have appellate Jurisdiction, both as to Law and Fact, with such Exceptions, and under such Regulations as the Congress shall make."[3] This power could be used to limit the Supreme Court from legislating from the bench and usurping the power of America's elected representatives.

Why don't the people rise up and demand that Congress do its job? Limit the courts and reign in the executive! A long succession of imperial presidents have stretched and molded a once limited role into that of an almost unlimited autocrat. Signing statements, which often declare that the executive's interpretation of a law is 180º from that of the legislators who wrote and passed it and executive orders, which have taken on the complexion of decrees from the throne have changed our chief representative into a term-limited Constitutional Monarch. The nine black-robed Justices sitting in their Temple of Law have become oligarchs handing down irrevocable edicts that are often irreconcilable with the letter and the spirit of the document they are charged to guard.

After telling us, "We hold these truths to be self-evident, that all men are created equal, that they are endowed by their Creator with certain unalienable Rights that among these are Life, Liberty and the pursuit of Happiness."[4] The Declaration of

Independence tells us the purpose of government, "That to secure these rights, Governments are instituted among Men, deriving their just powers from the consent of the governed."[5] This is the premise of our founding, the genius behind our devices, and the formula for our freedom. However, the Framers knew what man is and what men needed when it came to maintaining a government of, by and for the people. James Madison said in the Federalist 51, "If men were angels, no government would be necessary. If angels were to govern men, neither external nor internal controls on government would be necessary."[6]

Paying debt incurred during the Revolution by Congress thus establishing the credit of the United States as a sovereign nation was one of the major reasons that many supported the ratification of the Constitution. The United States was born with a debt. The national debt has never been paid off. [7] The lowest the national debt has ever been since the founding of the nation is $33,733.05 in 1835.

With all countries this is a normal state of affairs as with most businesses a revolving debt is carried, but as long as payments are made, as long as assets outweigh debts cash flow equals solvency. However debt can become overwhelming. Individuals declare bankruptcy. Businesses declare bankruptcy. Independent nations do not declare bankruptcy. Instead, they either repudiate the debt or pay it off with inflated currency. Greece, Spain, and others in Europe are crashing now because they have surrendered their power to do either of the state solutions and now must bear the brunt of reality: they have borrowed more than they can repay. Any government that borrows more than they can repay is robbing from the future to inflate the present.

We the People have every constitutional and moral right to petition government for the redress of grievances yet petition after petition, poll after poll demanding an end to ruinous deficit spending are ignored. Thus enumerated rights are rendered impotent.

The right of Judicial Review, which is the cornerstone of the power of the Supreme Court and the Federal judiciary, is not mentioned in the Constitution. It came about as the result of a deal struck between our third President, Jefferson, and the second Chief Justice, Marshall in the case of Marbury v. Madison[8] in 1803. Thus powers not given are usurped by the central government.

According to the 14th Amendment Section 4 it is illegal to question the validity of the National Debt. This section says, "The validity of the public debt of the United States, authorized by law, including debts incurred for payment of pensions and bounties for services in suppressing insurrection or rebellion, shall not be questioned."[9]

In contrast to the sanctity of the National Debt enshrined in the 14th Amendment Thomas Jefferson said,

> Then I say, the earth belongs to each of these generations during its course, fully and in its own right. The second generation receives it clear of the debts and encumbrances of the first, the third of the second, and so on. For if the first could charge it with a debt, then the earth would belong to the dead and not to the living generation. Then, no generation can contract debts greater than may be paid during the course of its own existence.[10]

And, "The conclusion then, is, that neither the representatives of a nation, nor the whole nation itself assembled, can validly engage debts beyond what they may pay in their own time."[11]

The lack of angelic intrusion on either side of the human governing equation mentioned above may be the reason the Declaration rounds out the wisdom quoted earlier as to the freedom of men and the reason for government saying, "whenever any Form of Government becomes destructive of these ends, it is the Right of the People to alter or to abolish it,"[12]

Dispatch Eleven

The Unlimited Blessings of Limited Government

The battles were over and the war won now the hardest task of all: how to secure the rights fought for while providing a government strong enough to endure. The Framers gathered in Philadelphia for the purpose of proposing amendments to the Articles of Confederation.[1] Within days they decided instead to frame a new government launching an experiment in centralized but limited government.

That they believed the people to be the source of legitimate authority is exposed in the Preamble[2] which begins, "*We the People.*" They based this belief upon the Enlightenment[3] concept of Natural Law: [4] that God endowed men with unalienable rights. Many people in Western Civilization believed in Natural Law realizing that these rights, though endowed by the Creator as inherent prerogatives, would not continue to exist in organized society unless protected by limitations on government power. The Framers believed Natural Law not only conferred rights it also established limits to the scope of government and man-made law. In their mind no legitimate law violated the possession and enjoyment of the rights of man. In declaring independence our ancestors proclaimed their purpose as assuming the station, "to which the laws of Nature and Nature's God entitle them."

Knowing all this was one thing, but devising a manner in which not only authority but also power could be conceded from society in general to a government which by the nature of organization consists of a much smaller number was quite another. How was this power to be limited? How were the rights of all to be protected from the power of the few? What was to stop the concentration of power into the hands of factions combined for their own benefit? How to provide a government with sufficient authority and power to ensure the security and order necessary for everyone to enjoy their natural rights, and yet restrained enough to allow them to do so? This was the problem which confronted those locked in Independence Hall[5] in 1787 devising a government strong enough to do good, yet limited enough to do no harm.

The concept of a written Constitution was the first step. England had no written constitution. It was and is to this day ruled by tradition and precedent. After the Revolution the Framers knew traditions and precedents can change. So they looked to a written Constitution to provide a framework and guide for the new government, thus setting boundaries and establishing them for all to see. They provided a means for change in the amendment process, but they made it difficult and cumbersome so that change would not be easy or readily accessible to the whim of a moment or the rulers of the day.

Beyond this primary recourse to a lasting written code the Framers sought to employ two vehicles for the limitation of government: a federal system wherein power is divided between the parts and the whole, and representation through which the voice of the people would speak. To accomplish these twin goals the States retain their sovereignty and provide a legislature[6] made up of two houses: the House of Representatives and the Senate. The House of Representatives was and still is popularly elected by all eligible voters. Every two years these closest of all national leaders return to the people for affirmation and a renewed mandate. And the Senate, which was originally elected by the states through their legislatures who were all at least partially elected by the public thus, ensuring both: more input from the people and the federal nature of the government. The President and Vice President[7] were and still are indirectly elected by the members of the Electoral College, which are chosen in accordance with procedures designated by the individual states, thus once again enhancing the federal nature of the government. The President, with the advice and consent of the Senate, chooses the judges of the Federal Courts.

This system, which we have come to call checks and balances, [8] originally provided that no law could be enacted without a majority vote by representatives elected directly by the people, representatives chosen by the States and signed by the President, whose election is a result of a combination of the people and the States. Thus the authority of the people was employed, the voice of the people was heard, yet the indirect manner in which it was applied and the muted manner in which it was heard sought to ensure a government insulated from the volatile passions of the day.

What the Framers sought was a government of reason. The Enlightenment thinkers believed through the use of reason people discover natural rights and natural law. They also believed reason is the source of a government capable of protecting those rights by enforcing that law. To this end they created a federal system to diffuse power and a representative republic to provide a voice for the people safeguarded from the emotions of the moment. They hoped that reasonable people working within a federal government divided between branches and surrounded by a written constitution would ensure the authority of the many would pass through the hands of the few for the blessings of all. At least that was the hope.

Dispatch Twelve

What Is Sovereignty and Who Has It?

Sovereignty is accepted as absolute uncontested authority. This definition of the concept of sovereignty emerged along with the nation-state. The nation-state has not always existed. Everyone tends to see the circumstances of their own times as the static normality of history. And contrary to the endless lectures of History teachers tied to politically correct text books and standardized tests, History is not static it is dynamic. It changes every day just because there has been another day. In addition, it is interpreted and re-interpreted every day by Historians, authors, teachers, and everyone else.

The concept of the nation-state emerged in the sixteenth century evolving from countries as the private property of monarchs, and however hard to envision, the nation-state will someday be replaced by something else.

If sovereignty is absolute uncontested authority, whether encased within a nation-state or otherwise, who has it? In England it is vested in Parliament. In

China it is vested in the Central Committee of the Communist Party. But in America sovereignty is not vested in any one place, it is defused. According to the working definition above there is no uncontested authority in a system of checks and balances, so does that mean there really isn't any? No sovereignty? How can that be? Since sovereignty is an absolute, it either exists or it does not, and it is a misapplied concept when striving to understand the American government as originally designed.

This does not mean that the United States is not a sovereign nation. The Federal Government represents the United Sates on the world stage. To the other countries of the world the Federal Government is the sovereign power with which they must deal. However, domestically we face a different situation. In some areas the Federal Government is sovereign, in some areas the States are sovereign, and in some areas the people are sovereign. Since sovereignty by definition is an absolutist concept and not one of degrees, either something is sovereign or it is not. In the United States there is no one legitimate source or center of sovereignty. The revolutionary theory the Framers advanced into practice is that several centers of power prevents the formation of an authority vortex swallowing all legitimate authority and paralyzing decision making, thus establishing the world's first viable system of disassociated sovereignty.

The Articles of Confederation, which preceded the Constitution as the foundational document and framework of organization of the United States, stated categorically in Article II, "Each state retains its sovereignty, freedom, and independence."[1] Nowhere in the Constitution is this retention of inherent sovereignty surrendered. The so-called sovereignty clause[2] found in Article Six[3] of the Constitution obviously gives precedence to the laws and treaties made by the Federal government. It does not however expressly say anywhere in the document that the States surrendered or forfeited their inherent sovereignty. If it had, it never would have been ratified. As expressly stated in the 10th Amendment[4] neither the States nor the people surrendered their sovereignty to the Federal Government they delegated it. There is a difference between these two actions. To surrender is to give entirely and irrevocably to another while delegation is a temporary action based upon continued agreement between the parties involved.

Another strong argument can be made that since all governments are the products of a social contract between those who govern and those governed, sovereignty ultimately resides in the people and governments are therefore merely agents of the people's will. According to this line of thought all governments wield delegated powers and can have no more power in and of them than the moon has light without the sun.

The Amendment process[5] is the only legitimate method for changing the Constitution. If the design calls for a decentralized diffused sovereignty in an asymmetrical system how was change achieved from that to the current system of highly centralized power and control? Was it by amendment or practice? Is it possible for an illegitimate practice to become a legitimate tradition? Is it possible for an illegitimate tradition to set a legitimate precedent?

All of these historically based academic discussions aside and for all intents and purposes, the argument about who is sovereign was forever settled by Abraham Lincoln. When the South attempted to succeed, an action not prohibited by the Constitution, they were beat back into submission to the Federal Government. Debate over. Question answered. The Federal Government is supreme. However, though this is the reality of our circumstance since the Civil War this is a reality imposed through the use of military force not to be confounded with the original condition based upon the voluntary agreement between the people, the states, and the national government in Constitution.

For years this question of who is sovereign has see-sawed back and forth. Today the Progressives and their two headed government party seek to make the exaltation of the central government permanent. If this stands unchallenged America has devolved from the defused model established under the Constitution to a centralized version reminiscent of its original absolutist definition. If this new normal is enshrined as reality, it will become increasingly obvious as States strive to assert their rights and people seek to preserve their freedom. For if the central government is now absolutely sovereign it will eventually crush all rivals. If the people are sovereign, in time they'll find their voice, reassert their power, re-establish the federal system, and return to the social contract as ratified in the Constitution.

Dispatch Thirteen

We Must Know Who We Are to Decide What We Will Be

Forget about the debate the government parties and the geriatric media want us to have, "Are you a Republican or a Democrat?" The debate we need to have concerns what we were meant to be, not who they tell us we should be. Instead we should discuss issues of substance such as, "Are we a Republic or a Democracy?" for this will lead us to the truth. In today's polarized political atmosphere conservatives shout "Republic!" while progressives scream, "Democracy!" In truth, neither term fully describes the boldest experiment to provide individual freedom and release human potential in the history of mankind. There is a third term needed if we are to grasp the qualities which makes us who we are.

The United States was birthed in the fire of revolution against the denial of personal freedom and the expropriation of resources by an authoritarian government. The first attempt to balance the rights of the people, the prerogatives of their local states and the need for a centralized structure to face other nations on the world stage, the Articles of

Confederation[1] proved inadequate. Then the Framers crafted a constitution establishing a democratic federal republic. All three terms democratic, [2] federal, [3] and republic[1] are needed to express the unique nature of the American Experiment. Not one of them conveys the strength of the three and therefore cannot stand alone. Together they outline the form of government and the manner in which it shall be chosen, yet even these loaded terms leave unstated the inner essence of the last best hope of humanity. For it is the separation of powers,[5] private property rights,[6] and the checks and balances[7] built into the system that has safe guarded liberty and unleashed the potential of the American people.

The fact that instead of a reasoned debate about who we are, where we came from, and how we got here we stand on opposite sides of barricades shouting slogans at each other highlights the need for all of us to educate ourselves in the history of the principles and values upon which our country was founded. The current public educational process is a government mandated system which forces teaching to a test that is forgotten as soon as it is passed. The teaching of American History has been presented as a boring jumble of names and dates for a few semesters in twelve years since before any of us were born. It is time for anyone who wants to understand what is going on in our rapidly evolving political landscape to dig in and educate ourselves. We cannot allow those who want to subvert the home of the brave and the land of the free, either to the right or the left, to sway us with slogans and catch phrases. We have to know enough to know when we're being conned by ideologues with a hidden agenda.

Ideologues reduce all things to the dimensions of their own thoughts. They oversimplify and overload words with meaning effectively blocking the channels of communication. They turn complex political, social, and economic principles into cat-calls, catch-phrases, and campaign slogans designed to move masses to emotional responses not individuals to reasoned reactions. It was the ideologue Karl Marx[8] who reduced history to a conflict between capital and labor, charged all problems to the inequalities of capitalism, projected a continually deteriorating situation, and then pointed to communism as the only answer.

We must resist the temptation to reduce our American experiment to an ideology. We cannot allow this bait-and-switch tactic to lead us to the mirage of a collectivist utopia. We need to understand this would deny and distort the constitutionally limited government we inherited. Ideologies start with a conception of mankind as made-up of interchangeable parts, projects, universally comprehensive answers, and ends with enforced uniformity in society. In contrast America has facilitated diversity, individualism, and a variety of life paths.

So, "Are we a Republic or a Democracy?" First of all, we need to understand these are not equivalent or interchangeable terms.[9] Today both republic and democracy have become loaded with ideological baggage as in the Democratic Peoples Republic, or Social Democracy.[10] To be specific: republic describes a form of government wherein representatives stand in place of others to deliberate, decide, and lead. Democracy means from the people. But there is always that third term that must be reckoned with if we're to understand America: federal. Federal means a form of government in which a union of states recognizes a central authority while retaining certain residual powers of government. Putting this all together, the United States of America was designed to be a federation of states with a republican form of government chosen through a democratic process.

Those who declare we are a democracy want majority rule while striving to build a majority of people dependent on the government tax, tax, tax, spend, spend, spend, elect, elect, elect. Those who say we are a republic have problems with the direction taken by the representatives whose very existence proclaims this to be a republic. This is where the third word fully impacts the other two. The federal nature of the American experiment declares to all that this is an elected representative government of limited power and separated authority. We are not a centrally-planned unitary government based on mob-rule. If we will learn who we are perhaps then we will see clearly who we will be.

Dispatch Fourteen

The Arrogance of Power

Americans have dealt with the arrogance of power before. From 1756 through 1763 a world war ravaged the globe from India to Europe and from the farthest reaches of the Pacific Ocean to the deepest woods of Ohio. England and France fought to see who would become the greatest colonial power.

For seven years, battles raged throughout the Colonies as the French and their Indian allies pushed the Americans back across the Allegheny Mountains and sought to over-run the fertile area from the mountains to the coast which held the majority of English settlements. After many massacres and defeats the American Militias, with a core of British officers and supplies, were able to not only repulse the enemy but also follow them home to Canada. Known as the French and Indian War [1] in America and as the Seven Years War in Europe when the final treaties were signed in 1763, with the lone exception of Florida, England became the master of North America east of the Mississippi.

After the war the politicians in England had to deal with massive debt. They also had a restive public tired of shouldering the burdens of war. The politicians knew raising taxes at home might lead to political problems, so they turned to the colonies as a source of plunder where the victims didn't get a vote. They justified their actions saying England had paid to defend the colonists and now the maturing colonies should pay their own way. The colonists however, felt that with the French gone there was no need to defend them. They also knew the taxes were bailing out the politicians without angering their voters thus birthing the classic rebel yell, "No taxation without representation!" When the taxes were ignored the British sent troops to enforce their will.

This explosive situation soon met the sparks which set it ablaze. As pamphleteers and patriots railed against the suppression of liberty ham-fisted British officers stumbled into debacles such as the Boston Massacre. The blood of Americans mingled with their economic self-interest and independent nature as the Boston Tea Party, Concord, and Lexington led to war. The Declaration of Independence, eight years of war combined with French allies and the American Republic, stood independent before the nations of the world. In a time of kings and landed aristocracy this was a bold experiment in freedom and opportunity birthed in a violent reaction to the arrogance of power.

In 1812, [2] a mere two decades after the birth of our nation the arrogance of power evoked another strong reaction from America. The Napoleonic Wars once again pitted England against a newly resurgent France ripping Europe apart. As the wars dragged on England was in desperate need of trained seaman to maintain the navy, which would eventually strangle France. Using the excuse of their blockade they stopped neutral merchantmen on the high seas. Using brute force they kidnapped sailors they said were deserters forcing them to serve in the British navy for the duration of the wars. Many of these men were native born Americans who would never come home again.

When we could bare the insult to our independence and the interference with our commerce no more, we declared war on the super power of the day. Like David against Goliath America with almost no Navy fought against the largest Navy the world had ever seen. With a rag-tag gaggle of militias led by a sprinkling of trained officers we stood toe-to-toe with the best trained and equipped army in the world. They sunk our ships. They invaded our land. They burned our capital. Yet in the end we handed them the worst defeat their arms had suffered in a thousand years at the Battle of New Orleans.[3] Andrew Jackson, leading militias from as far away as Kentucky, joined a hastily gathered force of irregulars and beat the best England had to offer. Again America stood up to the arrogance of power.

When Mexico, [4] which was considered the greatest military power in the New World, disputed the Texas border we challenged the arrogance of their dictator Santa Anna[5] and won the Southwest. When the German Empire declared unrestricted submarine warfare[6] against our merchant fleet and tried to incite Mexico[7] to stab a knife in our back America stood against the arrogance of power. When the Japanese Empire struck like a thief in the night[8] and Hitler sought to build a Thousand Year Reich[9] we stood against the arrogance of power. When the Communist slave masters of the Soviet Union [10] sought to subjugate the world we stood against the arrogance of power.

In America today our own government as caricatured by the Democrat Party of Barak Obama, Nancy Peolosi, and Harry Reid has decided they know best. Even though the vast majority of Americans said loudly, "We don't want what you're selling!" This trio of Progressive leaders is forcing a socialized, collectivist agenda down our throats. With the only bi-partisan feature of their cradle-to-grave nanny state being the opposition of both Republicans and Democrats they have succeeded in gaining legislative victory after legislative victory, sometimes only by one vote, but victories none-the-less.

But Americans know how to stand against the arrogance of power. Now is the time for all lovers of liberty to rally around the limited form of government the Constitution was meant to guarantee. Without violence, within the traditions of our great Republic, we must stand together or we will all hang separately. Read the Declaration of Independence, [11] the Articles of Confederation and the Constitution.[12] Look to American History for the key to America's future. We must educate ourselves in what this country was founded to be so that we know what we want it to become. Look into the eyes of these totalitarian[13] wannabees[14] and all together now shout, "NO!" to the arrogance of power. Keep the peace. Keep the faith. We shall overcome.

Dispatch Fifteen

What Comes Before a Fall?

That the slow-motion revolution non-partisan serial "bail-out" is more about government control and central-planning than about keeping the economy afloat becomes more apparent every day. When some of banks who were pressured[1] into accepting bailout funds by the Republican statists[2] saw the magnitude of control the central-planners at Treasury want to exert they saw the error of their ways. When they sought to return the money the Democrat statists refused to accept.[3] If it is all about maintaining financial institutions for the good of the economy what could be a better example of banks ready to stand on their own then ones seeking to repay tax-payers money? The government is showing their colors. They are more concerned with controlling the financial institutions and the economy than they are with saving them.

Capitalism and the individual freedom it requires is under assault by a pi-partisan clique of statists who are determined to ignore the advice of the former communist slaves from Russia and Eastern Europe who warn us we should not voluntarily place the links of collectivist chains upon the wrists of America.

Where are we right now in this process of selling our birthright for a bowl of bailouts? How far have we wandered from the path won by the sacrifices of the Revolution and mapped out by the Framers? Recently one of the main characters in the statist grab for power, Senator Chuck Schumer of New York, made some revealing statements. Senator Schumer is the senior Senator from the State of New York. Since 2006, he's been the Vice Chairman of the Senate Democratic Caucus making him the third-ranking Democrat in the Senate.

On the Rachel Maddow show Senator Schumer showed his utter disdain and disregard for the Republicans in Congress and for any Americans who believe in our country as we have known it when he said, "The world has changed. The old Reagan philosophy which served them well politically from 1980 to about 2004 and 2006 is over. But the hard right which still believes when the federal government moves, chop off its hands, still believes that, you know,"[4] here Schumer pauses to give a big patronizing smile and makes exaggerated Air Quotes as he continues, "traditional values kind of arguments and strong foreign policy, all that is over. So they have nothing other than to say no."[5] This may be a shock to Mr. Schumer but when the question is "Is it all right if we abandon traditional values and adopt a weak foreign policy?" The answer from millions of Americans is "NO!"

And how does Senator Schumer interpret the President's sincerity as he seeks to move his program through Congress? "I think President Obama has a pretty smart strategy. He is going to talk bipartisanship to the American people. But realizes until the Republican grassroots pushes their people over, if that ever happens, we are not going get change in the House or Senate. So the answer is 60 votes."[6&7] To these revolutionary collectivists seeking to change the traditional course of America the answer is to "talk bipartisanship" and work for enough votes to ram through anything without the need for any Republican support at all.

But until the statists manage to get a few more votes in the Senate the lunging left have another strategy as pointed out by Maddow, "Why not use the Budget Reconciliation[8] rules for more legislation even though that is not precedent?"[9]

The smiling Schumer agrees "I think that is the direction we are going to move in. I would support that. ... we are going to give Senator Baucus, Senator Conrad a chance to pass health care legislation with 60 votes. But it would be my view that if they can't do that by a certain time, August, we then move to reconciliation where we need 51 and it will be hard enough to pass national health care with 51 votes."[10] In other words if the rules of the Senate get in the way go around them and do whatever you have to do to ram this radical collectivist agenda through.

While the weakness the statists obviously perceive on the traditional side might seem depressing I believe this type of in-your-face public acknowledgment by Senator Schumer of their collectivist goals, his clear revelation of the calculated duplicity of the President, and the willingness to impose their will upon the nation by bending the rules of Congress betrays a sense of arrogance that's staggering to behold. So sure are they of their ability to fundamentally change America from a Republic of free citizens into a centrally-planned collectivist democracy dedicated to spreading the wealth around[11] they no longer feel the need to hide their agenda or their tactics behind their usual mask of politically-correct rhetoric.

Perhaps this is what comes before a fall?

Dispatch Sixteen

You Say You Want a Revolution

Our revolution changed the world. Our Declaration of Independence[1] proclaims self-evident truths. That all men are created equal, they are endowed by their Creator with unalienable rights, among these are life, liberty and the pursuit of happiness. These words shook a world held in the vise-grip of hereditary privilege inspiring people around the globe. Our Constitution established a representative republic with a limited government of the people, by the people and for the people.[2]

We have watched as our constitutionally limited government grew until today it's leviathan[3] running amok like Godzilla in Tokyo smashing things and scaring boy scouts. Today the Federal government is the largest employer[4] in America, states are the largest employers[5] in the states, and counties are among the largest employers[6] in the counties. Get the picture? Government's on a rampage and unless Mothra is going to fly in to save the day we'll have to deal with Frankenstein-on-the-Potomac ourselves.

Such brazen power-plays as the Executive branch issuing the Legislature an ultimatum,[7] either pass Cap-N-Trade[8] or we'll impose it administratively through command-and-control[9] make the dramatic changes in our political culture[10] shockingly apparent. Has our balance of powers[11] melted away under the glare of executive orders, signing statements, and now ultimatums? Some people say this is evolution. To others it's devolution. Our hard-won and dearly-paid-for Republic is devolving into a command-and-control all-encompassing central-state. With political dynasties bequeathing congressional seats like hereditary fiefdoms it's becoming hard to explain why we left the British Empire. Today we not only have taxation without representation[12] as congressional party-line voters ignore their constituents we also have representation without taxation[13] as the perpetually re-elected Lords and Ladies represent the illegal immigrants,[14] the professional welfare hammock-riders, and now Khalid Sheikh Mohammed[15] and his band of war-criminals.

These big government social planners may believe they have achieved their community organizing goals fulfilling Historian Will Durant's paraphrase of Lincoln's famous quote, "It may be true that you can't fool all the people all the time, but you can fool enough of them to rule a large country."[16] They may believe their revolutionary administration will fundamentally change

America, [17] however if they would step 20 miles outside the Beltway obviously there is a counter-revolution[18] brewing. The Tea Party[19] is overtaking the Republican Party in popularity.[20] It has already supplanted them at the grassroots of the conservative movement. By 2010 an avalanche of voters will throng the polling places demanding their country back.

Following the tactics of Saul Alinsky[21] brought the Obama[22] –Acorn [23]-SEIU[24] coalition control of the Democratic Party and the country, but following the Cloward/Piven Strategy[25] for overwhelming the system to impose an alternative system is going to lead to a complete repudiation of this radical departure from traditional American politics and economics. We aren't Venezuela.[26] Even after decades of legislative efforts to progressively create a permanent underclass of government dependents who'll follow the leader to the next looting of productive members of society, the majority in this country still want freedom and opportunity not cradle-to-grave mediocrity.

We can and should stage a counter-revolution against this growing tyranny. A peaceful, lawful revolution at the ballot box, and if you're talking about destruction, you can count me out. The last thing we need in this crowded theater full of combustible emotions is either a match or someone shouting fire. Any incident right now would trigger a massive response. Just as the executive is using the United

States Environmental protection Agency (EPA) to impose the onerous restrictions of a Cap-N-Trade style economy stunting strangulation regulation, he's also using United States Immigration and Customs Enforcement (ICE) to change the enforcement of immigration policy [27] without any messy debate. Ruling by decree is hardly compatible with constitutionally-limited government. We're told the administration has solutions. A solution to heal the greatest health care system in the world, a solution to save or create jobs while we lose jobs every month, a draconian solution for the man-made global warming hoax, a solution for endless wars for elusive peace. You say you have a solution. We'd all love to see the plan.

They say they want a contribution. Back in the good old change we could believe in days the dialogue of class warfare[28] repeated that no one making under 250,000, or was it 150,00[29] or was it ...anyway only the evil rich would have to pay a dime of new taxes. Watch out! You might find out you're rich[30] come next April 15th. Everyone has known, [31] since at least the days of that tax-cutting wild man JFK, [32] that cutting taxes increases revenue to the government and raising them lowers revenue. Since the government knows raising taxes lowers revenue and since they're raising taxes to increase revenue what are they really trying to do?

Complicated tax codes are used as a way to incentivize and de-incentivize behavior.[33] If you want more widgets give tax breaks for buying widgets. If you want less widgets tax widgets. Using that for a guide notice what's being pushed and what's being pulled? Taxes on producers and tax breaks for non-producers, what will you encourage and what will you discourage? Imagine tax cuts for people who don't pay taxes and tax increases for those who do. Taking the money of producers to bailout the greedy, reward the cronies, and support the lazy. It's time to tell the statists at the ballot box if they want money for things we hate they're going to have to wait.

Executive orders[34] and signing statements[35] have been used in Republican and Democrat administrations for years to change the constitution without changing the constitution. Now sweeping new powers by regulators threaten to make Congress irrelevant as an all powerful executive branch grows like a malignant tumor. Do not lose heart, do not despair, don't you know it's going to be all right? Keep the faith, keep the peace, organize, and win the day.

Dispatch Seventeen

Culture Kampf and the Kamikaze Congress

There is a culture war raging in America. It has wreaked havoc in our national psyche since the Summer of Love elevated the ersatz individualism and limousine liberalism of the Boomers from childhood fantasy to national fever-dream. This is a historically traceable event with vast implications for the future. He who controls the past shapes the present and creates the future. If history doesn't help us live in the here and now what good is it?

Instead of heeding history Congress reads the New York Times, the Washington Post, Time magazine, or some other reflecting pool of Liberal philosophy. Or they tune to the satirical news of John Stewart, Stephen Colbert, Keith Olbermann, or Rachel Maddow. Take Virginia's Senator Jim Webb as an example. He ran as a conservative Blue Dog Democrat. He only won because the Corporations once known as the Mainstream Media created a scandal based on a one time use of what his opponent said was a nonsense word from his childhood, "Macaca." Once in the Senate Mr. Webb avoided the Summer of Tea Party

Protests by traveling overseas instead of meeting with his constituents, which was probably a good idea since all he seems to do is talk right and vote left.

In a recent form letter sent in response to a personal note he states, "Together with 60 of my colleagues, I voted in favor of proceeding to debate the proposed health care reform legislation. I have yet to decide whether I will support final passage of the bill." After all his deciding he voted in lock-step with the party of power to pass the health care monstrosity the Obama-Reid-Pelosi triumvirate manages to bribe and bully to the floor of the Senate along with that anonymous group of 60 co-conspirators.

In the House, the Speaker rules with an iron hand like Nurse Ratched on steroids. She does whatever necessary to force her San Francisco version of reality down the throat of an unwilling nation. With all the integrity of Charles Rangel, the personal magnetism of Barney Frank, and the future of James Traficant the House Leadership whip their herd of lemmings towards the cliff and poof suddenly our two-day-a-week Congress works weekends passing bills no one reads.

The conventional wisdom of the chattering class tells us the Democrats have long been known to favor circular firing squads, and the electorate will pull the trigger in November 2010. Do not believe it. These Blue Dogs and Progressives have not been convinced to commit Hara-kiri for their emperor. There is something else going on here. As our self-serving representatives look to self-preservation I believe their leadership has finally begun to at least paraphrase a Founding Father, "We either hang together or we hang separately." Meaning if they bite the bullet and pass the entire liberal legislative agenda, health care takeover, cap-n-trade energy tax, endless amnesty/open borders import-a-voter immigration reform with a few omnibus/stimulus pork roasts thrown in to buy votes, ACORN will not need to steal they will experience a pre-defeat reincarnation as the perpetually re-elected.

Americans by the thousands who never heard of Saul Alinsky have now read his book *Rules for Radicals*. Suddenly the scales fall from our eyes and we see how a determined group of ultra-radicals organized their way to power. At last we have been roused from our media-induced trance and understand the radical plan to remake America before the next election. We were napping while the forces of Mordor searched for Sauron. We were watching the game while the hijackers were aiming their ACORN powered SEIU financed ship at the twin houses of Congress. We were concentrating on making a living and raising our families while the progressive paymasters, casino capitalists, and greed merchants turned Pleasantville into Pottersville. We have watched in amazement as we tighten our belts and Washington adds a few more notches.

Feverishly, we are trying to rearm after the Pearl Harbor of November 2008. The tide of battle is rushing over us like a torrent. Every day new regulations, more debt, and radical legislation are being spun over America like threads over Gulliver. The Tea Party Patriots and born-again community organizers of the right believe it is not too late to mount a D-Day at the ballot box on November 2010. The talking-heads tell us this is a Kamikaze Congress ready to go down in flames. Do not believe it. They know it is now or never. Impose their centrally-planned collectivist clap-trap over the Land of the Free before Americans get a chance to vote them out of the Home of the Brave.

I believe the Obama-Reid-Pelosi regime sells this Charge of the Blight Brigade to the backbenchers by assuring them their Acorn-Steal-the Vote and Immigration-import-a-Voter strategy will assure them of everlasting electoral life. They are saying, though it may be the Endless Great Recession for the rest of us, its Happy Days are Here Again for them. These Kamikazes plan to live to fly another day. But then again, no plan survives first contact with the enemy. Keep the faith. Keep the peace. We shall overcome!

Dispatch Eighteen

Too Many Rights on the Left

The United States was founded as a representative republic inspired by the soaring philosophy of the Enlightenment. As humanity clawed its way out of the depths of the Dark Ages thoughts of freedom found root and germinated in the minds of thousands. Rising from this rebirth or Renaissance came the realization that humanity inherently possess certain rights and that among these are the right to life, liberty, and property. These foundational rights are not conferred by government they are endowed by God. A godly government acknowledges them. An ungodly government claims to be the arbiter of rights. These fundamental rights are part of the original design and necessary for humanity to reach its full potential. Without them we are but a shadow of what we're meant to be. The leader-molded citizen of any earthly tyranny is restrained from success in ways alien to the free citizen of nature and of nature's God.

The fundamental qualities of these rights speak for themselves:

Who can possibly obtain the legitimate possession of the life of another? How would they obtain that possession? Over thousands of years of darkness many societies granted the right to own the lives of others. The dismal slave blocks and markets of shame, and the wasted lives and stunted relationships of both slaves and masters attest to the fraudulent nature of this barbarous custom. According to the Theory of Natural Rights, the life we hold we hold in trust. It has been endowed, and it is unalienable, which means even the legitimate possessor does not have the right to discard it or count it as a commodity to be sold or bartered away. This being true, how could any third party ever legitimately advance the idea that they can own the life of another? Life is sacred and without the right to life no other rights have any meaning.

Without liberty there is no ability to choose one's own course of action or to make real-time decisions pertaining to relationships. Without liberty individuals are but pawns in the game of others: grist in the mill of history. Without the freedom to choose, society is locked in a culture of command which restricts the free flow of ideas and materials thus throttling creativity and erecting artificial bottlenecks. In societies where bureaucrats try to replace the free choices of individuals there are always shortages, because no one can accurately predict how many widgets others want.

They can only decree how many should be made to fit what they believe will be the demand. In other words, person A can never really know the thoughts or desires of Person B. They can only estimate and guess, thus a command economy and a regimented society always have maladjustments of production and distribution. Without liberty life is stunted and prevented from reaching its full potential.

Without the full and free use of property life and liberty are held within a death grip which leads to a mere caricature of reality, shadows of people pretending to be motivated, marching to the leader's arbitrary drumbeat and saluting the flag. Or as the hopeless drones of the USSR used to say, "We pretend to work because they pretend to pay us." This necessity for the full and free use of property in order to make meaningful life and practical liberty possible is absolute. It can operate at 50% but then it is only 50% effective while at the same time being 50% defective. As the right to use the property we create or earn is taxed and regulated away so is meaningful life and practical liberty. If the state has abrogated to itself the power of God to decree what portion of life and liberty is applicable to that portion of humanity within its grasp, then it will gradually take more and more of the properties of its citizens until only serfs are left. Partial tyranny begets absolute tyranny just as sure as night follows day, for once the plundering begins its appetite is never abated until it has drunk the dregs.

These are the three fundamental and unalienable rights, life, liberty, and property. These are the rights recognized and enshrined by our founders. These are the rights meant to stand as the guardians and facilitators of American society. And for hundreds of years they have done so. The blight of slavery, which obviously ran counter to the ideals upon which this country was founded, was abolished; the rights proclaimed by our constitution were eventually guaranteed to all, and today all but the unenlightened seek to judge each by the content of their character and not by the color of their skin. These three rights provide the fertile soil that birthed the greatest nation ever to exist, the one nation all the world seeks to either immigrate to or to imitate.

However, today a glut of imagined rights advanced by demagogues to ply the emotions of hyphenated voting blocs threatens to smother the three which make everything else possible. The Progressives have actively attempted to push these bogus rights upon the nation since FDR in his fourth Inauguration speech proclaimed a Second Bill of Rights to include;

> The right to a useful and remunerative job in the industries or shops or farms or mines of the nation; the right to earn enough to

provide adequate food and clothing and recreation; the right of every farmer to raise and sell his products at a return which will give him and his family a decent living; the right of every businessman, large and small, to trade in an atmosphere of freedom from unfair competition and domination by monopolies at home or abroad; the right of every family to a decent home; the right to adequate medical care and the opportunity to achieve and enjoy good health; the right to adequate protection from the economic fears of old age, sickness, accident, and unemployment; the right to a good education.[1]

All of these sound good and it would be wonderful if everyone had them, but this is a classic case of putting the cart before the horse. These self-proclaimed rights are benefits which may flow from the exercise of our three unalienable rights, but they are not rights in and of themselves. If they are rights then government must violate the three real ones to provide the rest of the imagined ones. To provide the laundry list of progressive rights, the life, liberty, and property of all must be suppressed to generate the funds and the power to manufacture and allocate these benefits for those who have not earned them on their own.

Leave the bogus rights of the progressives to be allocated by tyrants to serfs who have no possibility of earning them for themselves because they have bartered their inheritance for a handful of promises. Instead give us the freedom and opportunity provided by our natural right to life, liberty, and property and America will be great again.

Dispatch Nineteen

Whose Responsibility is It?

Having spent time describing the three unalienable rights of life, liberty, and property upon which our Republic was founded and from which all others flow, it is necessary to speak of the natural responsibilities which form their inverse image. Peering through the looking glass at original intent we try to make sense of the present wonderland where rights and responsibilities are never what they seem.

There are five natural responsibilities. First, we are responsible for our actions. No one can make us do anything. Even when forced it is still us who must make our muscles move and make our voices speak. We are responsible for the validity of our word, and it should be our bond that we will do what we have said we will do when we have said we will do it. Second, people are responsible for their own sustenance. We should provide for ourselves not expecting others to meet our needs or supply us with the comforts we desire. Third, we are responsible for our children. It is the duty of every parent to provide for the physical, emotional, and spiritual support of our children until they are old enough to care for themselves. Fourth, we are responsible for the fulfillment of all contracts we have freely accepted.   And fifth, everyone has a responsibility to a social system which provides them freedom to use their own talents and energy for their own goals.

As stated earlier, these natural responsibilities are directly linked to the natural rights of humanity to life, liberty, and property. A person's right to life inherently carries a responsibility to provide for them self and for their family without making demands upon the goods or time of others. This responsibility to care for our family extends existentially in both directions. Just as it is incumbent upon all of us to care for our own children, each of us, initially claims the support of our parents, therefore it is equally incumbent upon us to care for our parents if they can no longer care for themselves. As we have the liberty to use our time and talents for our own improvement we are inherently responsible for how we use them and for any consequences that flow from their use.   And since legitimate government exists to protect our natural rights we are responsible for contributing to its ability to fulfill this function. This would include reasonable taxes and public service.

This is the extent of our natural responsibilities. Once we move beyond these we enter into the realm of moral or religious responsibilities.   While natural responsibilities, like natural rights, are objectively arrived at by the nature of humanity moral or religious responsibilities are by their nature subjectively learned. Consequently the fulfillment of natural responsibilities flow logically from life, while in most cases, unless moral or religious obligations are personally perceived and agreed upon, they must be fulfilled through the application of law and its ability to compel compliance.

As these secondary type responsibilities are most properly the purview of a moral code or religion and as each moral code or religion may carry different obligations it is presumptuous of government to impose upon its citizens what should instead be a free choice. For, the imposition of one moral code or religion could possibly transgress or ignore the moral obligations of another and the sanction of one moral code or religion over another inherently restricts the citizen's enjoyment of their unalienable rights.

Today our ever-expanding government invents new responsibilities and then force feeds them to a powerless public. These include responsibilities to the nation and the world. On a daily basis we hear of our responsibility to the poor, the uneducated, or the uninsured. And these new responsibilities do not just extend to our fellow Americans. Through the continuous imposition of these constantly proliferating rights internationalists seek to transfer the wealth of the United States to the third world as their open borders policy invites the third world to come here to claim it. Using our tax money the government seeks to care for everyone's needs from cradle to grave. The inefficiencies of bureaucracy ensure that a large percentage of these resources get flushed down the sewer while we fall deeper into debt.

These newly invented responsibilities are not natural, and our government must violate the natural rights of its citizens to fulfill them. They do this by expropriating our property and the enjoyment of the fruits of our labor which diminishes our lives from all they could be to what they allow them to be. In addition, the only way the government can expropriate these things and distribute them from who earned them to who they believe deserves them is to increase their power by diminishing ours.

If not from nature where do these government enforced responsibilities originate? They spring from ideology and the quest for power. By preying upon the gullibility of the uninformed, the culpability of the greedy, and the lethargy of the uncaring the Progressive clique has gained control of the American experiment. It has used the ideology and terminology of extreme socialism, "From each according to their ability to each according to their need" to construct a conveyor belt transferring wealth from producers to consumers. The Progressives buy votes and continued support by dividing the swag from their plunder of

American capitalism. Even though the government's propaganda arms drone constantly about these enforced responsibilities, still the majority of Americans instinctively know the difference between natural responsibilities and government mandated ones. If we don't demand a stop to this proliferation of imagined responsibilities and the expropriation of resources needed to fulfill them we will lose our natural rights and the ability to fulfill the natural responsibilities which flow from them.

Dispatch Twenty

Snatching Defeat from the Jaws of Victory Again

Never since the mid-1970s when the Water Gate Congress insisted on abandoning our South Vietnamese allies after the war had been won[1] have I seen defeat snatched from the jaws of victory in such a bold and decisive manner.

As I survey the scene in America today I am beginning to wonder if we would be in any worse shape if we had lost the Cold War. From sea to shining sea Americans watch as the once greatest industrial nation on earth board up our factories and ship our manufacturing capacity to other countries. It seems like every other day the last investigative journalist in America, Glenn Beck, exposes one more Marxist in President Obama's inner circle. That big lovable fuzz-ball Rush Limbaugh is judged a racist based on manufactured quotes and lies repeated by the President's trained peacock and the rest of the establishment media while America watches these non-substantiated accusations of racism and other forms of political correctness used to squash any criticism of Barak H*@%$*n Obama. Freedom of speech dissolves as we learn it is racial profiling for some to mention the man's middle name while at the same time school children are taught to memorize songs using his middle name extolling his Nobel sized accomplishments mmm mmm mmm.[2&3]

Like Iran we are nearing critical mass. With uninformed voters not knowing who they are voting for and uninformed politicians not knowing what they are voting for does anyone wonder why America's in trouble? It was bad when our elected representatives voted for bills they have not read, now under the inspired leadership of Nancy Pelosi and Harry Reid they are voting for bills they have not written yet. In their infinite wisdom they have figured out how to score a bill evaluating its impact on our budget before the official language meets the paper. Now that is economy of effort.

At least according to the corporations once known as the Mainstream Media the Great Recession is finally over. And at least according to Never-had-a-real-job-in-his life Joe Biden the stimulus is working better than expected. After diligent searching I have finally located those shovel-ready jobs the perpetually re-elected dangled in front of our eyes so we would not pass-out when they coughed up 787 billion of our dollars so that unemployment would not get over 8%. After driving past two miles of orange cones and seeing nothing but perfectly good road and a few guys using shovels as partners to dance the Chitown Hustle, I came upon one of those $2000 "Putting America to Work" signs that informed me the whole thing was a snow job, and the only shovel-ready thing about it was the politicians ready to shovel the billions to their pet interest groups to buy votes.

People who once had good paying jobs are selling lotto tickets at the Quicki-Mart to people who still believe that is their only hope for change. By the time the dust settles how many of us will be standing in front of our boarded-up economy asking, "Brother Can You Spare Some Change?" The President says he is looking at any way possible to create jobs. How about setting America free and getting out of the way? Does anyone doubt that if the Federal Government declared an income tax holiday and let everyone keep their gross for a year they would not spend it? Does anyone doubt if corporate taxes were cut and capital gains lowered people would not invest in expansion? Does anyone doubt that if we were allowed to choose any insurance company we wanted and there was real tort reform medical insurance rates would not go down?

This is not rocket science. It is political science and economics. Two arcane pseudo-sciences that just about anyone who takes the time to read can understand. Free people in a free economy will outperform any collectivist regime ever devised no matter how many songs praising the Dear Leader the school children learn to sing. Remember the Cold War?

The Communists with their bureaucratically strangled centrally-planned command economy said they would bury us while their workers joked, "They pretend to pay us so we pretend to work." Instead our capitalistic system of individual freedom and personal opportunity buried them. We won the war and declared a peace-dividend we wasted playing policeman of the world nation-building for people who hate us.

Today, with our economy on the ropes mired in wars we refuse to win, with our industry exported or government-owned people ask "Who won what?" The Soviets also said our own grandchildren would raise the red flag from the White House. They may not have raised a flag, but the place is now filled with Marxist advisors[4] and a media-made messiah president who listens to them. Who won Communism or Capitalism? In America today that may be a difference without a distinction: a place where honesty forces us to say if there's no difference there's no difference.

Dispatch Twenty-one

How We Got From Where We Were to Where We Are

The Virginia Assembly, ignoring the destruction of the State in 1865, the interruption of sovereignty during Reconstruction, and its reincarnation in 1870 as an equally diminished state within the post-Civil War re-constituted Washington-centered United States, claims to be the oldest continuously operating legislative body in the Western Hemisphere. While that may be true it would be a mistake to believe Americans invented the republican form of government.

Our Founders stood upon the shoulders of generations of unknown heroes who battled for years against tyranny slowly turning England away from absolutism towards a constitutional monarchy. When our ancestors came to America they set up representative assemblies to deliberate, vote, and to make as many decisions as possible dealing with local affairs. Such things as the Mayflower Compact[1] and the Fundamental Orders of Connecticut[2] set the stage upon which the Founders wrote the Constitution instituting a limited, representative republic based upon democratic suffrage and dedicated to securing the natural rights of man: life, liberty, and the pursuit of happiness.

This was the American tradition. And this was what the progressive proponents of social democracy had to overcome if they were to navigate America from where we were to where we are. For generations schools have taught us America is a democracy. While democratic principles have always been part of the American tradition it was never meant to be the whole of it. The electoral franchise has institutionalized popular choice as a fundamental building block in the foundation of our country. However, this single block does not change the design or form of the structure. A representative republic does not become a direct democracy merely because voting is involved in the selection of representatives even when the franchise has been expanded from its original proscribed form to its current all-inclusive one.

As it is presented and used today democracy is more an ideology than a process. Using positions of power in education and the media, Progressives spread the impression that becoming a direct democracy has always been America's goal. From the beginning of their movement in the 1890s the Progressives have championed evolutionary innovations and changes in the American system. These changes are always presented as vehicles designed to make government more responsive to the will of the people as expressed in elections. Initially outsiders, the Progressives railed against the entrenched Classical Liberals clinging tenaciously to the governmental structure received through the Constitution from the Founders. While on the outside railing against the power of government, the Progressives triumphantly inserted the initiative, referendum, and recall into the American system. Since first attaining the presidency under Teddy Roosevelt they have turned their efforts to using the power of government to evolve the structure from the top down by expanding government and imposing collectivist goals through law and regulation.

The major thrust of these reforms has been to re-enforce the belief that the equal opportunity to vote will bring forth the truest form of American Government where social entitlements fund the equality of outcome they call a level playing field. One progressive innovation moving America away from a federal system to a centralized government was the adoption of the seventeenth amendment taking the election of senators from the legislatures of the states and giving it to the voters. The House of Representatives was designed to speak for the people, the Senate to represent the States maintaining the dual levels, which made us a federal government.

When the form as well as the function of government is held in the hand of the people the goal of all government action soon becomes the voting of ever expanding benefits from the treasury. Especially when the sixteenth amendment changed the Constitution so that individual, progressive taxes made it possible to tax some for the benefit of others. Combined with gerrymandered districts enshrining a repeatedly re-elected hierarchy a populace convinced the ability to vote equals freedom and here we are.

The Framers of the Constitution worried about Mobocracy: masses of uninformed people overwhelming those who by diligence and hard work made themselves stakeholders in society. Or as age-old wisdom tells us,

> A democracy cannot exist as a permanent form of government. It can only exist until the voters discover that they can vote themselves largesse from the public treasury. From that moment on, the majority always votes for the candidates promising the most benefits the public treasury with the result that a democracy always collapses over lousy fiscal policy, always followed by a dictatorship. The average of the world's great civilizations before they decline has been 200 years. These nations have progressed in this sequence: From bondage to spiritual faith; from faith to great courage; from courage to liberty; from liberty to abundance; from abundance to selfishness; from selfishness to Complacency;

from complacency to apathy; from apathy to dependency; from dependency back again to bondage. [1]

Now Nancy Pelosi's San Francisco wants to allow illegal immigrants to vote. Moving from motor voter[2] to if you have a pulse you can vote. Convicted felons? Sure let them vote too. While we're at it ACORN-by-Any-Other-Name counting the census and the vote and presto change-o the fears of the Framers have come home to roost in a People's Democratic Republic. Education featuring the false teaching that direct democracy has always been the goal of the American experiment helped get us here, and its self-education and knowledge applied to action that will get us back to where we came from: a representative federal republic. Keep the faith, keep the peace, we shall overcome.

Dispatch Twenty-two

The Hand Writing is on the Wall

In a Bible passage so powerful even those who do not believe the Bible unknowingly quote it, an arrogant young ruler is so enamored with his exalted position he thinks he can disregard the traditions of his predecessors with impunity. In the midst of a celebration of his greatness, the proud young man calls for the sacred vessels captured when his father conquered Judah so that he can drink toasts to himself. Suddenly before a stunned king and his smug courtiers a hand appears in mid-air writing on the wall of his palatial palace. Never having seen a teleprompter the king had no idea these words would come to define his reign. He called for the wisest man in his kingdom to tell him what they meant.

When Daniel arrived he told the haughty king, "The writing reads: 'Mene, Mene, Tekel and Parsin.' The meaning of the words is this: Mene: God has measured your sovereignty and put an end to it; Tekel: you have been weighed in the balance and found wanting; Parsin: your kingdom has been divided and given to the Medes and the Persians."[1] That same night through an unperceived chink left by neglect in their previously impregnable defenses Babylon was conquered, the king was overthrown, and the rest is history.

If History does not help us in the world today it is useless. We might as well study tea leaves if we cannot learn from the past, to live in the present, and shape the future. There are numerous old sayings which attempt to pass this wisdom along to the oblivious young who always act as if youth was a new invention or something clever they have personally devised instead of a fleeting possession most of us squander. These sayings include; "Those who fail to learn from History are doomed to repeat it."[2] "The past may not repeat itself, but it sure does rhyme."[3] Or, my personal favorite, "It's like déjà vu all over again."[4] However you say it, if we fail to do it we have sown the wind and will reap the whirlwind.

History tells us that on New Year's Eve 1991 the Soviet Union ceased to exist. A Cold War which had often blazed hot ended in the unequivocal demise of one super-power and the undeniable triumph of the other. What lesson did we learn? What truth did we walk away with that would allow us to avoid the dust-bin of history which had devoured them?

Before the dust had a chance to settle the joy of victory over the agony of defeat was turned to political maneuvering, military mission creep, and economic chicanery. The same people who wanted us to unilaterally disarm during the darkest days of the fifty year confrontation, since it was obviously our belligerency causing the Soviet dictators to follow their oft announced plan to bury us, wanted to cash in the peace dividend the people who had ignored their previous advice had earned. After George the First shot himself in the foot by going back on his no new taxes pledge the man from Hope was only too eager to comply since he had been one of the people marching in the streets and leading the charge to disarm in the face of aggression. Cutting defense and expanding government, the Clinton administration partied its way across the stage of history leaving us weaker then they found us. George the Second rallied the world to punish the terrorists who assaulted us on 9-11. Then instead of declaring victory and coming home he opened a second front, and frittered away the admiration and allegiance of the world and our truncated military capacity in a pre-emptive war he knew how to win but did not know how to conclude. Now ignoring the fact that it was in large part a humiliating defeat in Afghanistan that set the stage for the collapse of the Soviet Union, our current commander believes we can win a war by dispatching more troops with a pre-announced date of departure.

Recalling the "Those who fail to learn from History are doomed to repeat it" truism here is a history lesson. Great Britain led the world into the Industrial Revolution becoming the number one manufacturer on earth by 1780. This led to over a century of British ascendancy. The United States over took Britain and became the number one manufacturer on earth after Europe committed suicide on the Fields of Flanders and assumed the acknowledged lead of Western Civilization after Europe administered the coup de grace in World War Two. If current trends continue, China will become the number one manufacturer on earth by 2011 while at the same time America is seeking a-cure-through-bleeding itself in two hot wars with no end in sight, open borders, and one-way free trade. Is there something we should learn here? Is there some remedy we could apply?

We must stop the hemorrhaging. We must stop the invasion. We must insist on fair trade. We must rebuild our industrial base. If we don't, one day we'll wake up to hear a mighty voice, saying, "Fallen, fallen, Babylon the great is fallen!"

Dispatch Twenty-three

The Bottleneck is Always at the Top

Why does bureaucracy cover the world? Because bureaucracy is the most efficient form of organization ever devised. Max Weber first pointed out the defining traits of a bureaucracy calling it the ideal type of organization because it's rational, efficient, and practical. Before his definition this form of organization was called common sense.

As with most things in life the foundational elements of bureaucracy, the things which make it good, can also make it bad. Division of labor, which allows the best adapted to concentrate on appropriate tasks producing efficiency, also produces people who can only do one thing. Layers of authority make it clear who is in command also deprives those below a role in decisions and facilitates the concealment of mistakes. Written rules and regulations which allow everyone to know what's expected also stifles individual initiative and imagination. Impersonality which reduces personal bias also makes people feel like faceless numbers and fosters feelings of alienation. Employment based on technical qualifications discourages favoritism and also discourages ambition. Maintenance of position as the primary occupation of office holder, which produces continuity also breeds stagnation. Promotion based on seniority institutionalizes stability, but it also brings those who can survive in the system to the top instead of innovators. All of which equals, the bottleneck is always at the top.

Spreading across the landscape inserting tentacles into everything from who does what to who gets what, the Leviathan of national government has grown far beyond anything our founders would or could have envisioned. Americans stand before the drones making up the business end of the federal bureaucracy hat in hand waiting for service. We are in the midst of a transaction wherein we're expected to trade in our freedom for cradle-to-grave security and individual liberty for bureaucratic regimentation. The problem is that when our Progressive collectivist leaders herded us toward giving them total control of our lives the American people have risen up in Tea Parties, Town Halls, and State governments declaring, "*We the People* will not go quietly into that dark night!"

The more the President flexes his media-enhanced, teleprompter-controlled, highly-reverberated communication skills the more people do not want what he's selling. Using procedure and manipulation the same 50+ 1 strategy candidate

Obama said[1] should not be used to pass health care was used to pass health care while the rest of the agenda stands waiting in the wings. With an overwhelming majority in Congress and enough votes to make the Progressive's evolution/revolution happen, watch as the total transformation of America metastasizes before the people get a chance to speak in November.

What a travesty! First the best Congress money can buy passes bills without reading them. Now we are bluntly told we do not get to know what is in them until they pass them. It is hard to imagine such arrogance. After taking control of GM, Chrysler, and the largest insurance company, the Progressives reformed America's medical system into who knows what and are now moving on to the financial sector. What will they bail-out (take over) next? The unions? The fossil press? This is no spur of the moment off the cuff solution to immediate problems. This is not just a case of one Imperial President passing collectivist legislation against the wishes of the electorate. Thousand page laws are not written overnight. This is the culmination of a long march by the Progressives. They've pretended to be one thing or another: liberals, unions, advocacy groups, or whatever it took to slip past the voters. And let us face it, they have been much more dedicated and disciplined than those who want a nation based on free enterprise and individualism.

From Teddy Roosevelt to Barak Obama we have had one Trojan horse after another: one more Federal mandate, one more dependency creating entitlement, and each one a step closer to total government control. Luckily the American spirit of individualism and tradition of liberty has not been completely cowed by 100 years of the Progressive's evolution/revolution. Not only are the Tea Party and the Town Hall Patriots continuing to stand up for liberty, many states are lining up to resist these naked power grabs. Congress refuses to have open debates on the implementation of legislation designed to fundamentally transform America. The Pelosi-Reid Congress following their leader have instituted what in effect is a one-party government seeking no input from the minority party and ignoring the outcry of citizens. They have bludgeoned their collectivist bills through to the President's desk, but to their surprise when he signed those bills he signed the marching orders for a legion of awakened voters. Voters who will troop to the polls and who will work to guide the way home to the America we have known and loved. The night may be dark, the way may be long, but if we keep the faith and keep the peace we shall overcome.

Dispatch Twenty-four

Return of the Swamp Thing

When the San Francisco über liberal Nancy Pelosi became the Speaker of the House she said she was going to drain the swamp of political corruption they claimed were created by twelve years of Republican control of Congress. Instead of draining anything Speaker Pelosi and her ham-fisted cohorts have brought slime time to prime time as they wallow in what they came to drain.

Representative Charles Rangel who has been in charge of writing tax policies for the Democratic Congress could not seem to pay his own taxes or even report millions of dollars of income. This of course is everyone else's fault. He has been forced to resign as chairman of the powerful Ways and Means Committee. Then there is the curious case of the Democrat Representative from New York who eagerly resigned rather than face an ethics investigation and then imploded on national television. Now the question turns to what did the Speaker know and when did she know it. Allegations have surfaced that her office was informed last year about Congressman Massa's tickle parties and Greco-Roman wrestling matches with male staffers but did not inform the ethics committee.

And the rot goes all the way to the top. Rep. Darrell Issa (R-CA), the top Republican on the House Oversight and Government Reform Committee charges the Obama administration may have broken the law by offering Rep. Joe Sestak (D-PA) a job if he wouldn't challenge Sen. Arlen Specter (D-PA) in a primary. Rep. Sestak admits the administration offered him a high-ranking government job if he would stay out of the race. Rep. Sestak made the accusation twice on national television. Democrats seem determined to prove Lord Acton's famous quote, "All power tends to corrupt; absolute power corrupts absolutely."[1]

Where will this cavalcade of corruption lead? Detroit is a picture of America's future. After decades of control by Progressive Democrats, what was once one of the greatest manufacturing cities in the world has degenerated to the point where banks are paying people to take abandoned houses, and the best idea they have is to downsize the city by converting empty lots into farmland. With a 75% dropout rate in their schools, and yes, Virginia, blatant corruption and low morals in high places, a collapsing economy and massive social dislocation, Detroit is a vision for the shabby world Progressivism creates.

When Detroiters lined up to collect what they called Obama Money they could not tell interviewers where the money they were waiting to receive came from all they knew was it was free, and someone was handing it out. This is where Nancy and her ethically challenged followers are leading America, a world where some people are bilked so others can receive freebees that never raise them out of poverty but instead encase them in it.

Is this shabby future inevitable? Is there any chance of avoiding the toxic embrace of this corrupt Swamp Creature? One more free election, one without the heavily Democrat illegal immigrant and convicted felon population voting and without His Honor Mayor Daley and ACORN counting the votes, and we will see America hand the Pelosi-Reid super majority their hat and show them the door. That will be the greatest victory for America since Saratoga and Yorktown. But what about the dreaded ever-living spawn of the Swamp Thing?

The damage that can be done before we show this crowd of Progressives to the back benches may hang on like a summer cold. The list of what will be imposed upon the American people during the progressive one-party rule will include:

Health Care Reform with thousands of pages of governmentese double-speak has the potential to become the pile of paper that devoured a nation. No entitlement once established has ever been repealed, and since we are not allowed to know what is in it until it passes who knows what anti-freedom anti-liberty provisions it will foist on us. Then it turns out that after it is passed even they do not know what is in it.

Cap-N-Tax cobbled together with various bits of legislation, executive orders, and bureaucratic regulation may lurch off the table and start pushing us towards seven dollar a gallon gas and the dislocations this would bring all in the name of discredited Al and his band of unethical cheating scientists. Millions of acres of potentially rich energy producing land may be seized and forever locked in the Fed's clinging claw while NASA is slated to become the eye-in-the-sky for the man-made Global Warming fanatics.

There are the President's on-going international apology tours and his We Are the World/Workers of the World Unite silliness that are daily depreciating the American brand.

And of course, the hockey stick curve that represents our national debt will weigh down generations of Americans.

The damage the Obama-Pelosi-Reid triumvirate causes before we drain their swamp will hang like a mill stone around the neck of our nation. It will take more than a stake of holly or a silver bullet to bring these Progressive policies down. It will take a populace educated in the founding documents of our Republic. A people determined to re-establish the last best hope of mankind. A people dedicated to resuscitating a nation, conceived in liberty, and dedicated to the proposition that all men are created equal. It will take citizens resolved that this nation under God shall have a new birth of freedom, and that government of the people, by the people, for the people shall not perish from the earth.

Dispatch Twenty-five

How True is the Truth?

Everyone wants to go to heaven, but nobody wants to die. In a similar fashion everyone wants smaller budgets and lower taxes, but nobody wants their services cut. Like all truisms these sound right, but are they?

Consider the various non-believers and believers along the trajectory of faith.

First think of the non-believers. Agnostics are not sure whether there is a God or not consequently they say there is no heaven and pray there is no hell so they have a vested interest in remaining above room temperature. Atheists are sure there is not any God and sure there is not any heaven so they want to hang on as long as they can since the alternative is not there.

Those positions make sense in that these two types of unbelievers don't know or believe there is anything beyond here so they want to stay here.

But what explains the hesitation of believers to leave the here and now for what comes after? They know there is a God and know there is a heaven, so why don't they want to die?

Some believers believe there is a God and believe there is a heaven but are not sure if they will make it in, so it makes sense they want to hang around at least long enough to earn enough points to get to where they want to go instead of any alternatives they may also believe in. The real puzzler is the believers who believe in God and believe in heaven and who also believe they know they are going to heaven. I know many people who fit into this category and without an exception none of them appear to want to die. Now if heaven is a better place and dying is the entrance fee wouldn't it make sense to want to die?

One of the principle leaders of the we know there's a God, know there's a heaven, and know we're going to heaven party once said if it was up to him he'd just as soon go to a better place, but since it would benefit others if he kept on keeping on he'd forgo the pleasure dying would bring and continue to live. Now a selfless choice to keep on living makes sense in that situation and I want to imagine that is what everyone fitting into this category is doing ,but I also imagine I should see a whole lot more "Benefiting of others" going on. So actually the saying should be, "Some people believe in heaven but for one reason or another nobody wants to die." That does not have the impact of the original does it?

Turning to the second truism, "Everyone wants smaller budgets and lower taxes, but nobody wants their services cut." Not everyone wants a smaller budget. Most people who work for government want bigger budgets if not across the board at least across their board. Most people who receive benefits want budgets raised if not for everyone at least for them. Most elected officials want bigger budgets (period). And among those who do want budgets cut it usually comes down to, "Take theirs don't touch mine."

If an environmentalist wants a smaller budget they want subsidies cut from big oil, but support subsidies to big ethanol. If supporters of military intervention want a smaller budget they may support cutting off the tree-huggers at the knees, but they want that latest weapons systems. Then there are those who want to increase the budget dropping pearls of wisdom like, "We've got to spend our way out of this recession."[1]

What about taxes? Doesn't everyone want taxes lowered? No! Taxation without representation may have worked to stir this country to rebellion but today there are many people who vote yet want taxes raised higher and higher. How can this be? In America today we have certain groups of people who are essentially exempt from taxes and recipients of direct benefits, and others who pay taxes and do not receive much from the government except next year's quarterly tax vouchers. The progressive tax system has achieved its goal: from each according to their ability to each according to their need.

Since people from the boomer-living-life-large-petal-to-the-metal generation are in charge budgets equate to, "If one is good ten is better." So if the milk cow rich finance our lifestyle now how about a bigger pay day? Let's milk them twice, three times, how about four times as much. Problem is we want more cheese than we have milk. As the national Visa bill grows and our foreign bankers want more interest the income level it takes to be considered one of the milk cow rich keeps getting lower. The long coddled poor still do not realize that the amount they receive in their monthly dole will eventually paint a target on their wallet to help the still poorer in our globalized village. The morbidly obese welfare recipient with three color TVs and two cars is one of the wealthiest people on earth, and this redistributionist plunder empire can only continue to survive with fresh victims to plunder. Have we changed our national motto to "Stand and deliver" yet?

How true is the truth? The definition of a truism is an undoubted or self-evident truth. We see from the short examination above, truisms often falter when they collide with scrutiny. What about these truisms, "We hold these truths to be self-evident, that all men are created equal, that they are endowed by their Creator with certain unalienable rights that among these are Life, Liberty, and the pursuit of Happiness." They acknowledge a creator and speak of life. They acknowledge liberty and a right to pursue happiness. Milk cows do not pursue happiness they only exist to give milk and they only live as long as they do. And that is the truth.

Dispatch Twenty-six

Red Emperors Exploit Red Ink

Where does our federal government get the right to put the chains of hopeless debt on our grandchildren to buy a better hammock for those who will not work? The 10th Amendment says, "The powers not delegated to the United States by the Constitution, nor prohibited by it to the States, are reserved to the States respectively, or to the people." If we never delegated the power to create a National Debt how did the government get it? The power to encumber is the power to destroy. This habit of charging the Visa to the MasterCard is selling us out to the rising red star in the East, and if we do not pull the brake we are heading for a cliff.

East is East and West is West and never the twain shall meet passed for wisdom in the days when information took more than a nanosecond passing between continents. Today they not only meet they compete, and the Red Emperors of the East exploit the red ink of the West. Today our Progressive leaders embrace the suffocating sameness of socialist conformity and collectivist confiscation while communist mandarins release the long pent up energies of their people.

Living behind the veil of a high-tech Forbidden City unseen by the outside world, Red Emperors abandoned the unattainable ideal of equality of outcome for the more economically successful model of indigenous industries and monetary policies designed to ensure a favorable balance of trade. Alexander Hamilton once recommended these policies and the early United States followed them. The unseen hand of Chinese leaders transforms Mao's Stalinist nightmare into the poster child for an economic miracle.

Transforming a cult of personality into an oligarchy, holding local elections monitored by the Carter Center and judged by them to be open and competitive, top leadership faces intraparty elections and peacefully transfers power from one leader to the next. They have jettisoned Communist economic policies, which inevitably lead to ruin, transforming themselves into a corporate-style authoritarianism resembling the Five Families of New York, or the Outfit and Machine of Chicago. An efficient arrangement that provides ample benefits for those who shut-up and go along to get along and ruthless whacks for any mole silly enough to poke its head up.

The tale of two civilizations: America slides into the decay of collectivism with oppressive regulations and confiscatory taxes discouraging the innovation and enterprise which made us great. China turns away from these tools of re-distribution and embraces capitalism without naming it. Today, business opportunities found in the shadow of Tiananmen Square are discouraged and penalized in the shadow of the Liberty Bell.

Today, Union Bosses no longer break your legs if you oppose them; instead they sell your stock short. Likewise the leaders of the People's Liberation Army openly urge that China dump American bonds to influence American policies: a naked example of Chinese power and American weakness. China knows they cannot face America militarily. However, due to crippling collectivist policies, the American economy is on life support propped up through massive borrowing from China making us vulnerable to extortion. In addition to the $798.9 billion in U.S. Treasuries[1] China holds it has also accumulated $2.4 trillion in foreign cash reserves that are mainly held in American dollars [2]. How are they using this economic arsenal? China buys American natural resources, [3] major stakes in American Icon companies, [4] and control of vital natural resources[5] around the world.

As the economies and social systems of Western Europe stumble and America lurches in the same direction, what type of system will rise from the abyss? Will dazed survivors of the coming crash shuffle off into a shabby future replicating the collectivist mistakes that drove us off the cliff adding totalitarian terror tactics to the mix, or will the re-booted West re-embrace the inspirational thinking of the Enlightenment? Though it's the excesses of casino capitalism protected and bailed-out by cronies in government inflating the bubbles of our drowning civilization, economic freedom and republican principles are blamed for the crime. The true engine of our decline is the collectivism of the Progressives slipping in one entitlement and one tax at a time regulating opportunity and predetermining outcomes. This undermined the economic and social forces of Western exceptionalism. As bewildered citizens become aware of what has happened to their countries they will gravitate to whoever promises the best example of success. It is an inescapable conclusion that China is well situated to provide that example.

    The Chinese master of war, Sun Tzu said, "To fight and conquer in all your battles is not supreme excellence; supreme excellence consists in breaking the enemy's resistance without fighting."[6] The debtor is slave to the lender, and he who pays the piper calls the tune. Whether it comes from the East or the West, wisdom tells us spending yourself into oblivion is not such a good deal when it comes time to pay the bill, and payday's coming someday.

Dispatch Twenty-seven

Polite Conversation

People avoid silence because they are afraid of what they might hear. Although we value our freedom of speech, polite conversation in America is subject to one crushing rule, "Don't talk about religion or politics!" Most of us were raised with this stifling warning in our ears. The purpose was to avoid arguments at the dinner table but the result is a population illiterate in the two subjects affecting life the most. I can only talk about the weather for so long, which displays the wisdom of memorizing sports stats and watching American Idol. With the two biggest topics off the table we are faced with either trivial pursuit or silence. Bored with the weather and having neglected my memorization and viewing options I propose a topic to stimulate vigorous conversation without causing any bickering: economics.

Barry, Harry, and Nancy know they have to take us through-the-looking-glass. With the reaction of voters staring them in the face Congress is moving so fast today their yesterday will be our tomorrow. With the addition of the funnyman from Minnesota, the ruling party can ram their agenda through without one opposition vote. Every revolution needs an emergency to justify radical surgery, and the economy is the emergency available. Consequently, these descendants of FDR and LBJ are about to shove a raw deal down the throat of a great society.

Almost everyone is in agreement that the first stimulus has failed. According to MSNBC, "In January of 2009, Obama's economic team predicted unemployment would rise no higher than 8 % with the help of $787 billion in new government spending."[1] However, according to the LA Times the unemployment rate in May reached a 25-year high of 9.4 %.[2] The Commander-in-Chief may see glimmers of hope, but Say-it Ain't-So Joe Biden says he cannot rule out a second stimulus telling us now the administration which ran on the slogan, "The worst economy since the Great Depression"[3] misread how bad the economy was. How bad is it? What's worse than the Great Depression? What is their answer to this baddest of the bad economies? What is their Plan B? Try Plan A again? I think what our leaders need as they drive the largest economy the world has ever known over the cliff is Economics 101.

Most people, including the best-Congress-money-can-buy, look at the economy as if it were controlled by magic having no idea where the rabbit goes or where the doves come from, and since I doubt I will convince any of our all-knowing leaders to enroll in freshman macroeconomics I want to offer a crash course in Economic Reality.

1. Government regulations distort markets and inflate bubbles.
2. Every generation experiences at least one bubble and at least one bust.
3. Every bubble bursts.
4. Every burst bubble is followed by a panic.
5. Panics inspire economic regulations.
6. Economic regulations reflect political ideologies not economic realities.
7. Economic regulations always regulate the excesses of the last bubble.
8. Economic regulations are always blind to the excesses of the next bubble.
9. Since consumption is the purpose for production, any economic regulation that ignores this fact always leads to the misapplication of resources and the misdirection of effort.
10. Depressions are recessions with government help.
11. It is impossible to spend yourself into prosperity.

12. It is impossible to tax yourself into prosperity.

13. Higher taxes lead to smaller revenue and black-markets.

The New Economy leads straight to the Second World, from freedom to conformity from capitalism to Obamanomics. Instead of a fair race with the rapidly transforming economies of Asia, America runs hobbled like a child in a three - legged race strapped to the stiff-legged ideas of collectivism.

Why would our leaders want us economically hobbled? What would they gain if we fall into the swamp of poverty engulfing most of the world? Wouldn't they be right there with us? Go to any Second or Third World country and you will see the rich and powerful behind walls in gated-communities where they live in the First World while everyone else sits in the dirt eating leaves. In America, we avoided this fate with the growth of a massive middleclass. Under assault with stagnant wages, rising prices, and disappearing jobs the middleclass is being outsourced. How is this being accomplished?

Remember the mantra of the Clintons? "It's the economy stupid!" That is still[4] the Liberal's strategy, riding like a flea on a rat, cradle-to-grave social engineering in the guise of economic policy. It is the divisiveness of class-warfare encouraged by the only people who win through America's split between red and blue, rich and poor, us and them. Who are they? If it isn't us I guess it's them.

Dispatch Twenty-eight

Chicago on the Potomac

Back in the Dream Time, elders were honored because of their accumulated knowledge, and if Pops knew a better way to saddle horses that knowledge helped Junior, since he saddled horses. Today if Pops knows how to tune-up cars what good is that when cars do not need to be tuned-up anymore? Now the old are relegated to exposing their own irrelevance while exclaiming, "I've never seen that before." Doddering ancients who use their cell phones merely to talk wonder why their grandchildren never answer their emails as Generation Z tweet each other: "Don't trust anyone over 15." The world is moving so fast not only is today tomorrow's yesterday the generations are living in different today's today. Generation X and Y parents with their once hip lap-tops under their arms stare in wonder as their pre-teen Generation Zs text with one hand while Wii skydiving in the backseat. For these new additions to middle-age who're just old enough to remember Star Trek imagine Captain Kirk visiting Captain Picard pointing at Commander Data and saying, "What's that?"

After years of being treated as if the Wisdom of the Ages were as relevant as Confucius in a fortune cookie, now that we have Chicago on the Potomac, the wisdom gained in the City that Works is suddenly spot-on. Of course George the Second's doctrine of pre-emptive war made one old saying make sense beyond the Southside, "Never start fights, but if you have to hit someone back first once in a while that's all right." Then again ACORN has shown the everlasting relevance of Chicago's best known adage, "Vote early, and vote often."

With the Obamacrats large-and-in-charge, Windy City Proverbs may help many believe what kind of change we have stepped in. Such as "Everybody cheats so if you don't cheat you're a cheater," or "What's mine is mine, what's yours is negotiable." Maybe the taxman could use, "They must not have wanted it they didn't have their hand on it." Looking at our Congress, "If you're going to get mad at thieves you'll never have any friends" comes to mind. Thinking of the new Green Home Efficiency Inspectors[1] we will soon deal with when buying or selling a home is reminiscent of the Chicago Fire Marshal conscientiously telling a business owner, "We'll save the city some gas money if we just do the inspection right here in my office," while patting his desk indicating where to place the money.

The Obama Administration started off with some Southside swag calling the biggest earmark in history[2] a stimulus bill, they continued the virtuoso performance calling ward-heelers czars, and followed a time-honored Second City tradition in the Minnesota recount by finding a bag of votes. Who says you can't go home again? They may turn the old neighborhood into Yuppie Heaven by knocking down the middleclass housing and putting up three-story imitation Victorians but right here right now the machine that gave no-show jobs to half the wise-guys on the corner as well as Michelle at the hospital is in the process of not just fixing tickets but fixing everything else. The political descendants of Big Bill Thompson, Richard the First, and Richard the Second parlayed community organizing into a national organization that should make the Five Families green with envy.

Having fixed the economy and with health care, hate-crimes, immigration, and cap-and-trade queued up to flow through the system before the voters get a chance to register their disapproval, Don Barak now has the opportunity to begin fixing the highest court in the land. In the Chicago justice system lawyers give out printed pricelists stating how much acquittals cost verses dismissals and the old saying concerning courthouses goes, "It may say justice on the outside but that doesn't mean there's any on the inside." Once the Democratic Machine and their Me-To Republican allies rubber-stamp President Obama's first few picks for the A-Team how do the prospects for judicial restraint and the Constitution look? Fine if you fit the profile for the protected or promoted classes, but not too good if you naively look for that lady wearing the blindfold and holding the scales.

Joining the sisterhood on the bench, Ms. Sotomayor feels her gender and her race make her uniquely qualified to reach wise decisions and believes international law should be consulted when weighing appeals. She should feel right at home with the former chief counsel for the ACLU who apparently believes American Citizenship is the right of all mankind. In one decision she said, "You would have a huge statelessness problem if you don't consider a child born abroad a U.S. citizen."[3] Then along comes Elena Kagan with no judicial experience and described as "No friend of Freedom,"[4] helping to tilt the Supreme Court away from limited government and towards the statist goals of the Progressive family from Chicago who has occupied the seats of power. Ah justice, what is it good for? Or as they say in Chi-town, "How much justice can you afford?" The difference between Chicago Prime and Chicago on the Potomac is in the original version mayors serve for life followed by a power struggle. Vive la Différence!

Dispatch Twenty-nine

I Got Some Transparency for You Right Here

President Obama promised[1] America he would establish the most transparent administration in history. He pledged all bills would be posted online for five days[2] before he signed them. It turns out that only applied to NON-emergency bills, [3] and everything is an emergency in our swiftly transforming America. As Rahm Emanuel, President Obama's Chief of Staff says, "never let a serious crisis go to waste."[4]

The first bill President Obama signed into law was the Lilly Ledbetter Fair Pay Act, which must have been an emergency since it did not qualify for the five day guarantee. We had to pass the pork-laden stimulus bill[5] before the Best-Congress-Money-Can-Buy could even read it, let alone post it online, otherwise unemployment might reach the unacceptable 8% range.[6] The stimulus bill had to be passed in such a hurry they passed it late at night on a weekend though most of the provisions would not kick in for months or years, and even though the Congress usually only works a few hours a week, but then again, that was an emergency.

Another bill too big to read is America's Affordable Health Choices Act, which fails to insure the uninsured[7] and does not slow the rising rates, [8] which are the two things it was supposedly designed to accomplish. And once again, even though most of the provisions will not overwhelm us until after the next presidential election it was an emergency. Adding insult to injury after saying, "There has never been a more open process,"[9] Nancy Pelosi crafted the health care take-over behind doors closed so tight they have been called an iron curtain.[10] Eventually she had the nerve to say "we have to pass the bill so that you can find out what is in it..."[11]

The American tradition was built upon the idea of limited and dispersed powers, and under the Constitution neither the people, nor the states, nor the federal government was given absolute power or complete sovereignty. Behind the veil of silence, mockery, and misstatements, and continuing a trend that has gone on through the reigns of many imperial presidents, the Obama administration is accumulating more power than any previous administration in American History.

Now the usual suspects are calling for the censorship of the media under the guise of protecting us all from hate speech.[12] After suffering through years of congressional blockade in the 1990s and presidential vetoes, the ruling Progressive CABAL has resurrected

Ted Kennedy's Hate Crimes[13] law which now hangs like a shroud on the body politic. These types of laws have been used in Europe and Canada to criminalize opinion and squelch any who do not repeat the catch phrases, which pass for free speech in the Progressive's mental gulag.

Mark Lloyd, [14] Diversity Czar at the FCC, seeks to gain greater control of broadcasting with the aim of curtailing[15] the daily drip-drip of conservative commentary by the likes of Rush Limbaugh and Sean Hannity. In cyber space Net Neutrality[16] is nothing but the patently unfair Fairness Doctrine[17] for the Internet. Political correctness has taken its toll of the spoken word.

We no longer know what to call anyone in this day of hyphenated-America and fractionalized interest groups when what is politically correct changes with the winds of doctrine. The fairness police choke freedom out of speech using peer pressure while the administration tries to malign and marginalize the only network that isn't acting as a fax service for their press releases. This is not exactly what I envisioned when I heard that pledge to be the most transparent administration in history. It is more like the smoke and mirrors that passes for representative government in a one party state like Chicago.

Our Progressive leaders are transparent in one thing: their contempt for the desires of the people. Even though President Obama gave speech after speech trying to explain why we needed to reform our medical system to death as the polls showed the majority of the American people wanted government to leave health care alone, he said people were only against it because they didn't understand it. The financial reform act combined with the previous takeover of auto and insurance brings a larger percentage of the American economy under government control than at any other time. Poll after poll consistently shows the popular sentiment solidly against these acts, but the bills were rammed through anyway. Obama the candidate denounced the Bush Administration as the most secretive in history. The Obama Administration is now denying Freedom of Information Act requests at a rate 50% above[18] the previous administration. I know we see through a glass darkly, but if this opaque obfuscation is transparency I would hate to see secrecy. Perhaps secrecy is what you call announcing in advance when and where the next offensive is coming in the shooting wars across the sea.

Those who believe the Constitution is a Living Document[19] they can self-amend at will continue to chip away at the traditional definitions of what it means to be free. In the New-Speak of the transformed

America, racial quotas are not racial discrimination, the take-over of industries are done to save free enterprise, and being in charge means it is always someone else's fault. If those of us who want to remain free do not use our remaining freedom to protect our freedom soon it may not be politically correct to even remind people that once we were free.

Dispatch Thirty

If the Voters are the Mob Who Brought the Thugs?

    The Obama administration's attempt to silence dissent is chilling. The San Francisco limonene-liberals led by the multi-millionaire Nancy Pelosi claim the protesters are carrying swastikas[1] clearly trying to label them Nazis without being so crass as to use the word. Do you think if there were pictures of any of these protestors carrying Nazi flags the Corporations once known as the Mainstream Media would have missed the chance to loop it continuously? The only demonstrator shown with a swastika was a person with a sign that showed one in a red circle with a line through it, which everyone knows is the international symbol for "No." And in this instance for "No Thanks. You can take these tactics back to the union hall or city hall, but not in my country you don't."

    The man who has a million-dollar fund-raiser headlined by the Commander-in-Chief in a primary when he has no opponent refuses to hold a public meeting to discuss Obamacare saying those citizens voicing their concern over the greatest power-grab in American history have run out of ideas and lost their manners. Mr. Reid, perhaps the long suffering, long silent American citizens have been inspired by this progressive revolution to turn off the tube, get off the couch, and demand their elected representatives listen to them.

And what does our glorious leader have to say? Is he defying those in his own party attempting to squash dissent, standing up for the commoners and against the House of Lords? After asking people to report to the Whitehouse website anything they hear in emails or casual conversations about Obamacare that's "fishy" he said, "I don't want the folks who created the mess to do a lot of talking"[2] blaming the victims of government's over-the-top intrusion into their lives for the crime. Later one of his Consigliere, deputy chief of staff Jim Messina told Democrat legislators who are afraid to face their constituents, "If you get hit, we will punch back twice as hard."[3]

In Texas, a town hall meeting was jammed by physicians who wanted an opportunity to express their opposition to Obamacare. After listening to the doctor's remarks Congressman Kevin Brady (R-TX) concluded, "The bottom line is that doctors don't want socialized medicine — another flawed health care system like Medicare. They don't believe it will lower the costs or improve quality. Medicare is already going bankrupt and (is) not quality care. It also shifts medical costs onto other paying customers. It needs to be fixed first."[4]

If the protesters are the mob, who brought the thugs? People, including news reporters, are being arrested for taking pictures, and for handing out flyers. Using the arrests as a reason to avoid facing their constituents some Democrats like Senator Claire McCaskill have begun cancelling their scheduled meetings citing a fear of violence.

Protests are flaring nationwide, from Michigan where Representative Dingle tried to defend Obabmacare to the jeers of an overflow audience, to Colorado where Speaker Pelosi was greeted with shouts of "We have healthcare now!"[5] In South Carolina a man who shouted "There's no way, shape or form we need to have a national healthcare system. No! Nothing! None! It's got to stop now,"[6] received sustained applause.

The Chicago thugocracy opened a branch office on the Potomac, but the Potomac is not the Tiber. There may be parallels but this is America not Rome. We fell asleep and allowed a group of statists to occupy the hallowed halls of freedom, but we are awake now and we will not go quietly into that dark night. There are many feeling like Neo in the Matrix. We have suddenly realized the Pleasantville we have been living in is really the Truman Show and that while we snoozed on the couch a gang of tinhorn Chavez wannabes came in the backdoor and are trying to convince Columbia she's the Material Girl. Like Rip Van Winkle it is time to rise from our slumber and take a cue from Howard, "I'm mad as hell and I'm not going to take it anymore!"[7]

Education is the key. There are libraries everywhere. Our leaders have tried to dumb us down into the lumpenproletariat[8] they have envisioned us to be so we must teach ourselves. Start with *Rules for Radicals* by Saul Alinsky. This is the playbook used where the acorn has not fallen far from the tree. If fiction is your thing read *1984*, *A Brave new World*, *Animal Farm*, and *It Can't Happen Here*. These should inspire you to read such things as *The Road to Serfdom* by Hayek, *Liberal Fascism* by Goldberg and of course the Constitution and the Declaration of Independence. Now is the time to stand up and be counted. Now is the time for all good men to come to the aid of their country, which should be more than a typing exercise. It should be a word to the wise and a caution to the tyrant.

Dispatch Thirty-one

If it Wasn't so Sad it Would be Funny

Lately the news reminds me of Monty Python. I keep waiting for President Obama to appoint a Czar of Silly Walks or Reverend Wright to resurface and declare piously, "Nobody expects the Spanish Inquisition!" If the situation was not so serious I could not take it seriously.

I mean seriously, Kevin Jennings, President Obama's Assistant Deputy Secretary of the Office of Safe and Drug Free Schools at the Department of Education, failed to report a case of statutory rape[1] involving a male sophomore who told him he was having sex with an older man. It does not end there. Mr. Jennings is also on record as praising Harry Hay[2] of the North American Association for Man-Boy Love Association (NAMBLA), which agitates for the legalization of sexual abuse of young boys by older men. Apparently not wanting to leave people with too little to uncover to unmask his agenda Secretary Jennings also penned the forward to a book some might find surprising for an educational administrator to promote entitled, Queering Elementary Education.[3]

I keep waiting for ex-sportscaster Keith Olbermann or Democratic Party Spokesman Chris Mathews to say, "wink wink, nudge nudge, say no more, say no more" when they deliver such classic lines as, "President Obama has appointed Mark Lloyd as the Chief Diversity Officer at the FCC" with a straight-face. Colbert and Stewart had better watch out or MSNBC will win the sweeps as the funniest thing on TV. Officer Lloyd left his perch at the Center For American Progress funded by the likes of George Soros where he co-authored a report entitled "The Structural Imbalance of Political Talk Radio" which offered this chilling bit of advice, "This analysis suggests that any effort to encourage more responsive and balanced radio programming will first require steps to increase localism and diversify radio station ownership to better meet local and community needs."[4]

Localism is a re-packaged Fairness Doctrine[5] designed to control conservative commentary. Officer Lloyd's goals are made clear in his book *Prologue to a Farce: Communication and Democracy in America*. In this book Lloyd states, "Too often Americans use the First Amendment to end discussions of communications policy."[6] He continued, "This freedom is all too often an exaggeration. At the very least, blind references to freedom of speech or the press serve as a distraction from the critical examination of communications policies."[7]

Drawing upon the revolutionary tactics of the philosophical father of the Obama Administration, Saul Alinksy, [8] Lloyd adds, ""We understood at the beginning, and were certainly reminded in the course of the campaign, that our work was not simply convincing policy makers of the logic or morality of our arguments. We understood that we were in a struggle for power against an opponent, the commercial broadcasters."[9] Leaving no doubt as to where he draws his inspiration Officer Lloyd comments, ""We looked to successful political campaigns and organizers as a guide, especially the civil rights movement, Saul Alinsky, and the campaign to prevent the Supreme Court nomination of the ultra-conservative jurist Robert Bork."[10]

And now for something completely different. What review of the Cavalcade of Czars would be complete without that zany guy President Obama appointed Administrator of the Office of Information and Regulatory Affairs in the Office of Management and Budget, Cass Sunstein. Remember all those gazillion page bills no one reads? This is the guy who interprets them and decrees how they are implemented. In other words he is the guy who fills in the blanks. The Administrator believes in Libertarian Paternalism[11] or the belief that people should have the freedom to make choices and government should encourage them to make the best ones. Here is where the nudge[12] comes in. Sunstein believes the government should guide people "by gentling nudging them in directions that will make their lives better."[13] Can the wink be far behind?

A few of the Administrator's wackiest quips highlight his madcap take on ideas for America. Speaking of free speech he says, "A system of limitless individual choices, with respect to communications, is not necessarily in the interest of citizenship and self-government."[14] He elaborates when commenting on broadcasting, "A legislative effort to regulate broadcasting in the interest of democratic principles should not be seen as an abridgment of the free speech guarantee."[15] That is democratic, as in a Democratic People's Republic.

When talking about taxes Mr. Sunstein says we need another holiday,

> In what sense is the money in our pockets and bank accounts fully 'ours'? Did we earn it by our own autonomous efforts? Could we have inherited it without the assistance of probate courts? Do we save it without the support of bank regulators? Could we spend it if there were no public officials to coordinate the efforts and pool the resources of the community in which we live?... Without taxes there would be no liberty. Without taxes there would be no property. Without taxes, few of

us would have any assets worth defending. [It is] a dim fiction that some people enjoy and exercise their rights without placing any burden whatsoever on the public. ... There is no liberty without dependency. That is why we should celebrate tax day.[16]

An advocate of adding to the rights of Americans, Administrator Sunstein seeks "to uncover an important but neglected part of America's heritage: the idea of a second bill of rights. In brief, the second bill attempts to protect both opportunity and security, by creating rights to employment, adequate food and clothing, decent shelter, education, recreation, and medical care."[17]

And who could forget this gem, "...The Second Amendment seems to specify its own purpose, which is to protect the "well-regulated Militia." If that is the purpose of the Second Amendment (as Burger believed), then we might speculate that it safeguards not individual rights but federalism."[18]

With Larry, Mo, and Curley already in place can the Czar of Funny Walks be that far away?

Dispatch Thirty-two

It's Never Too Early to be Too Late

If no one has told you this yet let me be the first, as you get older time goes faster. If you are under thirty you are thinking, "This old coot has finally gone off his rocker! Everyone knows an hour is an hour. So how can time go faster as you get older?" If you are between thirty and forty you are thinking, "Who has got time to think about time and who cares? I have got to go to work!" If you are between forty and sixty you are thinking "He might have something there" as you day-dream about those endless summers when you were in High School. If you are over sixty you are hoping time does not end before you finish reading this paragraph.

Besides being a dimension, time is a concept that's inextricably intertwined with our material reality as in the space-time-continuum, $E=MC^2$ and all that. It took the genius of Einstein to find a way to prove what every old man knows, time can move at different speeds for different people. Knowing all this is little comfort when confronted with reality. The last wave of the Millennial Generation has entered college. I now teach History to students born after the end of the Cold War, adults who've never known a day without a personal computer, the internet or a cell phone. Most have never used a telephone with a cord or worn a wrist watch.

When the weapons of the superpowers became too terrible to use the Lost Generation, those who fought World War One and led the world through the Great Depression and World War Two gave America the Cold War. For those too young to remember this was a 50 year conflict marked by bellicose rivalry and our first modern limited war in Korea. Not to be outdone, the Greatest Generation, those who grew-up in the Great Depression and fought World War Two and Korea, gave us escalating tensions, naval blockades, and another limited war in Vietnam. They finished with a flourish by winning the Cold War and then doing a hundred day encore in the Gulf.

The Boomers hit the White House like guest hosts on Saturday Night Live with a snappy monologue and a party in the Oval Office. They tried to keep the limited war train rolling by occupying Bosnia, losing a Blackhawk in Somalia, and bombing Serbia for Kosovo. Then Boomer George met Osama in New York. Enter the first post-boomer president and a War on Terror becomes a law enforcement problem just as Korea with 55,000 dead was a Police Action. Have we refined limited war to the point that we aren't sure whether it's a war or a series of unrelated unfortunate incidents? As all combat troops leave Iraq (except for the ones that remain behind) and as the Taliban await our exit from Afghanistan these unfortunate incidents have developed into a distressing pattern: barge in then bow out.

A friend who optimistically believes every cloud has a silver lining hopes the tragedy at Fort Hood was merely the work of a volunteer in the Insane Clown Army and not a terrorist attack on an American Army base in our supposedly safe Homeland. This struck me as symptomatic of the age we've entered: call it the Reality Show at the End of an Era. In the land of the free and the home of the brave the best we can hope for is a demented mass murderer because the alternative is too frightening to face. If home-grown Jihadists are beginning to kill the brave in the bosom of the Heartland it won't be long before check-points and internal passports begin restricting the free in the byways of the homeland.

Have you ever noticed that after Pearl Harbor we did not declare war on sneak attacks? Instead, we declared war on those who attacked us. In America today we are constrained by the emasculating cult of Political Correctness from even naming our enemy. Our leaders blather on about religions of peace when people hold street dances to celebrate 9-11 and mobs murder and burn in reaction to an offensive comic strip. Now we have a person doing his best to enlist as a foot-soldier in Osama's army while serving in Obama's, shouting the catch phrase of the 9-11 bomber pilots as he murders more than a dozen unarmed innocents at an army base and the Corporations Once Known as the Mainstream Media pussy-foot around trying to give us the false hope that he's merely a homicidal maniac.

It is time to understand that if we do not stand for something we will fall for anything and that until you admit you have a problem there is no chance of finding a solution.

Time is slipping into the future. Are we going to stand complicit in our silence as wars without limit fought by people who proudly proclaim they love death more than we love life shoot our unarmed citizens in the name of God? Will we allow apologists for evil to blame the second amendment instead of telling us the truth?

It is time to rise up and say enough is enough! We know who our enemies are and we know who we are! If the brave want to keep their land, the free cannot sit at home chasing the remote. Whatever speed time is moving its going too fast to wait. It is never too early to be too late. Let's roll….

Dispatch Thirty-Three

Obama's War(s)

A war here, a war there, everywhere it is war, war, war. General Douglas McArthur wanted to invade China because they offered a safe haven for our enemies during the Korean War. In testimony before the Senate the first Chairman of the Joint Chiefs of Staff General Omar Bradley said, "It would be the wrong war in the wrong place at the wrong time." Today we face endless wars for elusive peace when we can't secure our own borders. We are committed to war in Iraq and Afghanistan; we have been rattling sabers in Iran's direction for years and one more for good measure.

The Corporations Once Known as the Mainstream Media have stopped covering the war in Iraq. Our Progressive leaders are throwing away the peace accomplished by the surge Senator Obama opposed but now takes credit for it. Our brave troops are withdrawing from hard-won positions as violence creates havoc and Al Qaeda seeks to spark a sectarian civil war. Iraqi Prime Minister Nuri al-Maliki, our strong man in Baghdad, seeks to steal an election he lost and

Iraq is selling their oil to China. Candidate Obama promised that he would immediately begin bringing the troops home at the rate of one to two brigades a month. Obama also stated he would call for a second constitutional convention in Iraq with this one run by his friends at the United Nations, which he would not allow to adjourn until Iraq's leaders reached a new agreement on political reconciliation. The fruits of the surge thrown aside, the same people running the Iraqi government in the same way and endless garrison duty in Iraq look likely.

Then there's Afghanistan, the war Candidate Obama told us was the right war in the right place, and the one we need to win, which we can only assume means there're some wars we don't need to win. While life goes on as normal here, heroic volunteers are in harm's way.

Since taking office, President Obama, after agonizing past recent election deadlines, has done what he opposed in Iraq: sending in a surge of troops to rescue a deteriorating situation. And for the first time in American history, or maybe in any history, he announced the surge while at the same time announcing the date of our withdrawal scheduled for July 2011? So as hard as our forces are fighting, as many victories as they gain, since our leader has already announced we're leaving on a date certain, do you think maybe the Taliban is waiting in the wings?

Do you think anyone in Kandahar or Kabul might think about what the Taliban might do once we leave? Saying we are going to persevere and not quit means little when we have already announced the date we are going to quit. If we send them to fight we need to let them fight to win or bring them home. They are not chips in games played by diplomats over Champaign glasses. They are the cream-of-the-crop, and the best America has to offer.

To top off this no-win strategy, the man we installed as president and continue to prop-up with dollars we don't have and heroes we do, courts Iran and says he might join the Taliban. He is doing this either to save face since we have acknowledged he is basically the Mayor of Kabul and at least related to the biggest drug dealer in the country, or he is doing it to wring concessions from his handlers. The tragedy is we are sending troops to fight and die for a surrender that has already been announced.

Iran has offered to ship half their low-enriched uranium to Turkey. True, the deal was not brokered or imposed by Hilary and her crew at State, and though it lacks the Obama Imprimatur it is basically the same deal he has demanded. If President Obama does not accept this deal he is signaling to the rest of the world that it is his administration seeking confrontation with Iran, it is he who refuses to throttle back the avalanche to war.

Then there is the war for good measure: the one against free enterprise, federalism and the traditional America we have known waged by a president who promised (or threatened) to fundamentally transform our nation. Those of us still clinging to our God and our traditions cannot ignore the one campaign our national community organizer seems intent on winning: the one against us. From Soros-backed front groups to pandering pundits of the captured media, from union bosses to academics and bureaucrats who have never held a regular job in their lives, day-by-day traditional America is being transformed before our eyes. The battle may seem long, the way may seem dark, but if we keep the faith and keep the peace we shall overcome

Dispatch Thirty-four

Please, Mr. Custer, We Don't Want To Go!

When the neo-cons, a group of liberal democrats realized Margret Thatcher was right in saying, "The trouble with socialism is that eventually you run out of other people's money"[1] they decided liberalism is as Michael Savage contends, a mental disorder.[2] In the 1970s and 80s they abandoned the Good Ship Democrat proclaiming themselves to be Born-Again Republicans. Generally they still carry the baggage of their former psychosis when it comes to social issues but when it comes to foreign affairs and military matters they sound like Errol Flynn playing George Custer in *They Died With Their Boots On*, "Don't wait for orders from headquarters. Mount up everybody and ride to the sound of the guns."

These neo-cons not only flew high into the circles of on-air talking-heads they swirled through the Bush White House leading us into Iraq. Now they are beating the drums for massive reinforcements in Afghanistan.

The War in Iraq was a preemptive war, meaning we hit them back first. Preemptive war has a long history. The Romans and the Germans used it, but this was the first time America climbed on the get-in-the-first-whack bandwagon. The mission of rolling the big rock up that steep hill has not yet been fully accomplished. Due to the tireless and valiant sacrifices of our heroic military, the Iraqi theater is winding down into a perpetual garrison to make sure our now friendly ally remains friendly joining the list of American military garrisons in over sixty-three countries.[3]

The War in Afghanistan is a completely different situation. The Taliban managed to subdue most of the country once the Soviet armies retreated in defeat. These purveyors of religious purity and peace killed, tortured, and maimed anyone with the chutzpa to disregard any of their religiously inspired rules such as little girls who tried to learn how to read or women who dared to leave the house without a male escort or without wearing a tent. Unable to curb their enthusiasm they did not forget to kill, torture, or maim any man who did not grow a long enough beard, boys who did not memorize their rule book fast enough, and of course any member of the Gay-Lesbian-Bisexual-Transgendered society who happened to be trapped in their society. Under these turbaned and bearded fascists Saturday night soccer games were transformed into ritual be-headings and mutilations. Then for fun they would destroy historic works of art and crush people under walls as they waited for the Sunday stoning.

Stoically we considered all of these barbarous atrocities their own affair and never made a move to clean up this cesspool of 13th century evil until after the 9-11 war crimes. Then we politely asked them to kick the culprits out and we would let them go back to their celebration of depravity, but they would not listen. They stood by their man and in retaliation we sent in the Special Ops, bribed anyone who would take a dollar in the hand in place of a bullet in the head and in short order drove Omar, Osama, and their disciples of peace into Pakistan to fester and plot an encore performance. A confusing post-invasion coalition[4] eventually morphed into the blatantly corrupt but ostensibly pro-American Karzai regime.[5]

Then our friends, the neo-cons, expressed their belief that the mistake we had made after the proto-Taliban Mujahedeen[6] we supported defeated the Soviets was that we did not stay and do some nation-building. So this time we stayed to do some nation-building, [7] and today the regrouped Taliban are using the surge strategy to overwhelm our scattered troops. We are trying to build a nation where none exists. Afghanistan is a fiction of western minds. We created it as a single entity instead of a region. We drew it on a map and piously repeat that it exists like a mantra or a fever dream. To the medieval tribal people who actually inhabit the region their loyalty[8] is to their family, their clan, and their tribe.

It is apparent to everyone, except seemingly the people American presidents ask for advice, that no matter how much we want a nation to be built we don't have the raw material as in identifiable citizens of a nation, the treasure, or the patience to invest another decade or two to get electricity outside Kabul or democracy in Kabul. The whole world knows we are going to eventually either bail-out, and declare victory à la Nixon or admit defeat à la Gorbachev and come home. Why should one more American lose their life for a cause that has been stretched out way past our initial victory into our present morass?

On the campaign trail Mr. Obama claimed this war for himself,[9] and since his inauguration he has repeatedly stated that Afghanistan is a war of necessity.[10] He's installed his own commanders and almost immediately sent more troops.[11] Now he hesitates to the point that everyone can see he does not have the desire or the will to do what would be necessary to win even going so far in the direction of military insanity as to announce a withdrawal date in the same speech as he announces a surge.[12] Let us hope he has the political courage to withdraw before Afghanistan becomes the Little Big Horn with our

Heroes as the Seventh Calvary. Please, Mr. Custer we don't want to go.

Dispatch Thirty-five

We Can Learn What We Don't Know

If the price of freedom is eternal vigilance[1] we deserve what we have since we took our eyes off the ball to watch the game. As economically our once strong Republic veers from Universal Empire to quasi-colony of China, as the Alinsky trained radicals from the 1960s and their second-generation clone army guide America to Amerika, from freedom to serfdom[2] so many of the sheeple are still asleep. The alarm bells are ringing, but the cracks in the fabric of our nation have muted the sound as the crack has silenced the Liberty Bell.

There's nothing more interesting than speaking to people across our land following the big Democrat win in the Congressional version of March Madness. The opinions, emotions, fears, and gloating are a wonder to behold. In these days of change, hope still burns eternal in the hearts of Patriots grimly facing the prospect of America becoming a European-style social democracy so that some of us can finally be proud of our country.[3] Fear for the fate of their children and grandchildren is in the hearts, eyes, and voices of the newly awakened as they imagine the shabby future we face in a de-industrialized debtor nation.[4] They see the constantly expanding debt, and they know eventually someone will have to pay the tab. And they know it will not be the professional politicians and community organizers who flushed trillions down the rat-hole. Instead it will be the previously comatose populace and their unsuspecting children. Gloating like a fat cat left alone with a Christmas turkey, Progressives are crowing because they can finally pull their red flags out of the closet to match their Che Guevara tee-shirts as they take a victory lap around the White House.

The art of magic is all about getting us to watch the left hand while the right hand produces the quarter from behind our ear. It was telling when in the midst of his first real interview with real questions since O'Reilly, President Obama kept pushing his hand in Bret Baier's face and telling him don't be concerned with the process, don't ask about the process. Smoke and mirrors have become the hallmark of the Obama administration. Look at the Democrat re-election slush-fund Stimulus bill.[5] Have a nation-wide debate about spending hundreds of billions while the Federal Reserve System pumps out trillions without any fanfare whatsoever.[6] The media enhanced dialog heats up and flares over imposing nationalized medicine without realizing we've shape-shifted from E Pluribus Unum Latin for "Out of Many, One," to Ex Uno, Plures "Out of

One, Many" as America splinters into shouting crowds and oblivious leaders.

Progressives always want to be judged by their intentions never by the outcomes of their actions. Foisting a war on poverty[7] on a country which has fostered more upward mobility than every other nation in the world combined and forty years and trillions of dollars later we have more poverty[8] than when we started, but they meant well. They have opened our borders until we are awash in illegal immigrants then they act as if natural and naturalized citizens are racists for not wanting to pick up the tab and give away the vote too. The Progressives have successfully changed the melting-pot into a smelting pot as America fractures into ethno-tribal factions poised to tear each other apart, but they meant well. They have embraced free trade and giving most favored nation status to countries with populations willing to work at a fraction of the American scale. Causing industry to flood out as cheap goods flood in, changing us from the Arsenal of Democracy into a source of raw materials and credit card wielding consumers, our economy is shattered, but they meant well. Bowing to kings and emperors, embracing dictators and shunning allies mired in endless wars with phantom tribesmen, our prestige and power fades, but they meant well.

Mistakes of this magnitude do not happen innocently. It is time to rip the mask from these defilers of constitutionally limited government and expose them for the charlatans and hucksters they are. For as long as the Progressives and their corrosive influence have sought to bring the blight of socialism to our shores they have hidden behind their supposedly pure motives. They only want to help the poor. They only want to make a level playing field. They only want to heal the sick, soothe the dying, and give everyone everything leaving the check on the table for the producers to pay. It is time for anyone who's interested in knowing what this is all about to educate themselves. Generations of Progressives have burrowed their way into our education system changing it into an indoctrination system. The stale, boring, and flat history force fed to us as helpless cogs in the public school systems left out all the good stuff. Read *Liberal Fascism*[9] by Jonah Goldberg, *New Deal or Raw Deal*[10] by Burton W. Folsom Jr., *Arguing with Idiots*[11] by Glenn Beck, and any of the eye-opening books by Pat Buchanan. Now look at the bibliographies in those books and read the books they've cited.

Find out who these Progressives really are. Learn what their goals have always been and the smoke and mirrors will lose their power to blind and the way will become clear. We cannot let the emotions of the battle cloud the thoughts of our minds. There's a way home, but first we must understand how we got here before we can know how to return there. Keep the faith. Keep the peace. We shall overcome.

Dispatch Thirty-six

Pop Goes the Culture

Culture to a human is like water to a fish. We move around in it constantly but we do not notice it very much. Unnoticed water can have profound effects on fish. Too cold and they freeze. Too hot and they boil. Not enough oxygen and they suffocate. Too polluted and they choke to death. In a similar fashion the culture in which we move shapes us in many subtle ways. If it is refined the world we perceive and the world we deal with is refined. If it is crude the world is crude. If it is toxic the world is toxic.

An Icon in our 21st century whiz-bang gotta-have-it-now-twitter-me-when-you-get-in-line world is associated through the cultural tags we have recently embedded in our minds, through computer screens and cell phones as stylized display figures representing the various functions or resources available on a particular piece of hardware. However, in the jargon of Cultural History an Icon is an image or figure which represents someone or something regarded as embodying the essential characteristics of an era or group.

The first universally accepted Icon in America for America was Miss Columbia. In 1697, Samuel Sewall wrote a poem which suggested a good name for Brittan's American Colonies would be Columbina a feminized version of Columbus. In 1775, Phillis Wheatley, a former slave, sent George Washington a poem invoking Miss Columbia as the spirit of the Revolution. During the War of 1812, many political cartoons featured Miss Columbia and by the mid-nineteenth century she became the standard figure representing America. She was popularized by Thomas Nast who also gave us other Icons such as the Democrat donkey, the Republican elephant, and the American Santa Clause.

Uncles Sam knocked Miss Columbia off her pedestal. Uncle Sam has his origins back in the early days of the Republic, but the final version of Uncle Sam that most people are familiar with today comes from World War I. In 1917 James Montgomery Flagg drew the famous "I Want You" recruiting poster and created the enduring image of Uncle Sam.

This is a brief history of the development of American national Icons from the day Hancock wrote his name until the advent of technology-driven mass-media. Since then we have alternated between embracing and fending off new Icons coming at an ever-accelerating pace. Like Lucy in the Chocolate Factory we are dealing with these images so fast we have become overwhelmed, and culturally neutered like the Hawki in F Troop.

Ever since Andy gave Barney a bullet, Mary Richards threw her hat in the air, and the Jeffersons moved up-town we have been trying to manage the swirling images of America. We cannot decide whether we are the *Brady Bunch* or *All in the Family*. Are we happy and contented knowing *Eight is Enough* or are we forever wallowing in the self-pity of *Married With Children*? In a simpler time John Boy wished Mary Ellen goodnight with the affection of a brother, and the Fonz was a hood with heart.

That Girl showed us women could be single, decent, and successful now we get *Sex in the City* and *Cougar Town*. Good guys used to wear white hats. Elliot Ness always won. Now Tony Soprano smiles as he drops off his neighbor's daughter from soccer practice then later shoots the girl's father in the back of the head without blinking an eye over a poker debt, then comes back the next day to take the daughter to soccer practice. It was just business. Larry David endlessly curbs his enthusiasm by making up intricate rules to live by and then expecting everyone else to live by them. *The Office* shows us how the corporate bureaucracy really works while *Parks and Rec* shows us how government would work if it was that honest or efficient and *30 Roc* shows us how the Media thinks we think it works.

Entertainment is entertainment and news is news, but once you see an image you can never un-see it. The Icons we fill ourselves with become the world we perceive. We get to choose what fills our minds. Is it positive or is it negative? But the masters of media also get to choose what they promote to portray America. Is it Columbia with flags waving leading us to freedom, Uncle Sam with a kindly face asking us to serve, or is it dogs barking at hooded prisoners and people being water-boarded that our media moguls constantly ram down our throat. Do they show the people delivering a Thanksgiving turkey or the homeless pushing a cart full of rags?

A picture is worth 10,000 words, so we need to be aware of what images say to us and remember we can choose the movies we watch, the shows we follow, and the things we read. And reaching back to that culture as water analogy, we've gone from a social compass that kept our ship afloat to whatever floats your boat from the Mayflower to the Love Boat and let's hope not the Titanic.

Dispatch Thirty-seven

What Causes the Result?

That America has changed is without question. No one gets to live in the world they were raised to live in. My father grew up in a house with a dirt floor and no running water. He plowed a field with mules just as his father did and his father and so on. My grandmother never heard of telephones, or airplanes, or electricity until after she was twenty one and had several children, yet I sat next to her in 1969 watching men walk on the moon. My grandfather's generation was the first in my family that learned to read, my father's generation was the first to grow up with shoes on, mine was the first that grew up in a city, my son's was the first to have a computer before they had a car, and my grandchildren are the first to grow up in an America that's the largest debtor on Earth like Blanche DuBois depending on the kindness of strangers.

While rummaging through the attic a friend of mine's grandchild found their first cell-phone from the early 90s. They ran downstairs and asked, "What's this?" When told it was a cell-phone they would not believe it as they exclaimed, "It is not!" Not too long ago I had to explain to a young person that a "Record" was sort of an antique CD. Yes, America is changing around us every day.

America sinks deeper into the Bizarro World of European-style "Excuse me it must be my fault" diplomacy and the cradle-to-grave nanny state with each passing propaganda piece in the mainstream media. Examples range from the President's on-going Surrender Offensive[1] to Turbo-Tax Tim Geitner's latest explanation of how going further into debt is actually a good thing.

In the morning we learn the faith-based initiative program is not only run by people known to be hostile to major denominations it has now expanded to include Community Organizations which already had a snout in the Federal trough.[2] By noon we hear our poorly informed Secretary of Homeland Security thinking the 9-11 terrorists entered from the Great White North,[3] is worried about the Canadian border, and only sees terrorists[4] when she looks at Americans[5] clinging to their guns and Bibles. For dinner the shill tells us about a tax-cut for 95% of Americans when only slightly more than 50% pay taxes.[6] Overnight, we win the war on terror by changing its name. Yes America is changing all around us.[7]

One day we have the right to keep and bear arms and the next our President is advocating a treaty that makes re-loading ammunition a crime, [8] and the Attorney General wants to ban American guns[9] to make it safer in Mexico. One day the American Navy rules the waves and the next four men in a row-boat hold us off for five days and our leaders consider a treaty giving dominion of the world's oceans to the UN.[10] One day we are the industrial giant of the world and the next we are the supplier of raw materials and food to those who make things. From Carter's malaise to Obama's surrender the years in between are beginning to shimmer on the horizon like a mirage. From morning in America to mourning for America we have squandered our birthright and thrown our pearls before swine.

Sometimes from one cause there can flow multiple results. Now that her husband is America's leader Michelle is proud of her country[11] for the first time, while for the first time I am ashamed of my country. It is not just the Obama-Pelosi-Reid Triumvirate. It is everyone who wants Uncle Sam to be Uncle Sugar, a Big Daddy War-Bucks who meets all our needs. An increasingly secular society believing this is all there is rolls out the barrels and prepares for the Party at the End of the Galaxy. However, there is a problem at the core of Liberal Social Democracies. They are unsustainable because at heart they are a Ponzi scheme always needing an ever increasing generational tax base to pay for the benefits promised to the generation before. In other words this is generational theft. We are passing a burden on to our descendants. Meaning they will have to live small tomorrow so that we can live large today

With declining birth-rates and abortion-on-demand if we have not reached the end of the line you can see it from here. The merry-go-round is about to stop and we don't have the golden ring. So the proponents of the welfare gravy-train tell us the answer is immigration, or as its out-in-the-open boosters now call it migration. Just import new workers to do the menial jobs our kids will not do and let their taxes buy our Winnebago and pay our way to retirement in the sun. Sounds good but when those who pour in are mainly illegals who do not pay taxes but instead get benefits it is a net drain.[12] Add that to the demographic problem mentioned earlier and the question is how do we continue our existence for more than a few generations? Meanwhile the number of anchor babies[13] is through the roof with the result that in those few generations we will not be us we will be them. Since our new roomies have no tradition of living in or maintaining a representative republic but instead come mainly from paternalistic oligarchies once called Banana Republics it's no surprise America is beginning to resemble a Banana Republic.

Yes, America has changed. Instead of a disaffected public not re-electing anyone and turning the rascals out, the rascals are importing a new electorate and America as we have known her is not even mentioned in our children's textbooks. What's the cause? What will be the result?

Dispatch Thirty-eight

Who Changed the Change?

The Framers moved beyond a loose Confederation of States creating the greatest experiment in freedom the world has ever known. They birthed a nation conceived in Liberty[1] and dedicated to the proposition that all men are created equal unleashing the creative power and energy of humanity in a way never before known and never since equaled. They launched a government of the people, by the people and for the people.[2]

If imitation is the sincerest form of flattery the Constitution should feel very flattered. Our founding document has been copied by almost as many countries as radio talking-heads trying to imitate Rush Limbaugh. Though it was the best set of compromises[3] the Framers could hammer-out, they knew as time passed it might need to be changed. By establishing a mechanism for amending the Constitution they made provisions for gradual evolution to occur without the Revolution they used to obtain change they could believe in or the Civil War their grandchildren fought to change that change.

How are we the descendants of the ascendant supposed to change the foundations laid hundreds of years ago into the structure we want today? To preserve and protect the representative nature and federal structure of the government they created, the Framers designed a process[4] through which legitimate change must involve the representatives of the people and the States through formal amendments. Outside of this the words as written and as meant were to be the law of the land. The idea that the words of the Constitution have to be re-interpreted every generation is ludicrous. The Federalist[5] papers, the notes[6] of James Madison the primary author, and dictionaries of the time exist to tell us what the words meant to the writers. If the words are re-interpreted with every generation all that has to be done to change the document is change the meaning of the words.

The Framers in Article Five provided two methods to propose amendments.[7] Congress may propose amendments with a 2/3 vote in both houses or the legislatures of 2/3 of the states can call a convention for proposing amendments. The second method has never been used though today we're only two states away from calling a Constitutional Convention.[8] When an amendment is ratified by either the legislatures or specially called conventions of 3/4 of the states it becomes part of the Constitution.

This is how we are supposed to go about changing the fundamental nature of our Republic. It is not by fiat, not by decree, not by clever re-interpretation, and certainly not by the whim of a fickle electorate every four years.

President Obama is not the first president to appoint unofficial advisers without submitting them to the Senate for confirmation. Back in the 1830s, with an official Cabinet of lackluster hacks confirmed by the Senate, President Jackson depended on an unofficial group of close personal friends and practical politicians for advice. Turning a good phrase the journalists of the day anointed this the Kitchen Cabinet. Thus the presidents fulfill the letter of the law moving less controversial non-entities through the confirmation process as figureheads to run bureaucratic departments while relying on others outside the glare of scrutiny as their sources of information: their compass.

Has this now become the means to change the nature of our government without using the amendment process? From Republican to Democrat both parties have used an ever growing number of appointments to staff their governments with people who are not accountable to anyone, who are not vetted by anyone, and many who could not get a security clearance if they were. Until today we have the Cavalcade of Czars.[9] There is a school-safety czar who led the way in introducing homosexual advocacy[10] in public schools, a pay czar who decides who gets what[11] at companies receiving government funds, and a technology czar forced to resign because of a bribery scandal[12] is replaced by one who has no education in technology.[13]

This growing shadow government being constructed alongside our traditional governmental structure combined with the administration's radical legislative program marks a rising to a crescendo of change that is hard to believe. This radical agenda includes nationalizing health care along with approximately 1/6th of the economy, the take-over of major industries, a cap-n-tax energy boondoggle that will cripple the economy, and comprehensive import-a-voter immigration reform.

Have we reached the tipping point? Will we stand idly by while slick politicians surrounded by people we would never elect turn us into what we would never willingly become? Will we cruise the remote while they fundamentally change America from what we've known to what we would never choose? Is this the change we were promised or has someone changed the change.

Will we leave our children in service to an ever growing centralized state with a planned economy and an obedient media singing songs to the Glorious Leader and wondering, "Why did they let freedom slip through their fingers?"

Dispatch Thirty-nine

What's a Conservative? What's a Liberal?
What does it matter?

   For the first two of these questions change the words Conservative and Liberal into Republican and Democrat and the average voter would immediately chase the cheese through the mental template the media wants us to use as a substitution for thought. However, there are Blue-Dog Democrats (Conservatives) and Republicans in Name Only (Liberals). In reality both parties are led by interchangeable Big-Government Tax-and-Spend whatever-you-want-to-call-them political hacks.

   According to the template, the two Big-Box parties are separated by their relative location on a straight line having a Right, a Left, and presumably a Center. This is taught using charts and graphs in every American Government class and by endless repetition in what passes for journalism in America today. However the fact is we have an over homogenized political establishment with boring elections between Twiddle Dee and Twiddle Dumber. What relevance does this artificial construct have in the post-Christian, post-Constitution America we find ourselves in today?

As America careens toward a centrally-planned economy, a videotaped public life, and a wire-tapped sense of security *We the People* sit silently as perpetual incumbents debate adding more taxes to gasoline[14] while giving thousand dollar-a-plate speeches about the "obscene" profits of the oil companies."[15] They tell us there is virtually "No inflation"[16] forgetting to mention they have removed food and fuel from the mix when figuring the inflation rate[17] while pumping trillions of new made-from-thin-air dollars into the economy. Does someone need to explain what inflation is[18] to our money managers?

The sons of the Pioneers drive to MegloMart to buy the latest Chinese-made necessity. We watch the latest ad for a Mexican-made car on our Korean television. Collectively we charge our Visa to our MasterCard because Discover is over the limit and wonder what happened.

I once called myself a Conservative, but there is precious little left to conserve. I have called myself a Classical Liberal[19] because I seek, as did the Liberals of the 1790s, liberty and opportunity for all. I have called myself a Revolutionary, because I advocate a return to Constitutional government, something, which I am more and more convinced, would take a revolution to accomplish. What I do not want to do is call myself a Victim as I watch Rome fall and realize that just as Khrushchev predicted, and in contrast to Rome, the barbarians are us.

Recently I sat and listened to 40 young people explain why the Obama administration makes them optimistic about the future. It left me very pessimistic. I look to the youth to save us from the rapid decline the boomer generation has purchased with the national charge card. All I heard was 40 young people repeating the campaign slogans of 2008 and pointing proudly either to things that have not happened or to things that are actually the opposite of what they think they are. I ended up feeling like I was in Denver hearing the chants of "Yes, We Can!" reverberating between the imposing looking Styrofoam columns and the ever-present teleprompters.

The Republicans are traveling the country with a listening tour[20] as if they need to learn what Republican stands for, so they can lead their dwindling tribe out of the wilderness. From the looks of things they will jettison the Conservative brand for something more up-to-date, unless they see that they can win more votes by continuing the pretense that they are conservatives (read – less liberal than their opponents). Meanwhile the Democrats have decided they're not Liberals anymore they're "Progressives."[21]

This is how the story looks on the nightly news as reported by the mainstream media. Yet when we look at more than one source of data we get a wider view and a different picture. A recent Washington Post/ABC News poll[22] tells us only 21 % of Americans identify themselves as Republicans, 35 % as Democrats, and 38 % as Independents. The subtext is usually about the death of the GOP and the efforts of party leaders to get away from the repudiated Conservative label. This is usually as far as the reports go in their balanced and objective effort to shape the mind of America. However, there's a significant difference between what party people identify with and what ideology they claim as their own.

In August of 2008 the Battleground Poll[23] found that 60 % of Americans identify themselves as Conservative and only 36 % as Liberal. Forget about Right or Left and choose instead Right or Wrong. If somehow those who want a return to Constitutional government, those who want a return to traditional values, those who want their children and grandchildren to live in the USA not the USSA could rise above their inherited party loyalties and coalesce into one group we could stand against the tide, reverse the slide, and return America to the Constitutional government which is their heritage. What's a Conservative? What's a Liberal? What does it matter? In the end it might matter quite a bit.

Dispatch Forty

Who Are The Barbarians?

The comparisons between Rome and America are legion. Recently I listened to a Bible scholar declare that Revelation Chapter 18,[1] which has traditionally been associated with a veiled prophecy of the fall of Rome,[2] is in reality a direct reference to the fall of America.[3] Google "Compare Rome and America" and it reveals a cottage industry dedicated to perpetuating or debunking the premise. Every segment of American society the church, education, business, Hollywood, and main street have been warned that the enemy is within the gates paraphrasing a Roman, Marcus Tullius Cicero who said, ""The enemy is within the gates; it is with our own luxury, our own folly, our own criminality that we have to contend." [4]

Most of us have a picture of the fall of Rome shaped by Hollywood and encouraged by the fact that even a well-rounded education today covers the first 6,500 years of Western Civilization in one semester. The words, "Fall of Rome" conjure up visions of oafish men the size of pro-wrestlers dressed in skins with horned helmets bursting through the gates and ravaging the effeminate Romans and their buxom women. The truth is by the time Rome fell hardly anyone noticed and few cared. The Barbarians had been running the place, manning the frontier, and managing the government for so long when they finally decided they did not need a powerless Roman Emperor for a front man anymore it probably seemed like honesty in government to proclaim Odoacer King of Italy.

Among the direct causes of Rome's demise[5] were constant wars and foreign military interventions, [6] which sapped the strength and the resolve of the Roman population. Unchecked immigration[7] allowed masses of people to enter the Empire who had no interest in becoming Romans. They were, instead, intent on maintaining their own culture and language while appropriating Roman property and civilization. A debased currency brought on runaway inflation[8] and undermined the economic system.[9] The rule of law was subverted by the expansion of executive power.[10] The legislature fell into the hands of self-serving aristocrats[11] who sought their own benefit and were willing to sell their vote to the highest bidder. A declining birth-rate combined with the avalanche of immigration eventually made the Romans a minority in their own country. And to these self-imposed secular weaknesses Gibbon in his *Decline and Fall of the Roman Empire* adds a spiritual dimension when he advances the idea that the adoption of a new religion, Christianity, contributed to the fall.

Does any of this sound familiar? Today the United States is a country at war with itself. Some have called it the culture war.[12] Pat Buchanan has tried to warn us for decades. His well-written and well documented books have given anyone interested enough ammunition to hold the beaches, but instead we have surrendered the high ground and retreated to the couch. America is not being murdered we're committing suicide.

In his farewell address[13] George Washington warned us to avoid overseas entanglements.[14] This timeless advice is still read into the Congressional record at the opening of every session. However, this advice has been ignored so often that a constant drumbeat of intervention[15] has sapped our strength and eroded our will. Ronald Reagan among others[16] have shared such obvious wisdom as, "A nation that cannot control its borders is not a nation."[17] Our self-absorbed leaders tell us we are fighting a war against terror and leave the back door open.[18] Today the cacophony of hyphenated Americanism descends into arguments over which kind of American deserves more pity or power. Does a Norwegian-American with a limp and a bad case of the shingles trump a Welsh-American with pink-eye? Teddy Roosevelt said, "There is no room in this country for hyphenated

Americanism" and "Our allegiance must be purely to the United States."[19]

The serial stimuli and billion dollar bail-outs our economically challenged leaders keep handing out like door-hangers in a campaign are building a mountain of horded cash that's eventually going to come crashing down on our economy burying us in hyperinflation.[20] The already accepted federal obligations exceed the GDP of the entire world.[21] This is unsustainable. The level of America bashing and outright anti-American propaganda[22] that is foisted on our youth and called education today is beyond belief.

As a teacher of Political Science and History I often feel as if I am in an occupied country when I see and hear what is force-fed in classrooms today. Executive orders, signing statements and the constant proliferation of shadow-government Czars are examples of an executive branch that is out of control.[23] Both political parties operate as twin heads on one bird of prey constantly nibble away at the idea of a balance of power. Craven legislators abdicate their authority to special interests and betray their trust for thirty pieces of silver.

The birthrate among native-born citizens[24] while the highest in Western Civilization is barely at replacement levels as a government unable to pull its constituents to the left import voters accustomed to third world economics and third world politics. And what of a new religion sapping our strength and resolve? The Cult of Global Warming leads us to declare economic war upon ourselves through the imposition of Cap-N-Trade while the rest of the world watches in disbelief as the greatest economic power of all time hobbles itself in a race for life. [25&26]

Some point to the Blame America First crowd[27] and echo the words of Jean Francois Revel, "Clearly, a civilization that feels guilty for everything it is and does will lack the energy and conviction to defend itself."[28] Or as Pogo said, "I have met the enemy and ... he is us."[29]

Dispatch Forty-one

The Key

Once an entitlement program is started it never stops.[1] It never shrinks. It never stands still. It always grows. According to the Mainstream Media it's merely rightwing spin to say Obamacare is meant to become a single-payer one-size fits all public option. However, President Obama's own words[2] plainly tell us this is his goal. When the Best-Congress-Money-Can-Buy returns they will pass something, calling it Insurance Reform, saying it will save money until signed by President Obama when it becomes National Health Care. It'll start small and grow. This is merely the beginning of the re-making of America. Then comes Cap-N-Trade, mandatory pre-K, paid volunteerism, the Fairness Doctrine by any other name, and of course the Key.

The Key to institutionalizing the Progressive's November Revolution is Comprehensive Immigration Reform.[3] When the Obama administration manages to get this through whether with legislation or regulation, America morphs into the Obamanation. Convincing the Blue-Dogs to rubberstamp legalization[4] for multiple millions of illegal aliens brings generations of majorities. In addition, the 2010 census[5] counts illegal aliens the same as citizens.[6] Since the original and primary purpose of the census is for the re-apportionment of the House of Representatives[7] this means the number of illegal aliens helps decide who gets how many representatives. This obviously violates the spirit of the Constitution which was written to limit not empower government. The idea that it was citizens who were represented and not uninvited guests was also part of the original design. If this isn't recognized as illegal and unconstitutional what will be? And if our community organizing bean counters can find the illegal aliens to count them why can't the INS find them to send them home? The door this key opens leads to a Brave New World.

Why do our central planning social engineers want to remake the greatest engine for human advancement ever seen into just another socialist sinkhole? Ask any of them, from the extra-constitutional czars in the White House to your Progressive brother-in-law across the table, why the hard-working should be harnessed, to the hardly-working and they'll say, because we must take care of the less fortunate.

If these hyper-concerned Liberal/Progressives want to help the less fortunate, what is stopping them? What's holding them back from giving of their own resources and volunteering their own time? Why can't they take in a homeless family or use their food to make meals and feed those in need? Maybe they need a Big Brother government to force them to help others, but many people do not. As a person who established several feeding programs in multiple locations feeding thousands and regularly providing groceries and other necessities for families without using government money, I know that coercion is not needed to inspire people to give and work to help those less fortunate. All that is needed is genuine compassion as opposed to a general feeling that someone should do something.

Surveys and studies consistently show Liberal/Progressives do not give of their own resources to charities and Conservatives do.[8] Books such as *Who Really Cares* by Arthur C. Brooks document, "that the average conservative-headed household gives 30 % more money to charity than the average liberal-headed one ($1,600 compared with $1,227), despite earning 6 % less annually."[9] For example, between 2000 through 2007, Barack Obama donated between 0.4% and 6.1% of his net income to charities. In the same years McCain gave 28.6% and 27.3% of his income to charities, [10] yet it is President Obama telling us piously, "I am my brother's keeper."[11] This inevitably leads to the crowding out issue[12] when government forces people to give their money for inept programs with unintended consequences more negative than the original problems, and they have less to give to private charities that work.

So what does charitable giving have to do with Comprehensive Immigration Reform? In their effort to subject the productive members of society to a New New Deal[13] the Obama administration knows they have to re-make America before *We the People* throw the bums out. As their poll numbers sink like a rock, they know that they will reap the same harvest as the Republicans in 2006 and 2008 unless they bring in a new electorate to sustain them. They know passing Comprehensive Immigration Reform is the key to institutionalizing their re-made America. From this key flow a new status quo and a new establishment.

The community organizers trying their best to re-make America into their vision of Utopia, level playing fields, and a quota generated court enforced equality of result should remember Saul Alinsky said, "History is a relay of revolutions; the torch of idealism is carried by the revolutionary group until this group becomes an establishment, and then quietly the torch is put down to wait until a new revolutionary group picks it up for the next leg of the run." [14] Revolutions breed counter-revolutions and the town hall meetings may be the key reminding us that no matter what to-good-to-be-true freebees the statists offer the whole world doesn't really lay waiting behind door number three.

Dispatch Forty-two

Prayers of the Downtrodden

We open with a Soviet-era prayer; "Lord you know I've been poor all my life. My family never has enough to eat. We don't even have a cow. My neighbor has a fine cow. It gives milk every day. It keeps his family happy and healthy. Oh Lord, kill my neighbors cow!" In a society obsessed with leveling the playing field until everyone was standing in line for food and had an equal right to get their name on a doctor's waiting list, this prayer expressed the citizen's reaction to collectivist policies meant not to bring everyone up but to bring everyone down, which is why there is no Soviet Union today.

Turning the Bully Pulpit into a bully, every day we're beat up with a doom and gloom version of hope and change. The chief political knee-capper Rahm Emanuel advocates not letting this emergency go to waste. The daily drip of panic combined with the blather from the maw of the lapdog media spreads the cacophony of catastrophe as a means to panic us into doing what they want. What do they want? To change the United States from a free-market country founded upon a rock-solid Constitution into a Western Hemisphere version of France floating on a living document that says whatever the ruling-class wants. Are we really buying this securitized derivative of a social contract? Many people are starting to wonder if this contract has a cancellation clause. Panic salesmen tell us "Hang yourself or I'll shoot you" bumper stickers say, "Honk if you'll pay my mortgage" and "Wave if you'll send my kids to college."

The razzle-dazzle continues as the Not-a-State-of-the-Union-Address announces increasing the number of soldiers, increasing the defense budget, expanding the war, universal education through college, and universal healthcare while cutting the deficit. The 11:59 flight of pigs is now leaving for a snowball fight in hell.

Standing O's greet each flight of fantasy as we learn the economic team goes through the budget line-by-line finding trillions in waste to cut. Has anyone bothered to tell our resident Constitutional scholar the President does not have line-item veto? I don't know what amazes me more, someone having the control to say this with a straight face, the poodle-press reporting it with a straight face, or many of my fellow citizens swallowing it without choking. These are the very people who put the budget together. Why did they put the waste in to begin with? Why did they have to discover things they put in the bill? Does anyone believe anything will be cut besides our own budgets?

How're these plans to remake America going so far? Put it this way, over in what should be the Amen Corner this move-on-dot-agenda is too liberal for Senator Byrd and George McGovern.

Now the Forget About It Choir sings a lament by the Crying Prophet, "Things I don't Hear Others Saying."

Forget about the Fairness Doctrine. The High Priests of Change only need three votes from the five-member FCC to define Localism in such a way that no radio station would dare air any syndicated conservative programming. This light rail train wreck we call Hope and Change is moving so fast the Rubber-stamp Senate already voted to enshrine Localism as an enforceable tenant of FCC policy.

Forget about revising the union stranglehold on the Big three. Look for the unionization of Honda, Toyota and anyone else who thinks they can get by without a union boss as a partner. Along with the envelopes full of cash, you'll need to provide four no-work electricians and three no-work carpenters or at least the W-2s if you want to do business in the Brave New Bizarro World of the Employee Free Choice Act.

Forget about these nickel and dime stimulus plans. While everyone's gazing at smoke and mirror debates about the latest porker for hundreds of billions, the Fed and Treasury pump trillions into the economy without a vote.

Forget about Global Warming. Cap-N-Trade is coming to save the day fighting the main polluter of the earth, carbon dioxide, by controlling emissions through what is essentially a new carbon tax shell game which creates a new commodity out of thin air. Businesses don't pay taxes consumers do. The price of everything will go up if this monstrosity ever lurches off the table. That's a hidden-tax on everyone using everything. We exhale carbon dioxide. Will the climate commissars start taxing us for that too?

Let's end with a new American prayer, "Oh, God let there be just one more bubble. In your mercy Lord let me cash-in on the right side of the next business-cycle, and if, Lord, this cannot be, may the Sanhedrin on the Potomac bail me out." Keep the faith. We shall survive. Amen.

Dispatch Forty-three

Why This When We Want That?

Now that the Health Care Summit is over could we have a Jobs Summit or an Economy Summit? And what a Health Summit it was. When Mitch McConnell, the leader of the Senate Republicans, pointed out a two for one disparity[1] between the time given to the Democrats and the Republicans Mr. Obama explained, "I don't count my time because I'm the President."[2] Senator McCain criticized the current democrat bills for backroom pay-offs and unsavory deals. President Obama quipped this was no time for campaigning since "The elections over."[3] Representative Cantor, the Republican Whip, complained of the excessive length of the health care bills.[4] The President told him displaying the massive bills was merely using them as a prop. Such dismissive mockery doesn't build agreement.

With the health care process finally out of the backrooms and on TV what did we see? Were we treated to hours of soaring oratory that the liberal hype-machine proclaims is the best in a generation[5] or were we bored to tears?[6] After a few minutes of the President's lengthy introduction it was painfully obvious that off his teleprompter the Moderator-in-Chief has a hard time framing a complete sentence or expressing a thought. There were more ums and ahs then in a freshman speech class.

Our Professor-in-Chief lectures us daily proving he and his teleprompter may be the greatest orator since Reagan but he's a poor communicator. How can anyone give hundreds of speeches over a year and then say the reason no one supports his program is because he hasn't made it clear enough for us to understand. Either he's saying he can't communicate or he's saying we're too dumb. Maybe instead of thousand page bills he could give us an outline or a PowerPoint? Perhaps it's time the professor hears what the people are singing, "Hey Teacher, leave those kids alone!"[7]

The vast majority of people want to keep the insurance coverage they have.[8] Sure it would be great to provide insurance for those who don't have any, but if that's the goal for much less than any of the trillion dollar projections for the nationalization of our health care system we could buy Cadillac plans for every person who needs it. So what's the point? Why wreck what 84.6% of the people have to insure the other 15.4%?[9] Buy them the insurance. Leave the rest of us alone! Come to think of it, if the poor among us already have health insurance through Medicaid,[10] and the youth are covered by CHIPS[11] who are these millions upon millions who are uninsured? Illegal aliens perhaps?

The State of the Union Speech told us our esteemed leader was pivoting away from the health care paradox to focus on reviving our flagging economy. Instead we see the President compulsively fixed on taking-over America's health care system. The question is why? Once the Feds take over health care, besides directly controlling up to 18% of the economy, it will also give the vast new army of wellness bureaucrats who will follow the power to interfere in the most intimate and personal aspects of our lives. What we eat, how we exercise, how we drive, what light bulbs we use, and where we can smoke all will become health care issues as America slithers towards totalitarianism, which is the total control of a population by their government.

People bought into the vision of "I'm Not Bush" standing between Styrofoam pillars spouting platitudes and avoiding specifics in the midst of an economic meltdown caused by lobbyist advanced cronies and casino capitalism. George II's answer to his pals sinking the economy with government forced bad loans and toxic derivatives were bail out the perpetrators with tax money from the victims. And what does Hope and Change do? Double down with a pork-filled stimulus boondoggle that's essentially a slush fund to re-elect Democrats in 2010. Now as an anemic recovery lurches towards a double-dip, instead of doing anything anyone believes would actually help, he's banging the health care drum like a political rain man reciting what the weather was like on November 8, 2008.

Is it credible to believe that a team of political operatives who cut their teeth in the swamps of Chicago, who had the finesse to sell an empty suit with smoke and mirrors can't hear hundreds of millions of Americans shouting, "We don't want this we want that!" This makes no sense. How do political savants turn into tone-deaf conductors, colorblind painters, and tangle-foot dancers overnight? Mistakes of this magnitude do not occur innocently. Almost every political pundit in the nation is endlessly chattering that the Democrats are following the President like lemmings off a midterm cliff, and yet the White House organization is focused like a laser on nationalizing health care. Leave it alone! Move on. Allow freedom to fix the economy before unsustainable debt sinks the ship of state.

Americans want the economy fixed. This isn't rocket science. Economic geniuses such as Hayek and Friedman and political leaders such as Coolidge and Reagan charted the course years ago. Fixing the economy is simple: cut taxes, cut the strangulation of regulation, and get out of the way. Europe is sinking under the weight of its version of socialism, and if we make America the haven of freedom, capital and talent will flock to our shores. If we don't all that capital and talent may well flock to the rising colossus of the East. Forget the health care take over, the photo-ops, and endless speeches. We don't want this we want that.

Dispatch Forty-four

What To Do Now That It's Been Done

You cannot beat good political drama. The Nuremberg rallies with all those glistening uniforms and snappy torch light marches. The May Day Parades with the Soviet gerontocracy standing on Lenin's tomb smiling at the grandchildren of the people they tortured riding on their shiny tanks and missile launchers. Even little North Korea stages some pretty impressive mass birthday parties for their Glorious leader. We may disagree with everything these totalitarian nightmare regimes stand for. We may abhor their gangster tactics and hellish fantasies about conquering the world, but you have to give them credit for knowing how to wow the crowd. They know how to stage a scene and then walk on as the Luke Skywalker of megalomania, wave to the great unwashed return to their castle of doom and continue living life large like Dr. No or in Kim Jong-II's case, Mini-Me.

The Denver acceptance speech with its Styrofoam Acropolis gave us a hint of the political theater to come. The Victory speech to the teaming masses in Grant Park let us know the curtain was rising. Like the

Perils of Pauline in a serial of sequels the suspense continues in the never-ending crisis. We must have health care and we must have it now! We're so far in debt we need to spend a massive amount quickly or we will go bankrupt. This is an emergency, there's no time to read the bill, hurry up and vote. We need this now even though it won't be implemented until after the next presidential election. Hurry up vote!!!

There is nail-biting suspense and edge-of-the-seat excitement as the plot thickens. What will it cost to buy Mary Landrieu's vote? [1] How much does Ben Nelson want for Nebraska's vote? [2] Ram it through no matter what the people want. Our lawyer-infested government knows better. Besides, who are we to question the only honest politician to emerge from the swamp of Chicago political corruption? Want to wake up with a horse's head in our bed? Just pay the big and shut up. They obviously know what's best. They've got 60 votes.

What a scene. The courageous iron-willed Nobel-prize-laureate makes his adorable little girls wait for Christmas while Daddy bludgeons a compliant Congress to pass anything they can call heath care reform so the Cavalcade of Czars can fill in the blanks later.

Every move they have taken since the November Revolution has been to seize control of the economy and society. Following the insurance, banking, and auto coups the health care take-over delivers another 1/6 of the economy into their clutches. Swiftly following will be Cap-n-Trade either by legislation or EPA mandate, Import-a-Voter-Immigration-Reform, and watch for the regime to begin acting as if whatever that was the Boss agreed to in Copenhagen is a ratified treaty committing America to the UN administered shake-down carbon tax to help prop up statists around the world.

The plan is to push through so many changes and to commit us to such enormous debt there will be no way back to the America we've known. They are also planning on maintaining their power in perpetuity through Acorn voter registration, manipulation of the census, and import-a-voter immigration reform. Echoing the question I hear every day as I travel around the country, the question I receive every day in emails from concerned Americans from sea to shining sea, "What can we do?"

They organized their way into power and we need to organize their way out. We laughed when someone had the audacity to list Community Organizer as his profession on a presidential résumé. Now we know that was not a joke. We could not believe it when someone from the most corrupt political machine in America was presented as hope for change. But the Corporations Once Known as the Mainstream Media pulled it off. Then after the Republican statists and their casino capitalist pals abandoned free market principles to save the free market[3] it was anti-climatic when a majority of American voters elected a one party regime with unstoppable majorities.

    We must organize. We must remain peaceful. But we must organize. The Tea Party movement blazed the way. Now a new organization, GOOOH, [4] or Get Out of Our House is growing on the American political horizon with the intention of vetting and backing candidates across the political spectrum. Others such as the Tea Party Patriots[5] and the Tea Party Express[6] are springing up bringing like-minded Americans together for education, encouragement, and inspiration. Using the Internet and the exploding social networks, these innovative groups are leading the way.

    Believers in free enterprise, personal liberty, and individual freedom are coalescing to out-organize the organizers. Constitutionally limited government will return to Washington for we shall not go silently into that long dark night. The arrogant career politicians, their media fellow travelers, and the entrenched technocrat bureaucracy may think they have won the final round. They may think the America we have known and loved is down for the count, but in reality all they've done is awaken a sleeping giant and filled him with a terrible resolve. Keep the faith. Keep the peace. We shall overcome.

Dispatch Forty-five

Is Limbaugh Really the Problem?

It is fashionable to point at Rush Limbaugh as the source of our descent into toxic politics. After the decent and humane way the Move-on-dot-Democrats and the lap-dog Mainstream Media treated President Bush for the last eight years it is disappointing that suddenly these paragons of fairness, civility, and truth are being subjected to such a withering attack by the Most Powerful Man in America. Mr. Limbaugh is a radio personality, an astute commentator on the politics, society, and economy of the country and he probably does need to keep half his brain tied behind his back just to make it fair, but he is not the Most Powerful Man in America.

Can you imagine back in the Bad-Old-Days when we endured Bush's outrageous 400 billion dollar deficits the uproar that would've ensued if it had been revealed Carl Rove held daily conference calls with Rush, O'Reilly, Hannnity, and Beck? Can you imagine the charges of conspiracy and collusion that would've worn us out in the twenty four hour news cycle? Just imagine the outrage of the fairness police, Pelosi, Reid,

Frank, and Dodd. The gnashing of teeth and the howls of injustice would have been enough to convince anyone with ears that blessed freedom itself was in danger of descending into cruel despotism.

However, when it was revealed President Obama's Chief of Staff Rohm Emmanuel holds a daily conference phone call for poodle press TV commentators and reporters such as ABC's George Stephanopoulos, and CNN's James Carville, and Paul Begala surprisingly the in-the-tank Mainstream Media did not even take time to roll their eyes and yawn Ho-Hum. This sinks below the obvious double-standard we have come to expect. Just imagine if Pat Buchanan made a disparaging remark about the Special Olympics. Does anyone believe the media screech would have turned into rhapsodies about his courageous apology within hours?

Coming from the political cesspool that is Chicago, everyone expected the highest level of integrity and fairness from the in-coming Obama administration. So imagine our lack of surprise when the first announced pick to share his power was another denizen of Daley's Kingdom of Darkness, Rohm Emmanuel.

Many of us know Emmanuel by his intimidating happy-face nickname Rhambo. When we think about him, we usually smile as we reflect on his sunny pit-bull demeanor and his get-it-done-or-else reputation that would make Don Corleone proud.

Here are a few of the reasons Rhambo is also known as Deadfish and why having him wake up every morning for a conference call about how to drag your name through the mud might not be such a pleasant experience.

When one pollster reported numbers Emmanuel did not want to hear, he received a large dead fish in the mail, not a horse's head in his bed but to the point. Emmanuel's fundraising has a distinctly Chicago flair. When working to help finance one of Richard the Second's ritual re-elections when receiving offers (in Chicago donations are a negotiation item, exactly how much police and fire protection do you want) he would tell people their amounts were so low they were embarrassing themselves as he slammed the phone down. Surprisingly many called back with higher offers. On the night after Clinton won in 1992, at a celebratory party, Emanuel regaled his fellow politically-correct liberals with a long rambling recitation of Clinton's enemy list. After shouting a name, he playfully stabbed the table with a steak knife while hissing, "Dead!"

However, the dark side is not Rhambo's only side, there is also sweetness and light. Mr. Emanuel is well known for treating his stable of regular supporters well, sending them cheesecakes, earmarks, and bailouts.

Now back to the gist of the Conference Call Cabal's attack against that loveable little fuzz-ball Rush. The much ballyhooed campaign of the Democratic National Committee against Rush led by Emmanuel and his crew with the help of their Mainstream Media fellow-travelers in the tank repeats over and over, "He wants President Obama to fail!" As one who actually heard the original statement, Mr. Limbaugh has never said he wants President Obama to fail no matter how the cut-and-paste tactics of the Mainstream Media tries to make it sound as if he did. What he said and what he says consistently is that he wants President Obama's collectivist agenda to fail. That's the real crime here. He's an unabashed supporter of free markets and the personal liberty which by nature accompanies this traditional American economy. That's why he's being pilloried.

Looking at those who want us to look at Rush might make this a little fair. Has any of the Cabal ever wanted a President or his policies to fail?

Prior to hearing of the terrorist attacks on the Twin Towers, James Carville, when referring to President Bush, told a group of pet reporters: "I certainly hope he doesn't succeed."[1] Democratic pollster Stanley Greenberg joined in saying his polls showed some people somewhere had misgivings about the new President. He was smiling as he continued, "We rush into these focus groups with these doubts that people have about him, and I'm wanting (sic) them to turn against him."² When the news of the terrorist attacks reached the two Democrat leaders Carville stood by his convictions and bravely said, "Disregard everything we just said! This changes everything!"³ The only thing that doesn't seem to change is liberals get a pass and conservatives get skewered.

The pivotal point here is that we are witnessing a private citizen being harassed by a White House attack-machine for political gain. The power of the executive branch is awesome. While Rush the entertainer often calls himself the most powerful man in America others often call the President the Most Powerful Man in the World. When I think that the President's Chief-of-Staff and his cadre of media hit-men hold daily rap-sessions seeking ways to attack a private citizen it chills me to the bone. What is next? A tax audits, FBI wire taps, or maybe they will send in a black ops team to bug his office.

Is Limbaugh really the problem? Or is an over-the-top Rabid Response Team led by a Chicago-bred political hatchet-man bent on silencing opposing opinions the problem? Freedom of speech is an important thing, and when we have a White House staff dedicated to brow-beating anyone who disagrees it is hard to imagine someone who appoints a political knee-capper like Deadfish does not know what he is doing. Then again, plausible deniability does rhyme with unindicted co-conspirator at least in the pages of history.

Dispatch Forty-six

The Fix is In

Falling like the staccato drumbeat of a pouring rain, the day-by-day assault by the ruling Progressives on the traditions and sensibilities of America has the no-longer-silent majority reeling. We were warned. The watchmen on the walls Buchanan, Limbaugh, Beck, and others told us what was coming. They tried to alert those willing to vote for an untried community organizer because they wanted change that the change would change once the organizer got organized, so none of these transformative changes should surprise anyone. Obama the candidate told us what Obama the president would do. He said he wanted to be a transformative president.[1] He told us his administration would be all about fundamentally transforming America. But it seems not many of the people who hoped for change were listening except to the hope and change part.

Today many of these erstwhile supporters, the casual voters who tune in for the last week of the race and then decide who to vote for based on emotion and those who even vote for the same party their father voted for, are beginning to wake up. They are beginning to see the sheer drop of the cliff we're being driven over. Suddenly the scales are falling off eyes and they see the emperor has no clothes. The Progressives are being exposed for the corporatists[2] and statists[3] they've always been. These Rip Van Winkle voters are now saying, "We were fooled" and "We didn't know." But they were warned. They just didn't listen. Which makes one wonder, when they're warned now about how bad this transformation is going to get, what are they hearing?

The Progressives long pursued dream of having the power and authority to implement their cherished Cloward-Piven Strategy[4] to collapse the economy is coming into focus as America watches in stunned horror. It is so hard to believe anyone really wants to kill the goose that laid the golden egg. The free American economy has created more wealth and spread it farther and faster than anything else in history. A key to the Progressive's plan to re-boot the system and impose their command economy is the destruction of our capitalist system. When General Cornwallis marched out of Yorktown his regimental band played "*The World Turned Upside Down.*" Perhaps this should be the dirge of the mourners for Mom, apple pie, and the American Way?

The 60s radicals who marched in the streets waving Viet Cong flags, burning draft cards, and calling licentious living free love have become the establishment. The silent majority has become the peaceful protesters who want their country back. Political correctness censors free speech in the name of free speech. Government mandated racial quotas enforce the most rigid racism since Jim Crow in the name of fairness. We apologize for our past, bow to foreign leaders of the present, and look forward to a future where China, [5] not the United States, [6] is the engine that drives the world economy. Is that the change we were hoping for?

George the Second abandoned free market principles to save the free market throwing a TARP[7] over the biggest boondoggle in history starting the serial hand-out binge the shills now call the Government Bailout Era.[8] The bursting of the housing bubble caused the economy to almost come to a halt. Listening to his Chief of Staff Rahm Emmanuel to "Never let a good crisis go to waste,"[9] President Obama set about fixing everything that was broken, or was that breaking everything he thought needed fixing?

First he fixed the economy as a whole with what he and his Progressive cohorts call the Recovery and Reinvestment Act. Subsequently many others call this bill the bailout for Democrat campaign contributors.[10] Then President Obama fixed the health care system assuring us there would be no rationing, costs would go down, and the federal government would never fund abortion.[11] Once again the bill was thousands of pages long, and no-one had a chance to read it before it passed since as Speaker Pelosi told us "We have to pass it so you can learn what's in it."[12] Or Representative John Conyers who laughingly said, "I love these members that get up and say, 'Read the bill!' Well, what good is reading the bill if it's a thousand pages and you don't have two days and two lawyers to find out what it means after you've read the bill?"[13] Now we learn it must of course include rationing, [14] of course it means costs will go up, [15] and it will fund abortions[16] but at least now it is fixed. The Dodd-Frank team[17] of congressional slight-of-hand artists handed President Obama the Financial Reform bill, which we are assured will fix the Banking system except for Fannie and Freddie which are exempt[18] this bill too is thousands of pages long. No one has had a chance to read it. Senator Dodd has had his chance at the microphone to tell us, "No one will know until this is actually in place how it works."[19] How could this go wrong? This sets up thousands of bureaucrats to stand on the throat of the financial industry, but at least it's fixed.

And that is not all. We are told every day that the energy industry is broken. That fix is on the way. Representative Waxman, the chairman of the committee writing the coming cap-n-trade tax bill, admitted he didn't know what was in the bill.[20] As a way of making an in-your-face demonstration of power, he hired a speed reader[21] to read his bill for those upset, because he wants to pass a bill that would make energy costs sky-rocket[22] without reading it. Be assured more fixes are coming. If we get one more free election, the Democrat party will pay for what they have done. But before the door closes on these fixers they will fix America until it is so broken all the king's horses and all the king's men won't be able to put America back together again.

The never-ending crises have not been wasted and everything is being fixed, or as we used to say in Chicago the fix is in.

Dispatch Forty-seven

Without Hope You're Hopeless

Marching out of Yorktown to surrender the British Army played the song "The World Turned Upside Down." As I drive to Mega Lo Mart to make my latest deposit of monopoly money in a Chinese savings account all I can do is mumble the final tag-line of the Wicked Witch of the West, "What a world? What a world?"

There is a massive unspoken problem in America today, floating like the iceberg in front of the Titanic waiting to sink the unsinkable ship. Founded by revolutionaries crying "No taxation without representation!" the Republic these revolutionaries devised has devolved into a society where 47% of the people pay no Federal Income Tax[1] and the number of people receiving government benefits is even higher.[2] What incentive would these non-paying receivers have to reign in an overbearing and intrusive government? This unseen and unspoken problem is a cancer in the body politic.

Self-serving professional politicians buy votes by exempting non-productive people from personal financial responsibility while providing ever-expanding benefits at the expense of the productive. This is not the right versus left, conservative versus liberal, democrat versus republican he-said-she-said endless debate that devours the chatocracy of cable's wall-to-wall talking-heads. This is not an academic exercise that pointy-headed political science and history majors with dueling pocket protectors debate for hours in their mother's basement as they post their latest scoop on their samizdat blogs.[3] If it is not any of these things what is it? It is a dagger pointing directly at the heart of our civilization.

Western Civilization awoke from the slumber of the Dark Ages enlightened and empowered by a belief that humanity has an innate right to be free and a natural right to excel. Rights and freedoms given by God not bestowed at the whim of some Legend-in-his-own-mind Leader. This civilization gathered steam in Europe exploding upon the world stage through an energetic period of exploration.

In America after a revolution fought by farmers and merchants against the greatest empire of the day, the Founders dared to declare, "We hold these truths to be self-evident, that all men are created equal, that they are endowed by their Creator with certain unalienable rights that among these are Life, Liberty, and the pursuit of Happiness."[4] After centuries of government thugs standing on the windpipe of everyday people these self-sacrificing giants observed that in a civilized world government was not imposed by the strong upon the weak it was instead built upon a social contract between the governed and those entrusted with the privilege to govern when they said, "That to secure these rights, Governments are instituted among Men, deriving their just powers from the consent of the governed."[5]

Today this bold and unique experiment in freedom is being devoured from within and challenged from without. Those who believe the collective should reign over the individual, those who believe in the suffocating sameness of socialism over the rough-and-tumble of capitalism have worked for generations building a culture of dependency. This has tempered the steel will of the pioneers into the sloppy demands of the couch-potato slacker waiting for someone to find their remote as they guzzle some refreshments and wait for the game as bread and circuses take the place of innovation and accomplishment. Schools teaching 2+2 might = 5, trophies for everyone, politically correct new-speak, and affirmative action promotions have sapped the vitality from the citizens of our Republic. Politicians and their fellow-travelers use a system of cronies and sweet-heart deals[6] to reward each other for siphoning trillions from the public treasury promising the dumbed-down[7] descendants of revolutionaries that they just might win the lotto before they have to declare bankruptcy, so they might as well re-elect the same old grafters once again.

There comes a time when those who are raising the sails and paddling the boat have to admit to themselves the ballast down in steerage weighs more than the cargo. There comes a time when even the most non-confrontational and loyal among us begin to ask, "Who is John Galt"[8] as Atlas tires of his thankless job and shrugs[9] the burden of dead-weight into the dustbin of history. As the perpetually-reelected and the propaganda spewing Corporations Once Known as the Mainstream Media trumpet, the inevitability of government rationed health-care, cap-n-trade industrial suicide, comprehensive import-a-voter immigration reform, and the surrender of sovereignty through treaties supposedly designed to deal with mythical global warming[10] there shines a light in a bell tower, one if by land and two if by sea.

Without hope you're hopeless and I refuse to allow the unbelievable changes currently assaulting our economy and our political system to bring about my own personal Great Depression. Those who believe in the devil believe he comes to steal, kill, and destroy. I believe if he can't steal your joy he can't keep your stuff, and weeping may endure for a night but joy comes in the morning.

Dispatch Forty-eight

Payday's Coming Someday

The Congressional proponents of behavioral economics and social change have caused the very problems we are struggling to survive and they are rushing headlong to solve. Many of the talking-heads who shape public opinion have forgotten the entire economic crisis we currently face was started by the problems at Fannie Mae and Freddie Mac before Lehman Brothers declared bankruptcy and Bank of America bought Merrill Lynch with a government credit card.

We are reminded constantly all our current problems find their cause in a lack of regulation and that the Bush administration was asleep at the switch if not in outright collusion with casino capitalists who bet all our money and lost. It is too bad the facts do not support that particular urban myth. There are 1,870,000 pieces of evidence in .32 seconds a mere one click away that documents Congress was amply warned by the Bush Administration, Greenspan, even "Me Too" McCain offered a bill to strengthen the oversight of Fannie and Freddie. These measures were blocked by the likes of Barney Frank, Charles Schumer, and the usual cast of characters. It is an old ploy of statists and wannabe collectivists to create emergencies that have to be addressed immediately. "There's no time to read the bill just VOTE! VOTE! VOTE!" screech the cheerleaders as the perpetually re-elected fume, fizzle, and posture before taking out a fifteenth mortgage from a Chinese bank. How could this ever go wrong?

Every generation has its challenges. My parents faced the Depression, Hitler, and Mutually Assured Destruction. We face an economic system that's melting down and the statists who have been empowered to deal with it. I am still not sure which is worse. I am sure which will have the most far reaching long-term effect. The business cycle has been going on since Ugg tried to corner the market on round rocks. Bubbles inflate as people think, "Wow the price of round rocks is going through the roof! I better get in on this." Then the price of rocks not only goes through the roof it goes into orbit and Ugg makes a big pile of banana leaves until people notice round rocks are really just rocks and everyone ends up with a worthless pile of rocks as Ugg moves on to corner the market on flat rocks and the whole cycle repeats itself. This current meltdown is terrible, and my heart goes out to all who're suffering through it especially the ones who never had anything to do with the round rock market. However, this too shall pass.

The revolutionary changes being tossed out on a daily and sometimes even an hourly basis by the Progressives will be with us until there is a counter - evolution at the ballot box. They are institutionalizing the statist principles of the Frankfurt School[1] and Saul Alinsky, the original Chicago Community Organizer. America like Gulliver will remain tied by the threads of the Lilliputians until these many collectivist measures are repealed in a radical return to Constitutional government.

From bailing out Ugg and his round rock scam to telling the tribe they need to fire Ugg is a quantum shift. Our government has lent money and made grants to businesses from the Federal Roads through the Rail Road, to Chrysler. However, when bureaucrats in Washington start deciding who works where and how much they're paid we've moved far to the left of where we began. However, anyone who thinks the train has reached the station and we can now get off in the Brave New World needs to sit down, buckle their legally required seat belt, put on their legally required helmet, and brace for the bullet train to spin off more paradigm shifting changes at the speed of lies. All aboard! Next stop Stimulus II, Cap-N-Tax, Trillion Dollar Deficits, Comprehensive Amnesty Voter Enhancement, the World Poverty Tax, and the end of American Exceptionalism.

How do those who want a return to Constitutional government proceed? It seems as if many are asking that question and there seem to be answers popping up all over the place. Using the Internet to reach everyone at once there are many sites offering education and unity for those opposing the imposition of central planning. These include the 912project.com, ourcaucus.com, goooh.com, resistnet.com, and others added daily. There're also countless local groups springing up spontaneously around the country. These groups of citizens remind me of the Committees of Correspondence which were catalysts of the first American Revolution. Our statist leaders believe they have built a cage of legislation strong enough to constrain the creativity and energy of the American people and their capitalist system like the goose that laid the golden egg. However, I believe there is a surprise coming and it might just start with thousands of tea parties across the country on tax day which reminds me of an old song, "Payday's coming someday."

Dispatch Forty-nine

Winners Write History
To The Victors Go The Spoils

Somewhere along the line maybe in 7th grade history or 12th grade Political Science we are told the story of the long and tedious debate between the Federalists and the Anti-Federalists. This highly sophisticated debate which took place in newspapers, which were the internet of the eighteenth century, went on for months and swayed the thinking of a nation is usually covered today in perhaps a paragraph. Lost to the sesame street sound-bite generation are the intricacies as well as the true nature of this debate.

If we are taught anything we are instructed that the Federalists wanted to convince people to vote for the Constitution that is presented as a good idea considering the many benefits which have flowed from them to us. The Anti-Federalists are of course portrayed as against all good. A few of us might know that Hamilton and Madison were among the anonymous authors of the federalist articles but even fewer would be able to name any of the Anti-Federalists. Their names are lost to history or at least to the consciousness of their descendants just as their arguments have been obscured and buried, because winners write history and to the victors go the spoils.

However, if we think about the reality of the argument, ignoring the prejudice of the labels, it becomes apparent that the Federalists were in reality nationalists in favor of a much stronger centralized government than that which existed. There is another detail lost in the shuffle of victory. America after the Revolution was not a rudderless nothing until the Constitution was ratified. There was a functioning government which had been established and agreed upon by the thirteen independent states, which had won their independence from England. They had asked a committee to recommend amendments and that committee had decided to write a constitution establishing another government.

The so-called Anti-Federalists were actually supporters of the then legal government, which was a federation of states agreeing to united action in certain proscribed and limited areas. These patriots chose pen names such as the Federal Farmer and a Republican Federalist, which might surprise many for at the time those, we are taught, were the Anti-Federalists actually themselves considered to be federalists since they supported the federal structure of the at-that-time legal government of the Confederation. Those we today call federalists were at the time recognized as nationalist who favored a stronger central government.

Then Hamilton, Jay, and Madison won the debate, and their subsequent admirers won the naming rights and the Constitution replaced the Articles of Confederation as a loose federation was replaced by a binding union. But even the proponents of a more centralized government feared a resurrection of the tyranny they had just fought America's longest war to divorce. Consequently they sought to limit the power of the Central government, preserve the prerogatives of the state, and ensure the liberty of the people.

Freedom of expression began to bow before the state with Alien and Sedition Acts under our second President. Nationalism trumped federalism in the Louisiana Purchase. Peaceful coexistence as a free nation among equals fell victim to Manifest Destiny and the Mexican War. Any resemblance to a voluntary union died in the Civil War. The tradition of no foreign entanglements was forgotten in the interventionism of the Spanish American War. The twentieth century with a few exceptions under Coolidge and Reagan was one long descent into centralized government. It is time to quit fooling ourselves with the myth that the Constitution effectively limited government and protected individual freedom until the evil Progressives began their insidious behind the scenes march towards collectivism.

The Constitution was written as a means to impose a stronger central government by those who felt the idea of a confederation of independent states linked by culture and self-interest was not appropriate to the furtherance of a unified continental economy and the peaceful enjoyment of the prosperity such an economy would hopefully create. It was written in secret, ratified only by promising to include additional safe guards to personal and states' rights, and it has been used as both a cover and a tool to expand government at the expense of both the states and the individual since day one.

It is time to re-examine the arguments of both those we know as the Federalists and those we have been taught were the Anti-Federalists. It is time to re-examine the arguments in favor of the Constitution and those against it.

The Federalists said that the document they had written would create a nation of limited government dedicated to the preservation of the individuality of the states and the freedom of the individual. They promised that the central government would be circumscribed by law and unable to usurp the unalienable rights proclaimed to be the natural heritage of humanity.

The Anti-Federalists said this would not be the case. Their contention was that a centralized government once created would inevitably grow. They foresaw that the limits which the framers of the document thought iron-clad would eventually rust and the manacles restraining the tyranny they all feared would fall from the wrists of future leaders. They predicted that the power to create an all-embracing continental economy would also become the power to control that economy to the detriment of the individual. In other words, all power corrupts and absolute power corrupts absolutely.   Who was right?   What has become of our limited government? Is it time to go back to the drawing board or at least back to the history books? Perhaps what we've been taught wasn't really what happened. Perhaps the spin started so long ago we've been trying to hit a knuckle ball all along and only by taking off the Constitution colored glasses will we be able to see our way back to where we started from?

Dispatch Fifty

The Last Best Hope

In the darkest days of the war when one stunning defeat followed another and the Union couldn't seem to find a general capable of standing up to Robert E. Lee and the Army of Northern Virginia Abraham Lincoln said, "We shall nobly save, or meanly lose, the last best hope of earth."[1] Today, we face a Leviathan of our own creation. Dr. Frankenstein, a literary creation so brilliant he brought inanimate flesh to life, had his name hijacked by his brutish creation. In like manner the noble experiment conceived by our Founders is now in the hands of those seeking to bring the collectivist dead back from the trash-heap of history.

You know Capitalism is in trouble when markets move more over government reports, programs, bailouts, interventions, and threats then they do over invention and productivity. Our once free nation is dissolving into a re-tread of the Corporate State[2] once so fashionable with their natty Black Shirts[3] and calendar starting at the year one.

These colossal boondoggles whether they're called stimulus, bail-outs, or cross-generational theft, are attempts by those elected to save the system to make the current crisis so bad we'll cheerfully put collars around our own necks. If our government really wanted to jump start the economy there are better ways to do it than strangling the baby before you throw out the bath water.

Instead of borrowed bailouts why not an immediate one year personal tax holiday. We wouldn't have to borrow money or pay interest, and it wouldn't cost any more than all the borrowing we're doing now. This would put money in every tax-payer's pocket immediately leading to increased spending stimulating the economy.

Everyone outside the black-hole beltway knows we need to simplify a tax code of over 60,000 pages. Let's do what the former Communists in Russia did and enact a Flat Tax.[4] This would be fair for all and it would free up an estimated 6.6 billion hours spent filling out tax forms for productive pursuits.[5]

We could make America business friendly again. Today we have one of the highest corporate tax rates in the world while Communist China has one of the lowest. We also have some of the most stringent regulations and the highest amount of government interference in business operations. According to the

Small Business Administration, small-businesses spend more than one billion hours each year filling out government forms at a cost of $100 billion. Let's cut the corporate tax rates, burn the paper work, and let people get back to work.

Our current leaders are self-confessed followers of John Maynard Keynes. Lenin said," The best way to destroy the capitalist system is to debauch the currency. By a continuing process of inflation, governments can confiscate, secretly and unobserved, an important part of the wealth of their citizens."[6] Which Keynes, the guru of the Administration echoed by saying, "Lenin was certainly right. There is no subtler, no surer means of overturning the existing basis of society than to debauch the currency. The process engages all the hidden forces of economic law on the side of destruction, and does it in a manner which not one man in a million is able to diagnose."[7]

Stop printing money and debasing our currency. Abolish the Federal Reserve System created in 1913 to stop the cycle of boom and bust by regulating the money supply. According to the Constitution, Congress alone is granted the power to coin money. Our government was created by the people not the other way around, and the power we've lent them isn't to be abdicated to the Federal Reserve or anyone else. Stop the presses now!

We're following the British Empire off the cliff into a sea of endless red ink chasing the phantom of Free Trade. As America reduces or eliminates all tariffs on incoming foreign goods, our goods are still subject to imposed fees when they follow the return route. No one calls them tariffs, instead they're equalization adjustments based on a Value-Added Tax. Not only are American goods entering other countries slapped with VAT adjustments, in addition foreign companies sending goods our way receive rebates from their governments. These aren't subsidies which our Free Trade Agreements outlaw they're rebates working just like subsidies.

In his recent virtual town-hall meeting, President Obama was asked when people can expect a return of jobs outsourced to other nations. The President said, "Many of the lost jobs in recent years involve work that was done by people getting very low wages and those with limited work skills."[6] I thought good paying factory jobs built the middleclass in this country, and our Leader believes all those jobs our policies sent overseas weren't worth having. I believe millions of former factory workers now flipping burgers and chasing carts might have a different point-of-view. I say it's time to re-industrialize America. We need to make things again. The Arsenal of Democracy has become a flea-market filled with people living on charge-cards.

Even one candle looks bright in the dark. It is time to stand- up before we fall down. Tell your family, friends, neighbors, tell that person standing behind you in the check-out line, "We will not go quietly into that dark night!" We will not sit up and beg for scraps from the collectivist table. We're Americans. We will not be the generation that lost the last best hope.

Dispatch Fifty-one

To Build a Better Mouse Trap

One of my favorite sayings usually garnered from some old grizzled denizen of rural America on a dusty road that travelers may call "The middle of no-where" but a place he calls home is, "You can't get there from here." This is where America has arrived. I do not mean the middle of no-where; I mean the paradox of you cannot get there from here.

In the opening decades of the 21st century a nation created as an experiment in individual liberty and corporate freedom has devolved into a nanny-state determined to protect everyone from failure at the expense of success. A nation once confident enough to tell a much more powerful Europe the western hemisphere was off limits for their game of colonial imperialism now stands helpless as its borders become hypothetical and its balance sheet nonsensical. Our leaders pay lip service to a Constitution meant to limit their power while using the so-called elastic clause[1] and mere figures of speech like "general welfare" to build a government apparatus of unlimited power.

Self interest groups on the right and on the left advocate for feeding their favorite hog while screaming that we gore their neighbor's ox. Once sectional divisions split this nation in a horrendous fratricidal blood bath the hearts of the sons turned from the father. Today the country is split not along sectional lines but lines of race, ethnicity, and class. The love of the mother has grown cold and every man does that which is right in his own eyes. Consensus has broken down and factions build majority coalitions whose main aim is to vote themselves benefits from the public treasury.

How do we get back to a government of the people, by the people and for the people? Sad to say the answer may be, "You can't get there from here."

Back in the dream time before the summer of love became the winter of our discontent I try to make what I consider to be my wisdom more powerful by attributing my witticisms to old sayings. One of which was, "You have to walk through the blast to sit by the fire." I attributed this variously to Indian chiefs, mafia dons, and traveling mystics. By this I mean you have to endure the suffering of the moment to reap the benefit of repose. As a nation I believe we have reached such a moment. Not only is there no way back to where we once were, there is no way out of the box we're in without cutting some tape and folding some cardboard.

First we have to cut the tape which binds us to what once was. After the first blush of war enthusiasm passed and the Germany of World war I saw that they had cast their lot with the hollow shell of an Austro-Hungarian Empire, a decrepit patchwork of feuding ethnicities, a common saying was that they were chained to a corpse. Is it time that those who believe in limited government and individual liberty admit that the idealized Constitution in our hearts bears little resemblance to the stained and tattered document the Progressives currently use alternately as bathroom tissue or as cover for their naked power grabs. Is it time that we move on from nostalgia for a past that may or may not have ever existed and ask if you can't get there from here how do we get there?

The Progressives have become masters at changing the Constitution without amending it. They change it by degrees and then point to precedent. They usurp power than call it tradition. From judicial review to executive orders and signing statements the elastic clauses and general welfares have turned whatever the Constitution was meant to be into what it is today: a historical document that has little bearing upon how we are ruled and to what extent.

Has the time arrived to declare that the Constitution is not a suicide pact and that we are not chained to a corpse? Has the time arrived when we must take destiny into our own hands and declare we will be free and we will secure for our posterity the blessing of freedom? The United States was never meant to become a cradle-to-grave welfare state. It is a perversion of the intent of our founders and the will of our citizens that the United States becomes a nanny-state dedicated to protecting us from failure at the expense of success. We have not voluntarily surrendered our inalienable rights in exchange for an illusion of security. We have not decided to erase our borders and debase our heritage. We have not approved a program of endless spending and endless debt.

The time has come to re-think this social contract. Our ancestors ratified a document: the Constitution to limit government and to secure the blessings of freedom for us, their posterity. Today we stand toe-to-toe with tyranny and perhaps the time has come to drop our blind allegiance to a document that has failed and reread one that succeeded.

> When in the Course of human events it becomes necessary for one people to dissolve the political bands which have connected them with another and to assume among the powers of the earth, the separate and equal station to which the Laws of Nature and of Nature's God entitle them, a decent respect to the opinions of mankind requires that they should declare the causes which impel them to the separation.

> We hold these truths to be self-evident, that all men are created equal, that they are endowed by their Creator with certain unalienable Rights that among these are Life, Liberty and the pursuit of Happiness. — That to secure these rights, Governments are instituted among Men, deriving their just powers from the consent of the governed, — That whenever any Form of Government becomes destructive of these ends, it is the Right of the People to alter or to abolish it, and to institute new Government, laying its foundation on such principles and organizing its powers in such form, as to them shall seem most likely to affect their Safety and Happiness. Prudence, indeed, will dictate that Governments long established should not be changed for light and transient causes; and accordingly all experience hath shewn that mankind are more disposed to suffer, while evils are sufferable than to right themselves by abolishing the forms to which they are accustomed. But when a long train of abuses and usurpations, pursuing invariably the same Object evinces a design to reduce them under absolute Despotism, it is their right, it is their duty, to throw off such Government, and to provide new Guards for their future security.[2]

Every honest contract has an escape clause. Only suicide pacts are irrevocable. The Civil War taught us that there is no way for individual states or even for a group of states to leave the Federal state. What we need to do is find the escape clause; just as if you want to catch a smarter mouse you need a better mouse trap.

Dispatch Fifty-two

Freedom From Tyranny Is Our Goal

When taxes become destructive they've surpassed the consent of the governed bending to the will of tyranny. When regulations strangle competition instead of securing it from evil combinations they have become counterproductive and defeat the very purpose for which they were proposed. When foreign entanglements bleed the nation but do not secure the peace or defeat the enemy they have become interventionist vehicles for vested interests. When spending becomes a hemorrhaging of assists leading to national bankruptcy those who continue to pile debt upon debt seek not the good of the nation but instead its destruction. When leaders selected to unite instead do all they can to divide they no longer advance the interest of the whole and are instead partisan leaders in a factional fight.

A social contract is one made between a people and their government. It is an agreement whereby the people surrender certain aspects of their independence for the guarantee of corporate security and the enjoyment of a general welfare. In the case of most countries this is an unwritten and unconscious arrangement built upon tradition and precedent as in the case of England. However in the United States we have an actual contract, the Constitution. This was ratified by the original states and the subsequent states were formed under it and admitted as full partners to it.

All contracts may be legitimately changed over time as long as there are mechanisms either within the document or established by the document to do so. Within our Constitution there is an amendment process, and it has been amended 27 times so far. Whether we agree with those amendments or not they have been legally ratified and accepted becoming part of the document. However, over the years our government structure has been changed and our manner of life transformed more by the informal changes than by the formal. Nowhere in the Constitution is the central government given the power to wage unending undeclared war. Nowhere is the central government given the right to ignore the requirement to protect the states from invasion. Nowhere is there found any basis for executive orders, signing statements, or bureaucratic regulations to have the force of law without legislative action by Congress.

Well-connected rabble rousers now say equality will not be achieved until everything is equal in everybody's house. Leveling the playing field has finally thrown off its cloak of deceit and exposed itself as from each according to their ability to each according to their need. The professional civil rights entrepreneurs who have extorted vast amounts of personal wealth with threats of boycotts and demonstrations have been unmasked as the true purveyors of prejudice seeking to keep race and gender differences alive for their own benefit. Union bosses build political empires using the legally forced dues of members with more money spent on political activity than on member service. The union bosses ride in limousine comfort from board meetings to political rallies while their members lose jobs. The pensions of the bosses are golden parachutes while the pensions of the members are underfunded.

The Land of the Free is held captive, locked in a two party system where both parties are merely two heads on the same bird of prey. Both parties are dedicated to more spending and bigger government. Both parties exploit gerrymandering of districts and overwhelming corporate donations to ensure a hierarchy of the perpetually re-elected using a system of seniority to enhance their power. Legal barriers exist at every turn to stop any new parties from gaining access that might deflect the central government from its ever increasing growth towards totalitarianism.

When will enough be enough? When will citizens rise in their righteous anger and demand not a New Deal, not a Great Society, a New Frontier, or a Fundamentally Transformed America but instead their original deal. The one we wrested from the hands of the tyrant King George. The one we have fought to establish and defend from Yorktown to Kandahar and the right of a people to be free to live as they choose, to work for their own benefit, and choose their own destiny. Free from the smothering governmental control which has been the lot of most people in most places since the beginning of time. When will the yoke of tyranny become too heavy to be borne? What will be the spark that lights the torches and brings the incensed villagers to the gate of the castle demanding, "Bring the monster out!" so that a stake can be driven through the heart of tyranny and freedom can return to the land?

When that day comes what will *We the People* do? Will we try to resurrect the government of old that ultimately brought us full circle, or will we be bold enough to forge anew the social contract and design better ways to ensure the beast of tyranny doesn't once again break the chains of restraint.

Arguments of the Anti-Federalists

The Anti-Federalists believed that the Constitution had some major problems. They saw no reason to abandon a form of government that had governed the country successfully through the Revolution and had established a nation moving swiftly towards prosperity. They also felt that the Framers had exceeded their authority in a secret meeting and were attempting to foist a revolutionary change on an unsuspecting country.

The Anti-Federalists used the language of the Revolution placing a major emphasis on the Republican virtues of local power and de-centralized authority. They believed that the Constitution was a major move away from the goals of the Revolution written by aristocrats for aristocrats.

The power of the President and the vague language of the document such as the statement in Article 1, section 8 which authorizes Congress to "make all laws which shall be necessary and proper for carrying into execution the foregoing powers, and all other powers vested by this Constitution in the government of the United States, or in any department or officer thereof."[1] was seen as a blank slate where anything could be eventually written to the detriment of the people and the States. This led them to believe that the extended power of the Federal government would eventually lead to the virtual end to the sovereignty of the individual states?

Another, inter-related problem was the equally vague power to be conferred upon the Federal Courts. This engendered a fear of tyranny through interpretation. Melancton Smith stated his apprehensions in this matter by saying, "It appears to me, this part of the system is so framed as to clinch all the other powers, and to extend them in a silent and imperceptible manner to anything and everything, while the Court who are vested with these powers are totally independent, uncontrollable and not amendable to any other power in any decisions they may make."[2]

Still another argument that was widely dispersed throughout the country and echoed in many of the state ratification conventions was to what has come to be known as the Supremacy Clause. This clause is found in Article VI, Section 2, of the U.S. Constitution which states, "This Constitution, and the laws of the United States which shall be made in pursuance thereof; and all treaties made, or which shall be made, under the authority of the United States, shall be the supreme law of the land; and the judges in every state shall be bound thereby, anything in the Constitution or laws of any State to the contrary notwithstanding."[3] The Anti-Federalists correctly deduced that this would mean that the federal government, in exercising any of the powers enumerated or interpreted in the Constitution, would always prevail over any conflicting or inconsistent state exercise of power.

This fear was later completely realized almost from the very beginning of the Republic. The theory as well as the application of federal supremacy developed under the second Chief Justice of the Supreme Court, John Marshall, who led the Supreme Court from 1801 to 1835. In Mcculloch v. Maryland, 17 U.S. (4 Wheat.) 316, 4 L. Ed. 579 (1819), the Marshall Court invalidated a Maryland law relating to the taxation of all banks in the state which included a branch of the national bank. Marshall ruled that although none of the enumerated powers of Congress explicitly authorized the incorporation of the national bank, the Necessary and Proper Clause provided the necessary authority for Congress's action. Once he established that the exercise of national authority was authorized under the vague wording of the Constitution, Marshall stated, "The government of the Union, though limited in its power, is supreme within its sphere of action."[4]

The Anti-Federalists saw that the individual sovereignty of the States would be swallowed by a Constitution whose vagueness would be interpreted by the very government it created. Warning of the future rapaciousness of the Supremacy Clause Robert Whitehall declared in the Pennsylvania Ratification Convention that, "This Article eradicates every vestige of State government and was intended so, it was deliberate."[5]

Many Anti-Federalists, who believed in what was known as agrarian republicanism sought to preserve the independence of the local against the encroachments of the center.

The major problem with the Anti-Federalist cause was that while they were united in their opposition to the Constitution they never laid out a coherent plan for an alternative. It was this lack of an agreed upon goal, besides the defeat of the constitution, combined with the Federalist's dominance in the seats of power and influence that doomed the Anti-Federalists cause to defeat.

Many of the leading patriots of the Revolution worked for the defeat of the Constitution including Samuel Adams, George Clinton, Patrick Henry, Richard Henry Lee, George Mason, and the future President James Monroe.

Melancton Smith, "Representation in Government"

> [W]hen we speak of representatives... they resemble those they represent. They should be a true picture of the people, possess a knowledge of their circumstances and their wants, sympathize in all their distresses, and be disposed to seek their true interests. The knowledge necessary for the representative of a free people not only comprehends extensive political and commercial information, such as is acquired by men of refined education, who have leisure to attain to high degrees of improvement, but it should also comprehend that kind of acquaintance with the common concerns and occupations of the people, which men of the middling class of life are, in general, more competent to than those of a superior class. To understand the true

commercial interests of a country not only requires just ideas of the general commerce of the world, but also, and principally, a knowledge of the productions of your own country, and their value, what your soil is capable of producing, the nature of your manufactures, the capacity of the country to increase both. To exercise the power of laying taxes, duties, exercises, with discretion, requires something more than an acquaintance with the abstruse parts of the system of finance. It calls for a knowledge of the circumstances and ability of the people in general a discernment how the burdens imposed will bear upon the different classes.

... The number of representatives should be so large, as that, while it embraces the men of the first class, it should admit those of the middling class of life. I am convinced that this government is so constituted that the representatives will generally be composed of the first class in the community, which I shall distinguish by the name of the natural aristocracy of the country...

From these remarks, it appears that the government will fall into the hands of the few and the great. This will be a government of oppression.

...A system of corruption is known to be the system of government in Europe...[and] it will be attempted among us. The most effectual as well as natural security against this is a strong democratic branch in the legislature, frequently chosen, including in it a number of the substantial, sensible, yeomanry of the country. Does the House of Representatives answer this description? I confess, to me they hardly wear the complexion of a democratic branch. [6]

George Clinton, "In Opposition to Destruction of States' Rights"

The... premises on which the new form of government is erected, declares a consolidation or union of all thirteen parts, or states, into one great whole, under the firm of the United States... But whoever seriously considers the immense extent of territory comprehended within the limits of the United States, together with the variety of its climates, productions, and commerce, the difference of extent, and number of inhabitants in all; the dissimilitude of interests, morals, and politics in almost every one, will receive it as an intuitive truth, that a consolidated republican form of government therein, can never form a perfect union, establish justice, insure domestic tranquility, promote the general welfare, and secure the blessings of liberty to you and your posterity, for to these objects it must be directed: this unhindered legislature therefore, composed of interests opposite and dissimilar in nature, will in its exercise, emphatically be like a house divided against itself...

From this picture, what can you promise yourself, on the score of consolidation of the United States into one government? Impracticability in the just exercise of it, your freedom insecure... you risk much, by indispensably placing trusts of the greatest magnitude, into the hands of individuals whose ambition for power, and aggrandizement, will oppress and grind you where from the vast extent of your territory, and the complication of interests, the science of government will become intricate and perplexed, and too mysterious for you to understand and observe; and by which you are to be conducted into a monarchy, either limited or despotic... [7]

Patrick Henry, "Need for a Bill of Rights"

This proposal of altering our federal government is of a most alarming nature!.... You ought to be watchful, jealous of your liberty; for, instead of securing your rights, you may lose them forever... I beg gentlemen to consider that a wrong step made now will plunge us into misery, and our republic will be lost, and tyranny must and will arise...

> The necessity of a Bill of Rights appears to me to be greater in this government than ever it was in any government before... All rights not expressly and unequivocally reserved to the people are impliedly and incidentally relinquished to rulers, as necessarily inseparable from the delegated powers...
>
> This is the question. If you intend to reserve your unalienable rights, you must have the most express stipulation; for, if implication be allowed, you are ousted of those rights. If the people do not think it necessary to reserve them, they will be supposed to be given up.
>
> [W]ithout a Bill of Rights, you will exhibit the most absurd thing to mankind that ever the world saw a government [i.e. state governments] that has abandoned all its powers the powers of taxation, the sword, and the purse. You have disposed of them to Congress, without a Bill of Rights without check, limitation, or control... You have Bill of Rights to defend against a state government, which is bereaved of all its power, and yet you have none against Congress, thought in full and exclusive possession of all power! [8]

This is just a small representation of the myriad of arguments published and presented through speeches by the group of Patriots who saw the ratification of the Constitution as more of a counter-revolution than as the culmination of the struggle for liberty. And if this seems like the anti-American argument we were all taught in school stop and think what the Constitution would be like without the Bill of Rights. This was the Constitution the Framers wrote. This was the Constitution the Framers sought to have ratified. It was only due to the arguments of the Anti-Federalists that the Bill of rights was added.

How Long Did the Limit Last?

In 1798, a mere ten years after the ratification of the Constitution, war with France seemed imminent. In reaction to opposition regarding the policies of the government John Adams, hero of the Revolution, co-author of the Declaration of Independence, one of the Framers of the Constitution, and only the second President of the United States Congress passed the Alien and Sedition Acts.

Congress eventually passed four of these laws in an effort to strengthen the Federal government against internal dissent. The former supporters of the Constitution, now known as Federalists, sponsored the legislation meant to silence political opposition which was coming mainly from the Democratic Republicans, and their leader Thomas Jefferson.

First Congress passed the Naturalization Act which required people to be residents of the United States for fourteen years instead of five years before becoming eligible for U.S. citizenship.

Then they passed the Alien Act which authorized the President to deport aliens, which the government determined to be dangerous or a threat to the peace and/or safety of the United States. It must be remembered that while many believed America was under a threat of war this law was passed and enforced during peacetime.

Seeking to extend the power of the central government even further Congress next passed the Alien Enemies Act. This third act allowed the arrest, imprisonment, and deportation of aliens who were from an enemy country.

Finally Congress added the Sedition Act, aimed at any action deemed by the government to be treason. This included the publication of any material judged to be false, scandalous, or malicious. No matter what the Bill of Rights said the government declared these activities to be a severe misdemeanor that was punishable by both fine and imprisonment.

Under these bills twenty-five men, including numerous editors of newspapers, were arrested. In addition, their newspapers were shut down.

The net of suspicion was spread so far that it included Benjamin Franklin Bache, Benjamin Franklin's grandson who was the editor of a Philadelphia newspaper. He was charged with libeling President Adams. This arrest elicited a mounting public reaction against all four of the Alien and Sedition Acts.

Many Americans questioned the constitutionality of these laws. Indeed, public opposition to the Alien and Sedition Acts was so great that they were in part responsible for the election of Thomas Jefferson, a Republican, to the presidency in 1800. Once in office, Jefferson pardoned all those convicted under the

Sedition Act, while Congress restored all fines paid with interest.

The unpopularity and questionable legality of these acts led to Adams being the first one-term president. And these actions by one of the foremost Framers and most vocal supporters during the ratification process used these oppressive laws to silence opposition. Here at the very beginning of the Constitutional republic one of the architects of the document believed it gave him and Congress the power to silence the people when the people disagreed. [1]

Jefferson and his democratic Republicans defeated Adams' bid for a second term by capitalizing on the public's disgust at what were perceived to be unconstitutional and repressive actions by the very people who wrote and led the fight for the adoption of the constitution. Now those who portrayed themselves as the protectors of liberty would make sure that the limits placed upon the federal government were strictly observed.

In 1803, during their long wars with England and in need of financial relief France offered to sell Louisiana to the United States. This caused a novel situation and became the cause of a grave constitutional question and a major problem for President Thomas Jefferson and his ruling party. Seeing the opportunity to double the size of the United

States President Jefferson immediately wanted to purchase the territory.

This was rather surprising in that Jefferson advocated a narrow or strict interpretation of the Constitution. And no matter how you read the document nowhere does it authorize the President or even the Congress to buy additional territory. President Jefferson did not debate this point nor did he dispute this limitation. He did however, feel the need to act quickly, and believe there was not time for the amendment process to legally change the Constitution.

This being the case, President Jefferson and his Democratic-Republicans merely passed legislation giving the President permission to sign a treaty obligating the United States to pay the money and to take possession of Louisiana. In addition, the Democratic-Republicans also appropriated the money to pay France for the territory. Where did Democratic-Republicans in Congress believe they acquired the authority to do this? They claimed to act under the provision of the Constitution (Article 5, Section 3) which gave Congress the power to regulate the territories.

The third President and a compliant Congress interpreted the Constitution to do what they wanted to do even though it violated their own previously stated position.[2]

As a third and final example of how soon the limited government promised by the Framers of the Constitution began to be encroached upon the liberty it was meant to preserve by the generation who wrote it, let us look at the Monroe Doctrine.

During the presidency of James Monroe there occurred several revolutions against Spanish rule in South and Central America. The United States quickly recognized these newly established countries. Believing there was a strong possibility that European governments would intervene and try to reassert their control over the former colonies, President Monroe declared the Monroe doctrine in 1823. This doctrine declared that from that time forward America saw itself as the dominant power in the Western Hemisphere. It also warned that European interference in the Americas would not be allowed. The Doctrine consists of three principles:

1. The United States would remain neutral in European wars unless American interests were involved

2. Both North and South America were no longer subject to colonization by European powers.

3. The United States would consider any and all attempt at European colonization in the New World as an "unfriendly act."

And although the United States did not have the military power to enforce these claims, the declaration had symbolic importance, announcing the United States' posture as the power to be reckoned with in the New World.

The Monroe Doctrine aggressively asserted the position of dominance claimed by the United States in the Americas, and it has been a cornerstone of American foreign policy ever since.[3]

An interesting point that is little mentioned or considered is that this doctrine (and every doctrine proclaimed since) is not law but merely a declaration of a presidential policy. It is this fact that persuaded Monroe that as President he was authorized, without any Constitutional authorization, to establish a foreign policy that commits the United States to military action without a declaration of war by Congress. Thus following in the footsteps of the second and the third, our fifth president moved well beyond the limits the Constitution had imposed.

So how long did the limit last? The Anti-Federalists were still active in politics as the warnings they gave were realized and the children of the Revolution took their first steps down the road to tyranny.

Conclusion

The Constitution Failed

As can be seen by the preceding dispatches from the *History of the Future* the United States has reached an existential crisis; a crisis that has moved beyond a constitutional crisis, because our nation is currently under the control of people who either ignore the Constitution or simply say that it means something besides what it clearly says. The proponents of "A Living Document" have triumphed. The judicial review power of the black-robed oligarchy makes precedence triumph over original intent and has extended this to include precedent set in foreign courts. The limits imposed by the original Constitution and the Bill of Rights have been exceeded, and today the Federal Government is the seat of limitless power. This shift has become so profound, so pronounced, and so entrenched that the study of the Constitution should be moved from Political Science to History.

In America today we are paying people to teach our own children that both the American system of government and free enterprise are evil. I have personally witnessed a teacher of Political Science in

America give the following assignment: watch Fahrenheit 9/11 by Michael Moore and then write an essay outlining how many ways President Bush lied and how many laws he broke while deceiving America into invading Iraq. If you don't find this assignment offensive you've already had you quota of Kool- aid. Please step away from this book and dial 911 because your love for your country should be on life support. Tell them someone is about to tell you the truth, and you aren't prepared for what that might do to your world view.

Conversely, when I stated in the introduction that it might be time to admit that the Constitution has failed, I am sure many who regularly read the History of the Future were ready to call the headquarters of the Vast Rightwing Conspiracy and report that poor old Dr. Owens has veered off the reservation.

Once I was hired to teach history in a high school devoted to promoting the Socratic learning style using the works of the Enlightenment in the hopes of molding another generation akin to the Framers of the Constitution: critical thinkers dedicated to the proposition that liberty is the fountainhead of achievement. I was fired before the semester started because I did not hold the Framers in enough reverence believing as I do that they were mere men and not demigods infallible and universally inspired. Remember the Framers wrote the Constitution and fought for its ratification without the Bill of Rights. It was only the opposition of the Anti-Federalists that forced the Framers and their faction to accept the necessity of including those ten precious sentinels of personal liberty as the first order of business for the new government.

Now do not misunderstand me. I do believe that the Founders of American independence and the Framers of the Constitution were a unique collection of political geniuses who did their best to craft the vehicle for their posterity's benefit and for this nation's greatness. The limited government they founded allowed the pent-up abilities and longings of humanity to burst forth into the flowering of American Exceptionalism: the brilliance of the American experiment.

However, that experiment quickly crashed upon the shoals when: President Adams sought to jail people who opposed him. When President Jefferson decided it would be good to buy our way across the continent. When President Monroe believed he had the authority to commit America to an endless series of interventions and petty wars without Declarations of War. And less than one hundred years after the Ratification when Abraham Lincoln and the newly birthed Republican Party decided to interpret the Constitution, which had been freely entered into by the sovereign States, to say that no State could ever voluntarily leave even though this is not found anywhere in the document. Having made that determination, this minority government used the overwhelming majority they had in what was left of the Congress to marshal the power of the Industrial North to crush the seceding agricultural South. Slavery, which cannot be divorced from its evil nor defended in any way provided the spark, the rallying cry, and the effective explanation for a war which shattered the myth of a Federal Republic composed of sovereign States.

Since that war between brothers our nation has inexorably grown from the vision of Jefferson for a commonwealth of freemen into what is rapidly being revealed as a statist express highballing on its way to the gulag of collectivist uniformity and shabby mediocrity. Gone is the meritocracy of the young Republic. Gone is the equality of opportunity smothered in the cold dead grasp of the equality of outcome. Gone is the blind justice of a nation of laws devoured by the politically correct insanity of social justice. The Progressives and their coalition of crony capitalists and mega-state lobbies have turned the protections of a Constitution written to limit government into a suicide pact wherein if the nationalist Federal Government chooses to leave open the borders they are legally bound to protect, the individual states are condemned for passing a law which requires the police to enforce the law.

It is time to think the unthinkable and to embrace the abhorrent conclusion that the Constitution has failed. It was meant to limit government. This is proven conclusively by the 10th amendment which states, "The powers not delegated to the United States by the Constitution, nor prohibited by it to the States, are reserved to the States respectively, or to the people." The 10th Amendment clearly says, and obviously means that only those powers expressly delegated or enumerated by the Constitution to the Federal Government would be legitimate. This would not include the endless multiplication of powers of interpretation which allows the Federal Government to intrude into every aspect of our lives as we see today.

The very reason for a written Constitution was and is to limit the government created by that document to the powers expressly delegated, and not to open the door for interpretation and precedent to expand infinitely until all limits are gone. If that was not the intent why have a written Constitution at all? And though many trace the diversion from republican purity to Theodore Roosevelt and the Progressive cult, the truth is Hamilton set the stage for a big government and fathered the movement away from a decentralized federation of free people agreeing to disagree so that compromise would leave enough space for liberty to bloom. John Adams took a step down this road from limited to unlimited governance. Even Thomas

Jefferson could not resist the temptation to use more than the means allotted to achieve the ends he desired. John Marshall, the second Chief Justice of the Supreme Court, manufactured the power of judicial review out of the morass of political factions thus clearing the path for the rule of unelected black-robed aristocrats with the power to turn a country of laws into a country of men.

While it is the Democrats currently shoving collectivism down America's throat, we must remember the Progressives amongst the Republicans also support nationalized health care, cap-n-tax, and other revolutionary changes such as comprehensive import-a-voter immigration reform. Instead of an enraged electorate replacing faithless representatives they want to import a new electorate addicted to entitlements and beholden to the Progressive party of power. Both parties relentlessly expand the Federal Government when in power. The two major parties are two heads of the same bird of prey: an oligarchy of power elites with its foot on the throat of America's traditional meritocracy. The Republicrats are both run by Progressives dedicated to the fundamental transformation of America.

Though the slide away from limited government started early in our nation's history, the current variation of the statist movement is controlled and guided by the Progressives. Progressivism in modern

America rises out of the 1890s. Leaders such as Theodore Roosevelt and Woodrow Wilson championed expanding government, military interventionism, and the curtailing of American rights to achieve their goals.

After an interlude of pro-freedom typified by Calvin Coolidge the Progressives once again gained power under Hoover and solidified their dominance under FDR. Since then it has been a patchwork of more or less progressives in the White House with the sole exception of Ronald Reagan who had to contend with large Progressive majorities in Congress. Even Nixon, the self-proclaimed nadir of liberalism, instituted cherished Progressive programs such as price controls and the EPA. He also followed Progressive monetary policy when he took America off the gold standard.[1] Then in 1971 he unmasked himself by saying, "We are all Keynesians now"[2] referring to the economic poster boy of the tax and spend aristocracy John Maynard Keynes. After the Reagan hiatus the Bush Dynasty hyphenated by Clinton and ratified by the community organizers of the Obama Administration have plunged headlong into the Progressive program seeking to take us from where we were to where they think we should be.

Who are these community organizers who are riding rough shod over the Constitution and acting as the pall-bearers of our great Republic?

Any history of modern American community organizing must start with Saul Alinsky. Alinsky built his organizing technique on confrontation. He also used the strategy of redefining well known concepts such as power and self-interest. In his book *Rules for Radicals*, he said, "Power must be understood for what it is, for the part it plays in every area of our life, if we are to understand it and thereby grasp the essentials of relationships and functions between groups and organizations, particularly in a pluralistic society," Speaking of self-interest, he decided that it is not the same as selfishness. He discarded the idea that altruism could be a valid motivation for the type of organization he was trying to create. In his mind organizations will ultimately fail if they ignore the perceived self-interest of its members. Conversely, Alinsky proposed that aligning the perceived self-interest of members with the stated interest of the organization creates a dynamic relationship that builds a self-sustainable and powerful entity.

Building upon the foundation provided by his redefined concepts of power and self-interest, Alinsky pioneered a radically different way for poor people to enter the political process. He stressed the ability of community organizing groups to take action as opposed to more traditional local groups which sought to provide services. In this way he left the work of providing to others who actually worked in a community while he advocated professional organizers to rally supporters willing to appear and agitate to that these professionals could speak for the community.

Tom Wolfe in his classic Mau-Mauing the Flack Catchers told us clearly how the Progressives set about building their vast army of agitators and the leadership needed to fundamentally transform America, and they were so brilliant, they got us to pay for it.

> To sell the poverty program, its backers had to give it the protective coloration of 'jobs' and 'education,' the Jobs Corps and Operation Head Start, things like that, things the country as a whole could accept. 'Jobs' and 'education' were things everybody could agree upon. They were part of the free-enterprise ethic. They weren't uncomfortable subjects like racism and the class structure – and giving poor the money and the tools to fight City Hall. But from the first that was what the lion's share of the poverty budget went into. It went into 'community organizing,' which was the bureaucratic term for 'power to the people,' the term for finding the real leaders of the ghetto and helping organize the poor.[3]

And in the election of 2008 the Progressives finally won a lock on the Federal Government. They won the presidency, an overwhelming majority in the House, and a filibuster-proof majority in the Senate. Their absolute control of the Senate was momentarily held in check after the death of Senator Kennedy and the election of a Republican to replace him. However when the first Republican Senator from Massachusetts joined the herd of RINOs the Progressives maintained a working filibuster-proof majority.

And what has this one-party government brought us?

Talk about a man-caused disaster.[4] Have you looked at the economy lately? Previously the nation's ruling elite under the Bush dynasty and the Clinton hyphen paved the way for a debacle of fiscal debauchery. The timely onset of economic collapse engineered by the Progressives themselves gave them the election of 2008. Through the use of serial bail-outs and massive take-overs the only thing growing is the government. Khrushchev predicted the Soviet Union would bury us and since they are now on the trash heap of history is the Liberal Politburo of leftwing academics, corrupt politicians, casino capitalist cronies, and their propaganda machine digging the grave instead? Which brings us to the question, have the Progressives staged a second revolution?

The Obama administration's takeover of America's health care system, the financial industry, the biggest player in the insurance industry, major manufacturing the long sought Cap-N-Trade boondoggle, and the drive for import-a-voter immigration reform is a direct assault upon the productive designed to hobble their economic power and limit their personal freedom. The statists know the economically prosperous and individually free people of America stand in the way of their plans to create a centrally-planned economy and the regimented society it requires.

The Progressives have a strategy and they have a set of tactics for their war against limited government. The Cloward-Piven Strategy for overwhelming the American Constitutional system of limited government by destroying the economic system through an exponential growth in spending was formulated in the game-changing 1960s. The leading tactician of the Progressive Movement, Saul Alinsky, embraced and promoted this strategy devising the practical methods for achieving the power to implement it on a national scale.

This strategy and these tactics are well known and publically embraced by the Progressive leaders. Richard Cloward and Frances Fox Piven, the authors of this strategy, became so influential they were invited to signing ceremonies for laws advancing their cause by President Clinton. President Obama taught Alinsky's[5] principles to ACORN and recently Chris Matthews in one of his softball interviews with a fellow liberal hailed Alinsky as "our hero." [6]

Applying Alinsky's methods the cabal of liberal community organizers, corrupt politicians, unions, and thinly veiled criminal organizations captured power. Using that power they have instituted programs designed to implement the Cloward-Piven Strategy. And now they labor to bring our system to its knees. America is staggering under runaway spending while the Federal Reserve System turns the dollar into monopoly money. The TARP rip-off[7] has turned into an inexhaustible slush fund[8] of crony capitalist corruption, the stimulus bill isn't stimulating, [9] and the uncertainty[10] of future governmental action discourages anyone from investing anything anywhere. Why would anyone want to overwhelm the system? So they can re-boot the system and establish something else in its place. They may still call it the United States of America, but it will no longer be the land that we love.

The contempt the power party, the Democrat/Republican Dualocracy has for the American people and the processes of a free people seems to know no bounds.

President Obama believes the Constitution is a flawed[11] document because it doesn't deal with the re-distribution of wealth. Speaker of the House Nancy Pelosi thinks it's a joke[12] when asked where in the Constitution she finds the authority for her actions. Representative John Conyers, a leading Democrat

Congressman mocked[13] people who dared ask that their representatives read the bank-busting game-changing bills they pass in the middle of the night, saying "Unless you have two lawyers and two days you can't understand them anyway."[14] In his contempt for the American people Representative Henry Waxman even went so far as to hire a speed reader to read a bill in Congress to the laughter of his colleagues.[15] Senator Harry Reid, the majority leader of the party that invented Jim Crow Laws and separate but equal, the party of Bull Connor has the nerve to compare anyone resisting his attempt to nationalize the greatest medical system in the world with those who opposed the end of slavery.[16] As the country sinks into the economic chaos their spending and regulatory strangulation cause, they cast themselves as the Framers of a new vision, the Founders of a new completely transformed America.

Today we are dealing with a small clique of Progressives (in both parties) who have gained control by fooling people, by pretending to be your standard garden variety political hacks when in reality they are left-wing ideologues intent on transforming America into a cradle to grave nanny-state. Finally they have gained sufficient control of the Federal Government and are rushing head-long for the finish line. However, due to their crass power grabs and vest nationalizations they have been unmasked. Even the vast majority of the people who have been electing them are beginning to see these are not just hacks these are revolutionaries. The Progressives know the game is up so they intend on accomplishing the transformation by December, 2010 when an aroused electorate shows them the door.

But as many have pointed out, we surround them and if we pull together, work hard, and stand by the traditional principles of freedom and opportunity that made us great we will be great again.

These Progressive agents of change have succeeded in destroying the economy and neutering the Constitution. In the face of an all-powerful Federal Government what now protects the freedom and opportunity of America? How do we re-establish a limited government, re-institute capitalism, and stop our slide into the incentive-killing swamp of collectivism?

It is easy to see a problem and much harder to find a solution.

The fact that I am not calling for dissolution of the United States is abundantly portrayed by the way in which I have used the term *We the People* throughout this work. Some of the more radical Anti-Federalists such as Samuel Adams riled at these words seeing them as the ultimate proclamation of what they termed "consolidation" or the centralization of America.

Adams went so far as to say, "As I enter the building I stumble at the threshold."[17] By the use of italics to highlight the term I am making an obvious reference to the opening line of the Preamble to the Constitution and an obvious reference to the fact that I see the United States as one nation and its citizens as one people.

We the People need to organize. We must educate ourselves, our children, our families, our neighbors. We must shine the light of truth of the corruption that is Progressivism. Use the social networks to communicate and connect. Support local patriot groups. It's critical that we remain peaceful but it's just as critical that we use our constitutional rights of assembly and petition to gather our strength and present our case for the re-institution of the traditional American system of limited government, individual freedom, and economic opportunity.

I know many people are afraid of a second Constitutional Convention, yet at present only two more states need to sign on for one to be called.[18] I recommend that instead of fearing this *We the People* should embrace it. People have feared this because the supporters of the Constitution believe:

> Once a Convention is called Congress determines how the delegates to the Convention are chosen. Once chosen, those

> Convention delegates possess more power than the U.S. Congress itself; if it were not so they would not be able to change the U.S. Constitution! [19]

And this makes sense. But why should we, the supporters of limited government fear this? The Constitution, no matter what its original intent or its original form has failed. The Federal Government is operating as an entity without limits. *We the People* should not fear the market place of ideas. In an open forum we should trust in the soundness of our ideas and the righteousness of our cause.

In a Second Constitutional Convention we could advocate for either a return to the document as written and amended with the inclusion of even stricter controls upon the power of the Federal Government. We could even offer the proposal that we return to the Confederation concept and reconstitute our nation as it was originally born: a league of independent States held together by mutual heritage and self-interest.

In an open and free debate the possibilities are endless. We would at least have a chance to re-establish limited government and preserve the liberty and opportunity which has always been the seedbed of American greatness. As the situation stands today, we face more elections composed primarily of pre-approved choices, either a Progressive with a "D" or a

Progressive with an "R" after their names. We have got to either change the game or change the rules, because this deck has been stacked and the fix is in. Keep the faith. Keep the peace. We shall overcome.

Robert R. Owens

Notes

Dispatch Two:

1. The Charters of Freedom. http://www.archives.gov/exhibits/charters/constitution_founding_fathers.html Retrieved 8-27-10

2. The Articles of Confederation http://www.usconstitution.net/articles.html Retrieved 5-8-10

2. The history of the Articles of Confederation http://www.publicbookshelf.com/public_html/The_Great_Republic_By_the_Master_Historians_Vol_II/articleso_fh.html Retrieved 5-8-10

Dispatch Three:

1. Declaration of Independence Online http://www.ushistory.org/declaration/document/index.htm Retrieved 9-23-10

2 The Social Contract or Principles of Political Right http://www.constitution.org/jjr/socon.htm Retrieved 8-17-10

3. Declaration of Independence Online http://www.ushistory.org/declaration/document/index.htm Retrieved 9-23-10

4. Bartleby.com
http://www.bartleby.com/73/753.html Retrieved 8-17-10

5. The Social Contract or Principles of Political Right http://www.constitution.org/jjr/socon.htm Retrieved 8-17-10

6. ThinkExist.com. http://thinkexist.com/quotation/i_would_rather_be_exposed_to_the_inconveniences/144520.html Retrieved 8-17-10

Dispatch Four:

1. Huffington Post http://www.huffingtonpost.com/2010/03/04/obama-to-progressives-thi_n_486426.html Retrieved 8-17-10

2. Progressive America Rising http://www.progressivesforobama.net/ Retrieved 8-17-10

3. Sweetness and Light http://sweetness-light.com/archive/obama-constitution-is-living-document Retrieved 8-17-10

4. The Social Contract and Constitutional Republics http://www.constitution.org/soclcont.htm Retrieved 8-17-10

5. Federal Republic.net
http://www.federalrepublic.net/?p=8/ Retrieved 8-17-10

6. National Review
http://www.nationalreview.com/articles/227823/our-founders-realists/rich-lowry Retrieved 8-17-10

7. The Economist.
http://www.economist.com/blogs/democracyinamerica/2009/12/when_too_much_democracy_threat Retrieved 8-17-10

8. Find Law
http://caselaw.lp.findlaw.com/data/Constitution/amendment17/ Retrieved 8-17-10

Dispatch Five:

1. U. S. Constitution. Net
http://www.usconstitution.net/consttop_cnb.html
Retrieved 8-17-10

2. Britannica.com
http://www.britannia.com/history/docs/magna2.html
Retrieved 8-17-10

3. The Washington Post
http://www.washingtonpost.com/wp-srv/politics/documents/byrd_to_obama.pdf Retrieved 8-17-10

4. U. S. Constitution.net
http://www.usconstitution.net/xconst_Am25.html
Retrieved 8-17-10

5. U. S. Constitution.net
http://www.usconstitution.net/xconst_Am25.html
Retrieved 8-17-10

6. The Washington Post
http://www.washingtonpost.com/wp-srv/politics/documents/byrd_to_obama.pdf Retrieved 8-17-10

7. The Legal Significance of Presidential Signing Statements http://www.justice.gov/olc/signing.htm
Retrieved 8-17-10

8. Politico
http://www.politico.com/news/stories/0309/20625.html Retrieved 8-17-10

9. The Powers that Be
http://dougpowers.com/2009/04/01/obama-names-new-gm-board-of-directors/ Retrieved 8-17-10

10. CBS News.com http://www.cbsnews.com/8301-503983_162-5012735-503983.html Retrieved 8-17-10

11. The Examiner
http://www.examiner.com/republican-in-phoenix/update-the-obamas-date-cost-taxpayers-250k
Retrieved 8-17-10

Dispatch Six:

1. U. S. History.org http://www.ushistory.org/declaration/document/index.htm Retrieved 8-17-10

2. Your Dictionary.com http://www.yourdictionary.com/law/equality-before-the-law Retrieved 8-17-10

3. The Stanford Encyclopedia of Philosophy http://plato.stanford.edu/entries/equal-opportunity/ Retrieved 8-17-10

4. The Founders Constitution http://press-pubs.uchicago.edu/founders/tocs/a1_9_8.html Retrieved 8-17-10

5. Bill of Attainder http://www.techlawjournal.com/glossary/legal/attainder.htm Retrieved 8-17-10

6. Charters of Freedom http://www.archives.gov/exhibits/charters/bill_of_rights_transcript.html Retrieved 8-17-10

7. The Literature Network http://www.online-literature.com/orwell/animalfarm/10/ Retrieved 8-20-10

Dispatch Seven:

1. The Free Dictionary http://www.thefreedictionary.com/egalitarianism Retrieved 8-17-10

2. Principles of Progressive Politics http://principles-of-progressive-politics.blogspot.com/ Retrieved 8-17-10

3. NECN http://www.necn.com/Boston/Politics/2009/06/20/President-Obama-Were-going/1245498900.html Retrieved 8-17-10

4. Who Runs Government http://www.whorunsgov.com/Profiles/Christopher_J._Dodd Retrieved 8-17-10

5. The Washington Post http://www.washingtonpost.com/wp-dyn/content/article/2010/06/25/AR2010062500675_pf.html Retrieved 8-17-10

6. The Wall Street Journal http://online.wsj.com/article/SB10001424052748703615104575328020013164184.html?mod=WSJ_hpp_LEADNewsCollection Retrieved 8-17-10

Dispatch Eight:

1. Declaration of Independence Online http://www.ushistory.org/declaration/document/index.htm

Dispatch Nine:

1. Britannia History http://www.britannia.com/history/docs/magna2.html Retrieved 8-17-10

2. Britannia History http://www.britannia.com/history/docs/petition.html Retrieved 8-17-10

3. The Charters of Freedom http://www.archives.gov/exhibits/charters/bill_of_rights_transcript.html Retrieved 8-17-10

4. The Laws of Nature and Nature's God http://www.lonang.com/exlibris/organic/1606-fcv.htm Retrieved 8-17-10

5. GPO Access http://www.gpoaccess.gov/constitution/index.html Retrieved 8-17-10

6. Meriam-Webster Dictionary http://www.merriam-webster.com/dictionary/presentism Retrieved 8-20-10

7. GOP USA http://www.gopusa.com/news/2005/july/0707_gonzales_court1.shtml Retrieved 8-20-10

8. Discover Magazine http://blogs.discovermagazine.com/cosmicvariance/2009/04/05/post-christian-america/ Retrieved 8-20-10

9. The Nation http://www.thenation.com/article/post-capitalist-future-possible Retrieved 8-20-09

10. NPR.org http://www.npr.org/templates/story/story.php?storyId=18489466 Retrieved 8-20-10

Dispatch Ten:

1. U. S. Constitution Online. "Amendment 10." http://www.usconstitution.net/xconst_Am10.html

2. America Betrayed http://www.americabetrayed-1787.com/elastic-clause.html Retrieved 8-17-10

3. U. S. Constitution Online http://www.usconstitution.net/xconst_A3Sec2.html

4. Declaration of Independence Online http://www.ushistory.org/declaration/document/index.htm

5. Ibid.

6. The Federalist 51. http://www.constitution.org/fed/federa51.htm

7. Treasury Direct http://www.treasurydirect.gov/govt/reports/pd/histdebt/histdebt_histo1.htm Retrieved 8-17-10

8. Thinkquest.org
http://library.thinkquest.org/2760/madison.htm
Retrieved 8-17-10

9. Find Law
http://caselaw.lp.findlaw.com/data/constitution/amendment14/ Retrieved 8-17-10

10. Thomas Jefferson on Politics and Government
http://etext.virginia.edu/jefferson/quotations/jeff1340.htm Retrieved 8-17-10

11. Thomas Jefferson on Politics and Government
http://etext.virginia.edu/jefferson/quotations/jeff1340.htm Retrieved 8-17-10

12. Declaration of Independence Online
http://www.ushistory.org/declaration/document/index.htm Retrieved 9-21-10

Dispatch Eleven:

1. U. S. Constitution.net
http://www.usconstitution.net/articles.html Retrieved 8-17-10

2. U. S. History.org
http://www.ushistory.org/documents/constitution.htm
Retrieved 8-17-10

3. History Wiz
http://www.historywiz.com/enlightenment.htm
Retrieved 8-17-10

4. The National Center of Constitutional Studies http://www.nccs.net/articles/ril17.html Retrieved 8-17-10

5. U. S. History.org http://www.ushistory.org/tour/independence-hall.htm Retrieved 8-20-10

6. U. S. Constitution.net http://www.usconstitution.net/const.html#Article1 Retrieved 8-17-10

7. U. S. Constitution.net http://www.usconstitution.net/const.html#A2Sec1 Retrieved 8-17-10

8. Checks and Balances http://www.mcwdn.org/GOVERNMENT/ChecksBalances.html Retrieved 8-17-10

Dispatch Twelve:

1. U. S. Constitution.net http://www.usconstitution.net/articles.html Retrieved 8-19-10

2. The Tenth Amendment Center http://florida.tenthamendmentcenter.com/2010/03/who%E2%80%99s-supreme-the-supremacy-clause-smackdown/ Retrieved 8-19-10

3. U. S. Constitution.net
http://www.usconstitution.net/xconst_A6.html
Retrieved 8-19-10

4. U. S. Constitution.net
http://www.usconstitution.net/xconst_Am10.html
Retrieved 8-19-10

5. The National Archives
http://www.archives.gov/federal-register/constitution/
Retrieved 8-19-10

Dispatch Thirteen:

1. U. S. Constitution.net
http://www.usconstitution.net/articles.html Retrieved 8-19-10

2. Government Structures
http://www.couplescompany.com/features/politics/structure1.htm Retrieved 8-19-10

3. The Free Dictionary
http://www.thefreedictionary.com/federal Retrieved 8-19-10

4. Your Dictionary.com
http://www.yourdictionary.com/republic Retrieved 8-19-10

5. About.com
http://americanhistory.about.com/od/usconstitution/g/sep_of_powers.htm Retrieved 8-19-10

6. Library of Economics and Liberty http://www.econlib.org/library/Enc/PropertyRights.html Retrieved 8-19-10

7. U. S. Constitution.net http://www.usconstitution.net/consttop_cnb.html Retrieved 8-19-10

8. The Stanford Encyclopedia of Philosophy http://plato.stanford.edu/entries/marx/ Retrieved 8-19-10

9. An Important Distinction: Democracy versus Republic http://www.lexrex.com/enlightened/AmericanIdeal/aspects/demrep.html Retrieved 8-19-10

10. Encyclopedia Britannica http://www.britannica.com/EBchecked/topic/551073/social-democracy Retrieved 8-19-10

Dispatch Fourteen:

1. U. S. History.org http://www.ushistory.org/declaration/related/frin.htm Retrieved 8-19-10

2. War of 1812 http://www.galafilm.com/1812/e/intro/index.html Retrieved 8-19-10

3. History Central.com http://www.historycentral.com/1812/NewOrleans.html Retrieved 8-19-10

4. Lone Star.net http://www.lone-star.net/mall/texasinfo/mexicow.htm Retrieved 8-19-10

5. Antonio Lopez de Santa Anna http://www.lsjunction.com/people/santanna.htm Retrieved 8-19-10

6. Unrestricted Submarine Warfare http://www.historylearningsite.co.uk/unrestricted_submarine_warfare.htm Retrieved 8-19-10

7. The National Archives http://www.archives.gov/education/lessons/zimmermann/ Retrieved 8-19-10

8. The History Place.com http://www.historyplace.com/worldwar2/timeline/pearl.htm Retrieved 8-19-10

9. History World http://www.historyworld.net/wrldhis/PlainTextHistories.asp?gtrack=pthc&ParagraphID=qhp Retrieved 8-19-10

10. History of Russians Abroad.com http://www.russiansabroad.com/russian_history_251.html Retrieved 8-19-10

11. U. S. History.org http://www.ushistory.org/declaration/document/index.htm Retrieved 8-19-10

12. U. S. History.org http://www.ushistory.org/documents/constitution.htm Retrieved 8-19-10

13. Totalitarianism http://www.history-ontheweb.co.uk/concepts/totalitarianism.htm Retrieved 8-19-10

14. Urban Dictionary http://www.urbandictionary.com/define.php?term=wannabee Retrieved 8-19-10

Dispatch 15:

1. Breitbart http://www.breitbart.tv/fnc-analyst-claims-bush-administration-committed-extortion-against-banks/ Retrieved 8-19-10

2. The Free Dictionary http://www.thefreedictionary.com/Statists Retrieved 8-19-10

3. The Wall Street Journal http://online.wsj.com/article/SB123879833094588163.html Retrieved 8-19-10

4. MSNBC http://www.msnbc.msn.com/id/30110064/ Retrieved 8-19-10

5. Ibid.

6. The Washington Post http://voices.washingtonpost.com/thefix/senate/senate-talk-of-60-fades.html Retrieved 8-19-10

7. MSNBC http://www.msnbc.msn.com/id/30110064/ Retrieved 8-19-10

8. The Budget Reconciliation Process http://www.rules.house.gov/archives/bud_rec_proc.htm Retrieved 8-19-10

9. MSNBC http://www.msnbc.msn.com/id/30110064/ Retrieved 8-19-10

10. MSNBC http://www.msnbc.msn.com/id/30110064/ Retrieved 8-19-10

11. The New York Post http://www.nypost.com/p/news/politics/item_iQRtIQHjYPcEoMZ0lJX0hI Retrieved 8-19-10

Dispatch Sixteen:

1. U. S. History.org http://www.ushistory.org/declaration/document/index.htm Retrieved 8-19-10

2. Abraham Lincoln Online http://showcase.netins.net/web/creative/lincoln/speeches/gettysburg.htm Retrieved 8-19-10

3. About.com http://economics.about.com/library/glossary/bldef-leviathan.htm Retrieved 8-19-10

4. United States Department of Labor http://www.bls.gov/oco/cg/cgs041.htm Retrieved 8-19-10

5. United States Department of Labor http://www.bls.gov/oco/cg/cgs042.htm Retrieved 8-19-10

6. Ibid.

7. Fox News http://www.foxnews.com/politics/2009/12/09/administration-warns-command-control-regulation-emissions/ Retrieved 8-19-10

8. The Washington Post http://www.washingtonpost.com/wp-dyn/content/article/2009/07/13/AR2009071302852.html Retrieved 8-19-10

9. Prison Planet http://www.infowars.com/epa-threatens-command-and-control-economy-to-push-climate-change-agenda Retrieved 8-19-10

10. Political Culture of the United States http://academic.regis.edu/jriley/421elazar.htm Retrieved 8-19-10

11. The Free Dictionary http://legal-dictionary.thefreedictionary.com/Balance+of+powers Retrieved 8-19-10

12. U. S. History.com http://www.u-s-history.com/pages/h640.html Retrieved 8-19-10

13. The American Thinker http://www.americanthinker.com/2009/04/representation_without_taxatio.html Retrieved 8-19-10

14. Separation of Powers http://97.74.65.51/readArticle.aspx?ARTID=15733 Retrieved 8-19-10

15. Fox News http://www.foxnews.com/story/0,2933,258817,00.html Retrieved 8-19-10

16. Think Exist.com http://tabacco.blog-city.com/thinkexistcom_quotations_re_fooling_people__includes_quote_f.htm Retrieved 8-19-10

17. The Arizona Sentinel http://thearizonasentinel.com/2009/08/31/obama-in-5days-we-will-fundamentaly-transform-america/ Retrieved 8-19-10

18. The American Thinker http://www.americanthinker.com/2009/08/beware_the_counterrevolution.html Retrieved 8-19-10

19. The Tea Party Partiots.org http://teapartypatriots.org/ Retrieved 8-19-10

20. The Huffington Post http://www.huffingtonpost.com/adele-stan/collapse-of-the-gop-tea-p_b_384618.html Retrieved 8-19-10

21. Discover the Networks.org http://www.discoverthenetworks.org/individualProfile.asp?indid=2314 Retrieved 8-19-10

22. Michelle Malkin http://michellemalkin.com/2008/06/25/the-acorn-obama-knows/ Retrieved 8-19-10

23. You Tube http://www.youtube.com/watch?v=8vJcVgJhNaU Retrieved 8-19-10

24. Breitbart http://breitbart.tv/uncovered-video-obama-leads-seiu-chant-after-vowing-to/ Retrieved 8-19-10

25. Cloward-Piven.com http://cloward-piven.com/ Retrieved 8-19-10

26. Fox News http://www.foxnews.com/story/0,2933,242780,00.html Retrieved 8-19-10

27. Human Events http://www.humanevents.com/article.php?id=34269 Retrieved 8-19-10

28. The New York Daily News
http://www.nydailynews.com/opinions/2009/03/08/2009-03-08_obamas_search_for_an_enemy_the_president.html Retrieved 8-19-10

29. Fax News
http://video.foxnews.com/v/3916896/250000-or-150000 Retrieved 8-19-10

30. You Tube http://www.youtube.com/watch?v=z-SavgJlBLA Retrieved 8-19-10

31. The Heritage Foundation
http://www.heritage.org/Research/Reports/2004/06/The-Laffer-Curve-Past-Present-and-Future Retrieved 8-19-10

32. You Tube
http://www.youtube.com/watch?v=aEdXrfIMdiU Retrieved 8-19-10

33. Business Dictionary.com
http://www.businessdictionary.com/definition/tax-incentive.html Retrieved 8-19-10

34. This Nation.com
http://www.thisnation.com/question/040.html Retrieved 8-19-10

35. The American Presidency Project
http://www.presidency.ucsb.edu/signingstatements.php   Retrieved 8-19-10

Dispatch Eighteen:

1. The Realignment Project

http://realignmentproject.wordpress.com/2009/07/04/fdrs-second-bill-of-rights-and-the-progressive-mission/ Retrieved 8-21-10

Dispatch Twenty:

1. America Won the Vietnam War!
http://www.americawonthevietnamwar.com/ Retrieved 8-21-10

2. Fox News
http://www.foxnews.com/politics/2009/09/24/lyrics-songs-president-obama/ Retrieved 9-23-10

3. You Tube
http://www.youtube.com/watch?v=yaWRXIdRcpI Retrieved 9-23-10

4. The Canada Free Press
http://www.canadafreepress.com/index.php/article/14452   Retrieved 8-21-10

Dispatch Twenty-one:

1. All About History.org
http://www.allabouthistory.org/mayflower-compact.htm Retrieved 8-21-10

2. The Fundamental Orders
http://www.constitution.org/bcp/fo_1639.htm Retrieved 8-21-10

Dispatch Twenty-one:

1. Famous Quotes
http://www.famousquotessite.com/famous-quotes-6934-alexander-fraser-tyler-cycle-of-democracy-1770.html Retrieved 9-23-10

2. Discover the Networks
http://www.discoverthenetworks.org/viewSubCategory.asp?id=808 Retrieved 9-23-10

Dispatch Twenty-two

1. Daniel 5:25-28, New King James Bible,

2. Said What?

http://www.saidwhat.co.uk/quotes/political/winston_churchill/those_that_fail_to_learn_from_2804 Retrieved 8-21-10

3. Quotes Daddy
http://www.quotesdaddy.com/quote/1040548/Mark+Twain/the-past-may-not-repeat-itself-but-it-sure-does-rhyme   Retrieved 8-21-10

4. Brainy Quote.com
http://www.brainyquote.com/quotes/quotes/y/yogiberra135233.html   Retrieved 8-21-10

Dispatch Twenty-three:

1. Breitbart http://www.breitbart.tv/obama-american-agenda-flashback-dems-should-not-pass-healthcare-with-a-50-plus-1-strategy/   Retrieved 8-21-10

Dispatch Twenty-four:

1. The Future of Freedom Foundation http://www.fff.org/freedom/0897f.asp   Retrieved 8-21-10

Dispatch Twenty-five:

1. The Hill http://thehill.com/blogs/blog-briefing-room/news/79039-clyburn-weve-got-to-spend-our-way-out-of-this-recession   Retrieved 8-21-10

Dispatch Twenty-six

1. About.com http://useconomy.about.com/od/worldeconomy/p/China_Economy.htm   Retrieved 8-22-10

2. Reuters http://www.reuters.com/article/idUSN101725412010 0210 Retrieved 8-22-10

3. Gerson Lehman Group http://www.glgroup.com/News/China-Is-Using-Its-Horde-Of-Dollars-To-Buy-Natural-Resources.-Is-This-Because-The-Chinese-Believe-That-The-US-Dollars--38786.html Retrieved 8-22-10

4. The Washington Post http://www.washingtonpost.com/wp-dyn/content/article/2008/01/27/AR2008012702380.html Retrieved 8-22-10

5. The Wall Street Journal http://online.wsj.com/article/SB10001424052748703594404575191671972897694.html Retrieved 8-22-10

6. Military Quotes http://www.military-quotes.com/Sun-Tzu.htm Retrieved 8-22-10

Dispatch Twenty-seven:

1. MSNBC http://www.msnbc.msn.com/id/31508658/ns/business-stocks_and_economy/ Retrieved 8-22-10

2. The Los Angeles Times http://articles.latimes.com/2009/jan/10/business/fi-jobs10 Retrieved 8-22-10

3. Reuters http://www.reuters.com/article/idUSN0749084220081008 Retrieved 8-22-10

4. The American Prospect

http://www.prospect.org/cs/articles?article=its_the_economy_stupid_but_not_just_the_current_slowdown retrieved 8-22-10

Dispatch Twenty-eight:

1. The Examiner http://www.examiner.com/sarpy-county-conservative-in-omaha/cap-and-trade-allows-strangers-to-enter-your-home-do-you-meet-the-national-building-code-standards Retrieved 8-23-10

2. The Washington Examiner http://www.washingtonexaminer.com/opinion/columns/TimothyCarney/Obama-Durbin-Blagojevich-and-K-Street-get-biggest-earmark-in-history-39548692.html#ixzz0xQnU8zJE Retrieved 8-23-10

3. Think Exist.com http://thinkexist.com/quotes/ruth_bader_ginsburg/ Retrieved 8-22-10

4. Capitalism Magazine http://www.capitalismmagazine.com/law/5984-Friend-Freedom-Obamas-Supreme-Court-Nominee-Elena-Kagan.html Retrieved 8-23-10

Dispatch Twenty-nine:

1. Politico http://www.politico.com/blogs/bensmith/0410/Most_transparent_White_House_ever.html   Retrieved 8-23-10

2. Politico http://www.politico.com/news/stories/0209/18441.html Retrieved 8-23-10

3. Politifact.com http://www.politifact.com/truth-o-meter/promises/promise/234/allow-five-days-of-public-comment-before-signing-b/ Retrieved 8-23-10

4. Human Events http://www.humanevents.com/article.php?id=31438 Retrieved 8-23-10

5. The Guardian http://www.guardian.co.uk/world/2009/feb/06/obama-senate-economic-stimulus-congress   Retrieved 8-23-10

6. The Hill http://thehill.com/homenews/administration/57335-white-house-defends-stimulus-despite-job-figures Retrieved 8-23-10

7. The Polijam Times http://polijamblog.polijam.com/?p=15560   Retrieved 8-23-10

8. The Heritage Foundation http://blog.heritage.org/2010/04/05/side-effects-obamacare-fueling-higher-insurance-costs/ Retrieved 8-23-10

9. The Hill http://thehill.com/blogs/blog-briefing-room/news/74389-pelosi-responds-to-c-span-there-has-never-been-a-more-open-process Retrieved 8-23-10

10. Human Events http://www.humanevents.com/article.php?id=35086 Retrieved 8-23-10

11. Breitbart http://www.breitbart.tv/nancy-pelosi-we-need-to-pass-health-care-bill-to-find-out-whats-in-it/ Retrieved 8-23-10

12. Arts Technica http://arstechnica.com/web/news/2010/05/should-the-government-keep-tabs-on-hate-speech.ars Retrieved 8-23-10

13. The Washington Examiner http://www.washingtonexaminer.com/politics/Dems-undermine-free-speech-in-hate-crimes-ploy-8371517-64046162.html Retrieved 8-23-10

14. The Examiner http://www.examiner.com/conservative-in-columbia/fcc-diversity-czar-proves-obama-gov-t-has-declared-war-on-america Retrieved 8-23-10

15. Newsbusters http://newsbusters.org/blogs/tim-graham/2008/11/06/obamas-new-fcc-transition-head-talk-radios-executioner   Retrieved 8-23-10

16. The Hill http://thehill.com/blogs//hillicon-valley/605-technology/63875-blackburn-net-neutrality-is-qfairness-doctrine-for-the-internetq   Retrieved 8-23-10

17. The Heritage Foundation http://www.heritage.org/Research/Reports/1993/10/EM368-Why-The-Fairness-Doctrine-Is-Anything-But-Fair   Retrieved 8-23-10

18. The Los Angeles Times http://articles.latimes.com/2010/mar/21/nation/la-na-ticket21-2010mar21   Retrieved 8-23-10

19. Sweetness and Light http://sweetness-light.com/archive/obama-constitution-is-living-document   Retrieved 8-23-10

Dispatch Thirty:

1. Real Clear Politics http://www.realclearpolitics.com/video/2009/08/05/pelosi_town_hall_protesters_are_carrying_swastikas.html   Retrieved 8-23-10

2. Breitbart http://www.breitbart.tv/obama-dont-want-the-folks-who-created-the-mess-to-do-a-lot-of-talking/   Retrieved 8-23-10

3. Politico
http://www.politico.com/news/stories/0809/25891.html Retrieved 8-23-10

4. Houston and Texas News
http://www.chron.com/disp/story.mpl/metropolitan/6563705.html Retrieved 8-23-10

5. The Denver Post
http://www.denverpost.com/ci_13011617 Retrieved 8-23-10

6. Reuters
http://www.reuters.com/article/idUSTRE5765QH20090807?feedType=RSS&feedName=topNews&rpc=22&sp=true Retrieved 8-23-10

7. New York Magazine
http://nymag.com/news/intelligencer/65501/ Retrieved 8-23-10

8. The Free Dictionary
http://www.thefreedictionary.com/lumpenproletariat Retrieved 8-23-10

Dispatch Thirty-one:

1. The Washington Times
http://www.washingtontimes.com/news/2009/sep/28/at-the-presidents-pleasure/?source=newsletter_opinion_headlines retrieved 8-23-10

2. The Washington Examiner http://www.washingtonexaminer.com/opinion/blogs/beltway-confidential/Obama-appointee-lauded-NAMBLA-figure-63115112.html Retrieved 8-23-10

3. City Journal http://www.city-journal.org/html/13_2_queering_the_schools.html Retrieved 8-23-10

4. American Progress http://www.americanprogress.org/issues/2007/06/talk_radio.html Retrieved 8-23-10

5. The Technology Liberation Front http://techliberation.com/2008/04/23/localism-is-the-new-fairness-doctrine/ Retrieved 8-23-10

6. CNS News.com http://www.cnsnews.com/news/article/55040 Retrieved 9-23-10

7. Ibid.

8. Midwest Free Press http://www.midwestfreepress.com/2009/05/07/who-was-saul-alinsky/ Retrieved 8-23-10

9. CNS News http://cnsnews.com/news/article/55040 Retrieved 8-23-10

10. Ibid.

11 Social Science Research Network http://papers.ssrn.com/sol3/papers.cfm?abstract_id=405940&rec=1&srcabs=957369 Retrieved 8-23-10

12. The Moderate Voice http://themoderatevoice.com/20616/sunsteins-nudge-choice-architecture-and-obama/ Retrieved 8-23-10

13. Who Runs Government http://www.whorunsgov.com/index.php?title=Profiles/Cass_R._Sunstein Retrieved 8-23-10

14. The American Thinker http://www.americanthinker.com/2009/07/enough_is_enough.html Retrieved 8-23-10

15. Google Books

.http://books.google.com/books?id=1oBUoJFjr8gC&pg=PA92&lpg=PA92&dq=sunstein++A+legislative+effort+to+regulate+broadcasting&source=bl&ots=Yccdt_bkpS&sig=gyEgTMErrIs8ivCBETBEzzEVQtQ&hl=en&ei=cvdyTLvzIuadIQfWpqWWDg&sa=X&oi=book_result&ct=result&resnum=6&ved=0CCoQ6AEwBQ#v=onepage&q&f=false   Retrieved 8-23-10

16. Stephan Holmes & Cass R. Sunstein, Why We Should Celebrate Paying Taxes, in The Chicago Tribune, at 19 (April 14, 1999) http://home.uchicago.edu/~csunstei/celebrate.html Retrieved 8-23-10

17. Cass Sunstein Quotes http://stopsunstein.com/media/pdf/Sunstein%20quote%20file.pdf Retrieved 8-23-10

18. Ibid.

Dispatch Thirty-four

1. Good Reads http://www.goodreads.com/author/quotes/198468.Margaret_Thatcher Retrieved 8-24-10

2. Amazon.com http://www.amazon.com/Liberalism-Mental-Disorder-Savage-Solutions/dp/1595550062 Retrieved 8-24-10

3. Global Search.ca http://www.globalresearch.ca/index.php?context=va&aid=5564 Retrieved 8-24-10

4. PBS http://www.pbs.org/newshour/extra/features/july-dec01/kabul_11-14.html Retrieved 8-24-10

5. Time Magazine http://www.time.com/time/world/article/0,8599,1920954,00.html Retrieved 8-24-10

6. About.com http://terrorism.about.com/od/m/g/Mujahideen.htm Retrieved 8-24-10

7. The American Conservative http://www.amconmag.com/article/2005/oct/24/00013/ Retrieved 8-24-10

8. The New York Times http://www.nytimes.com/2001/12/17/world/nation-challenged-identity-loyalty-rural-afghanistan-places-tribe-before-country.html Retrieved 8-24-10

9. Counterpunch http://www.counterpunch.org/herold08062008.html Retrieved 8-24-10

10. The Los Angeles Times http://articles.latimes.com/2009/aug/18/nation/na-obama-vfw18 Retrieved 8-24-10

11. The New York Times http://www.nytimes.com/2009/02/18/washington/18web-troops.html?_r=2 Retrieved 8-24-10

12. Our Changing Globe http://www.ourchangingglobe.com/announcing-an-early-withdrawal-date-from-afghanistan-was-a-huge-blunder/ Retrieved 8-24-10

Dispatch Thirty-five:

1. Quote DB http://www.quotedb.com/quotes/2283 Retrieved 8-24-10

2. Google Books
http://books.google.com/books?id=qg61T_I1mwsC&printsec=frontcover&dq=road+to+serfdom&source=bl&ots=3bgmAhUJVG&sig=hyTL8CEvtV_pNGfFWUrAsYjCdHo&hl=en&ei=h0OtS5GbAoWglAez0aWQAQ&sa=X&oi=book_result&ct=result&resnum=8&ved=0CEgQ6AEwBw#v=onepage&q&f=false Retrieved 8-24-10

3. You Tube
http://www.youtube.com/watch?v=LYY73RO_egw Retrieved 8-24-10

4. Harvard Magazine
http://harvardmagazine.com/2007/07/debtor-nation.html Retrieved.

5. Big Government
http://biggovernment.com/vderugy/2010/03/26/politics-democratic-stimulus-haul-is-almost-double-republicans/ Retrieved 8-24-10

6. The Washington Post
http://www.washingtonpost.com/wp-dyn/content/article/2009/03/18/AR2009031802283.html Retrieved 8-24-10

7. Human Events
http://www.humanevents.com/article.php?id=16860 retrieved 8-24-10

8. Freedom Works http://www.freedomworks.org/publications/the-war-on-poverty-turns-40 Retrieved 8-24-10

9. Amazon.com http://www.amazon.com/Liberal-Fascism-American-Mussolini-Politics/dp/0385511841/ref=sr_1_1?ie=UTF8&s=books&qid=1269515140&sr=8-1 Retrieved 8-24-10

10. Amazon.com http://www.amazon.com/New-Deal-Raw-Economic-Damaged/dp/1416592377/ref=sr_1_1?ie=UTF8&s=books&qid=1269515193&sr=8-1 Retrieved 8-24-10

11. Amazon.com http://www.amazon.com/Arguing-Idiots-Small-Minds-Government/dp/1416595015/ref=sr_1_1?ie=UTF8&s=books&qid=1269515302&sr=1-1 Retrieved 8-24-10

Dispatch Thirty-seven:

1. The Wall Street Journal http://online.wsj.com/article/SB124044156269345357.html Retrieved 8-24-10

2. CNS News http://cnsnews.com/public/content/article.aspx?RsrcID=46192 Retrieved 8-24-10

3. Fox News http://www.foxnews.com/politics/2009/04/22/napolitano-riles-canadians-suggesting-terrorists-crossed-border/ Retrieved 8-24-10

4. Fox News http://www.foxnews.com/story/0,2933,509655,00.html Retrieved 8-24-10

5. The Washington Times http://www.washingtontimes.com/news/2009/apr/16/napolitano-stands-rightwing-extremism/ Retrieved 8-24-10

6. The Wall Street Journal http://online.wsj.com/article/SB123958260423012269.html Retrieved 8-24-10

7. The Washington Post http://voices.washingtonpost.com/44/2009/03/23/the_end_of_the_global_war_on_t.html Retrieved 8-24-10

8. Gun Owners of America http://gunowners.org/a042109.htm Retrieved 8-24-10

9. ABC News http://abcnews.go.com/Politics/story?id=6960824 Retrieved 8-14-10

10. Small Government Times http://www.smallgovtimes.com/2009/04/the-law-of-the-sea-treaty-is-back/ Retrieved 8-24-10

11. The Boston Herald
http://news.bostonherald.com/news/national/politics/2008/view.bg?articleid=1074519&srvc=home&position=0 Retrieved 8-24-10

12. Renew America.com
http://www.renewamerica.com/columns/kellmeyer/060406 Retrieved 8-24-10

13. The American Resistance
http://www.theamericanresistance.com/issues/anchor_babies.html Retrieved 8-24-10

Dispatch Thirty-eight:

1. Abraham Lincoln Online
http://showcase.netins.net/web/creative/lincoln/speeches/gettysburg.htm Retrieved 8-25-10

2. Ibid.

3. Constitutional Compromises
http://www.google.com/search?q=constitutional+compromises&hl=en&client=firefox-a&rls=org.mozilla:en-US:official&hs=FiP&tbs=tl:1&tbo=u&ei=XGD1SoHCFZn48Qaa36ShAQ&sa=X&oi=timeline_result&ct=title&resnum=11&ved=0CB4Q5wIwCg Retrieved 8-25-10

4. U. S. Constitution.net
http://www.usconstitution.net/constam.html Retrieved 8-25-10

5. The Federalist
http://www.constitution.org/fed/federa00.htm Retrieved 8-25-10

6. Library of Congress
http://www.loc.gov/rr/program/bib/presidents/madison/memory.html Retrieved 8-25-10

7. The National Archives
http://www.archives.gov/federal-register/constitution/article-v.html Retrieved 8-25-10

8. Freedom Phoenix
http://www.freedomsphoenix.com/Feature-Article.htm?InfoNo=042460 Retrieved 8-25-10

9. Congress.org
http://www.congress.org/congressorg/bio/userletter/?id=3181&letter_id=4164753236 Retrieved 8-25-10

10.
    Chttp://www.congress.org/congressorg/bio/userletter/?id=3181&letter_id=4164753236 Retrieved 8-25-10

11. The Washington Post
http://www.washingtonpost.com/wp-dyn/content/article/2009/06/10/AR2009061001416.html Retrieved 8-25-10

12. The Washington Post http://www.washingtonpost.com/wp-dyn/content/article/2009/06/10/AR2009061001416.html Retrieved 8-25-10

13. Newspatriot.com http://newspatriot.com/?p=2536 Retrieved 8-25

14. Fox News http://www.foxnews.com/story/0,2933,339589,00.html Retrieved 8-25

15. CNN http://www.issues2000.org/Archive/2008_Late_Edition_Energy_+_Oil.htm Retrieved 8-25-10

16. Reuters http://www.reuters.com/news/video?videoId=98951 Retrieved 8-25-10

17. Library of Economics and Liberty http://econlog.econlib.org/archives/2008/06/inflation_why_w.html Retrieved 8-25-10

18. How Stuff Works http://money.howstuffworks.com/question737.htm Retrieved 8-25-10

19. NCPA http://www.ncpa.org/pub/what-is-classical-liberalism Retrieved 8-25-10

20. Politico http://www.politico.com/news/stories/0509/22056.html Retrieved 8-25-10

21. Corrente http://www.correntewire.com/the_difference_between_liberal_and_progressive Retrieved 8-25-10

22. The Washington Post http://www.washingtonpost.com/wp-srv/politics/polls/postpoll_042609.html Retrieved 8-25-10

23. The American Thinker http://www.americanthinker.com/2008/08/the_biggest_missing_story_in_p.html Retrieved 8-25-10

Dispatch Forty:

1. The Apocalypse Project http://www.apocalypseproject.com/index.php/revelation-18/ Retrieved 8-25-10

2. Ibid.

3. Is Babylon America? http://revlu.com/Rev18.html Retrieved 8-25-10

4. Liberty Tree http://quotes.liberty-tree.ca/quotes_by/marcus+tullius+cicero Retrieved 8-25-10

5. Rome Info http://www.rome.info/history/empire/fall/ Retrieved 8-25-10

6. Absolute Astronomy http://www.absoluteastronomy.com/topics/Military_history_of_ancient_Rome Retrieved 8-25-10

7. The Free Library http://www.thefreelibrary.com/How+immigration+destroyed+Rome.+Oxford+historian+Peter+Heather+has...-a0141907543 Retrieved 8-25-10

8. About.com http://ancienthistory.about.com/od/fallromeeconomic/a/econoffall.htm Retrieved 8-25-10

9. The Cato Journal http://www.cato.org/pubs/journal/cjv14n2-7.html Retrieved 8-254-10

10. The Imperial Index: The Rulers of the Roman Empire http://www.roman-emperors.org/impindex.htm Retrieved 8-25-10

11. Craig Space: Historia: The Roman Senate http://pages.interlog.com/~gilgames/senate.htm Retrieved 8-25-10

12. Real Clear Politics

http://www.realclearpolitics.com/articles/2009/07/20/culture_wars_will_endure_97535.html Retrieved 8-25-10

13. Washington's Farewell Address 1796
http://avalon.law.yale.edu/18th_century/washing.asp Retrieved 8-25-10

14. History News Network
http://hnn.us/blogs/entries/3572.html Received 8-25-10

15. Google: History of American overseas involvement

http://www.google.com/search?q=history+of+american+overseas+involvement&hl=en&client=firefox-a&channel=s&rls=org.mozilla:en-US:official&hs=PS&tbs=tl:1&tbo=u&ei=ipFxSo3pBI38tgeclKmNBA&sa=X&oi=timeline_result&ct=title&resnum=11 Retrieved 8-25-10

16. Citizens for Immigration Law Enforcement

http://www.citizensforlaws.org/index.php?option=com_content&view=category&layout=blog&id=37&Itemid=80 Retrieved 8-25-10

17. Good Reads
http://www.goodreads.com/author/quotes/3543.Ronald_Reagan?page=2 Retrieved 8-28-10

18. Desert Invasion. US http://www.desertinvasion.us/ Retrieved 8-25-10

19. Theodore Roosevelt http://www.theodore-roosevelt.com/trpresident.html Retrieved 8-25-10

20. Investopedia.com http://www.investopedia.com/terms/h/hyperinflation.asp Retrieved 8-15-10

21. WorldNet Daily.com "Federal obligations exceed world GDP" http://www.wnd.com/index.php?fa=PAGE.view&pageId=88851 Retrieved 8-25-10

22. The NEA's Anti-American Agenda Threatens Our Nation http://www.natall.com/american-dissident-voices/adv031393.html Retrieved 8-25-10

23. The American Thinker http://www.americanthinker.com/2009/07/enough_is_enough.html Retrieved 8-25-10

24. Finding Dulcinea http://www.findingdulcinea.com/news/Americas/August-08/U-S--Fertility-Rate-Falling--Census-Data-Shows.html Retrieved 8-25-10

25. The National Defense Magazine https://www.nationaldefensemagazine.org/ARCHIVE/2009/AUGUST/Pages/Cap-and-TradeTheTriumphofPoliticsOverEconomics,Science.aspx Retrieved 8-25-10

26. The Heritage Foundation http://blog.heritage.org/2009/07/08/epa-admits-cap-and-trade-won%E2%80%99t-work/ Retrieved 8-25-10

27. Real Clear Politics http://www.realclearpolitics.com/articles/2007/03/the_blameamericafirst_crowd.html retrieved 8-25-10

28. The Quotations Page http://www.quotationspage.com/quote/34469.html Retrieved 8-25-10

29. I Go Pogo http://www.igopogo.com/final_authority.htm Retrieved 8-25-10

Dispatch Forty-one:

1. Helium http://www.helium.com/items/316120-a-history-of-american-entitlement-programs Retrieved 8-25-10

2. You Tube http://www.youtube.com/watch?v=p-bY92mcOdk Retrieved 8-25-10

3. Numbers USA
http://www.numbersusa.com/content/news/june-19-2009/president-obama-committed-comprehensive-immigration-reform.html   Retrieved 8-25-10

4. The New York Times
http://www.nytimes.com/2009/04/09/us/politics/09immig.html?_r=2   Retrieved 8-25-09

5. Fox News
http://www.foxnews.com/politics/2009/03/18/acorn-play-role-census/   Retrieved 8-25-10

6. The Wall Street Journal
http://online.wsj.com/article/SB10001424052970204908604574332950796281832.html   Retrieved 8-25-10

7. U. S. Census Bureau
http://www.census.gov/population/www/censusdata/apportionment/history.html   Retrieved 8-25-10

8. The New York Times
http://www.nytimes.com/2008/12/21/opinion/21kristof.html?_r=1&hp   retrieved 8-25-10

9. Real Clear Politics
http://www.realclearpolitics.com/articles/2008/03/conservatives_more_liberal_giv.html   Retrieved 8-25-10

10. Topix "Charitable giving: McCain Vs. Obama"
http://www.topix.com/forum/city/jacksonville-fl/TOC2ERP9CMGVA1PKV   Retrieved 8-25-10

11. PBS
http://www.pbs.org/wnet/religionandethics/blog/2008/01/barack-obama-i-am-my-brothers.html   Retrieved 8-25-10

12. Investopedia
http://www.investopedia.com/terms/c/crowdingouteffect.asp   Retrieved 8-25-10

13. Cornell University Press
http://www.cornellpress.cornell.edu/cup_detail.taf?ti_id=5458   Retrieved 8-25-10

14. Bahoowah
http://bahoowah.blogspot.com/2008/03/saul-alinsky-interview.html   Retrieved 8-25-10

Dispatch Forty-three:

1.   The Washington Times
http://www.washingtontimes.com/news/2010/feb/26/obama-listens-at-health-summit-but-mostly-hears-fr/   Retrieved 8-25-10

2.   Real Clear Politics

http://www.realclearpolitics.com/video/2010/02/25/obama_at_health_care_summit_i_dont_count_my_time_because_im_the_president.html   Retrieved 8-25-10

3. Business Week http://www.businessweek.com/news/2010-02-25/obama-tells-mccain-election-s-over-as-he-presses-health-plan.html Retrieved 8-25-10

4. Bearing Drift http://bearingdrift.com/2010/02/25/cantor-runs-afoul-of-obama-at-healthcare-summit/ Retrieved 8-25-10

5. The Sunday Times http://www.timesonline.co.uk/tol/news/world/us_and_americas/us_elections/article5114841.ece Retrieved 8-25-10

6. The Sunday Times http://www.timesonline.co.uk/tol/news/world/us_and_americas/article7041663.ece Retrieved 8-25-10

7. You Tube http://www.youtube.com/watch?v=M_bvT-DGcWw Retrieved 8-25-10

8. Fox News http://www.foxnews.com/politics/2009/06/24/obama-pushes-national-health-care-americans-happy-coverage/ Retrieved 8-15-10

9. The New York Daily News Dhttp://www.nydailynews.com/money/personal_finance/2009/09/10/2009-09-10_number_of_americans_without_health_insurance_rises_to_463m.html   Retrieved 8-25-10

10. Department of Health and Human Services http://www.cms.gov/home/chip.asp Retrieved 9-23-10

11. Ibid.

Dispatch Forty-four:

1. ABC News http://blogs.abcnews.com/thenote/2009/11/the-100-million-health-care-vote.html   Retrieved 8-25-10

2. Reason.hit & Run http://reason.com/blog/2009/12/19/ben-nelson-gets-a-basket-of-go   Retrieved 8-25-10

3. Breitbart http://www.breitbart.com/article.php?id=081216215816.8g979810   Retrieved 8-25-10

4. Get Out of Our House http://goooh.com/ Retrieved 9-23-10

5. Tea Party Patriots http://www.teapartypatriots.org/ Retrieved 9-23-10

6. Tea Party Express http://www.teapartyexpress.org/ Retrieved 9-23-10

Dispatch Forty-five:

1. Associated Content
http://www.associatedcontent.com/article/1555110/james_carville_i_certainly_hope_he.html Retrieved 8-25-09

2. Fox News
http://www.foxnews.com/politics/2009/03/11/flashback-carville-wanted-bush-fail/ Retrieved 8-25-10

3. Ibid.

Dispatch Forty-six:

1. The New York Times
http://www.nytimes.com/2010/06/02/opinion/02dowd.html Retrieved 8-25-10

2. WordIQ.com
http://www.wordiq.com/definition/Corporatism Retrieved 8-25-10

3. WordIQ.com
http://www.wordiq.com/definition/Statism Retrieved 8-25-10

4. The American Thinker
http://www.americanthinker.com/2009/02/the_clowardpiven_strategy_of_e.html Retrieved 8-25-10

5. The New York Times http://economix.blogs.nytimes.com/2010/07/01/the-g20s-china-bet/ Retrieved 8-25-10

6. The Fox Nation http://www.thefoxnation.com/business/2010/06/25/geithner-us-can-no-longer-drive-global-growth Retrieved 8-25-10

7. Real Clear Markets http://www.realclearmarkets.com/articles/2009/04/the_stunning_level_of_tarp_was.html Retrieved 8-25-10

8. The New York Times http://www.nytimes.com/2009/12/15/business/economy/15bank.html Retrieved 8-25-10

9. You Tube http://www.youtube.com/watch?v=QrrRWDclbYA Retrieved 8-25-10

10. The Spectator http://spectator.org/archives/2009/01/27/acorns-stimulus Retrieved 8-25-10

11. Yid With a Lid http://yidwithlid.blogspot.com/2010/03/ten-obama-promises-about-health-care.html Retrieved 8-25-10

12. You Tube http://www.youtube.com/watch?v=gsV7tWCnlxg&feature=related Retrieved 8-25-10

13. The American Thinker http://www.americanthinker.com/2010/04/does_anybody_really_understand.html Retrieved 8-25-10

14. Breitbart http://www.breitbart.tv/obamas-budget-director-powerful-rationing-panel-not-doctors-will-control-health-care-levels/ Retrieved 8-25-10

15. The New American http://www.thenewamerican.com/index.php/usnews/health-care/3387-obamas-hhs-concludes-his-healthcare-reform-will-increase-costs Retrieved 8-25-10

16. Operation Rescue http://www.operationrescue.org/archives/obama-violates-own-executive-order-funds-abortions/ Retrieved 8-25-10

17. Ricochet http://www.ricochet.com/conversations/Dodd-Frank-Fannie-Freddie-the-Axis-of-Evil-Headed-for-your-Wallet Retrieved 8-25-10

18. MSNBC http://www.msnbc.msn.com/id/38250967/ns/business-eye_on_the_economy/ Retrieved 8-25-10

19. The Washington Post http://www.washingtonpost.com/wp-dyn/content/article/2010/06/25/AR2010062500675.html Retrieved 8-25-10

20.	Michelle Malkin http://michellemalkin.com/2009/05/21/waxman-clueless-about-his-captrade-bill-youre-asking-me/ Retrieved 8-25-10

21.	Climate Progress http://climateprogress.org/2009/05/21/the-speed-reading-clerk-waxman-marke/ Retrieved 8-25-10

22.	You Tube http://www.youtube.com/watch?v=HITxGHn4sH4 Retrieved 8-25-10

Dispatch Forty-seven:

1.	Money.com http://money.cnn.com/2009/09/30/pf/taxes/who_pays_taxes/index.htm Retrieved 8-26-10

2.	Ludwig von Mises Institute http://blog.mises.org/6597/study-more-americans-receive-government-benefits-than-do-not/ Retrieved 8-26-10

3.	Russian Past and Present http://russiapastandpresent.blogspot.com/2009/07/banned-dissident-literature-of-soviet.html Retrieved 8-26-10

4.	U. S. History.org http://www.ushistory.org/declaration/document/index.htm Retrieved 8-26-10

5. Ibid.

6. Business Insider http://www.businessinsider.com/senate-says-senator-dodds-sweetheart-loans-were-okay-2009-8 Retrieved 8-26-10

7. The American Thinker http://www.americanthinker.com/2009/08/liberalism_and_the_dumbing_dow.html Retrieved 8-26-10

8. Working Minds http://www.working-minds.com/galtmini.htm Retrieved 8-26-10

9. Atlas Shrugged http://atlasshrugged.com/ Retrieved 8-26-10

10. Global Warming Hoax http://www.globalwarminghoax.com/news.php Retrieved 8-26-10

Dispatch Forty-eight:

1. The Frankfurt School http://filer.case.edu/ngb2/Pages/Intro.html Retrieved 8-26-10

Dispatch Fifty:

1. Abraham Lincoln Online http://showcase.netins.net/web/creative/lincoln/speeches/congress.htm Retrieved 8-26-10

2. Library od Economics and Liberty
http://www.econlib.org/library/Enc/Fascism.html
Retrieved 8-26-10

3. Spartacus Educational
http://www.spartacus.schoolnet.co.uk/SPblack.htm
Retrieved 8-26-10

4. The Heritage Foundation
http://www.heritage.org/Research/Commentary/2003/03/Russias-Flat-Tax-Miracle   Retrieved 8-26-10

5. The Tax Foundation
http://www.taxfoundation.org/blog/show/348.html
Retrieved 8-26-10

6. Lew Rockwell.com.
http://www.lewrockwell.com/orig3/hein6.html
Retrieved 9-23-10

7. Ibid.

8. CBS News

http://www.cbsnews.com/stories/2009/03/26/politics/100days/economy/main4894616.shtml   Retrieved 8-26-10

Dispatch Fifty-one:

1. About.com
http://americanhistory.about.com/od/usconstitution/f/elastic.htm   Retrieved 8-26-10

2. U. S. History.org http://www.ushistory.org/declaration/document/index.htm Retrieved 8-26-10

Arguments of Anti-federalists:

1. U. S. Constitution.net http://www.usconstitution.net/const.html#Article1 Retrieved 8-26-10

2. Main, 156.

3. U. S. Constitution.net http://www.usconstitution.net/xconst_A6.html

4. The Free Dictionary http://legal-dictionary.thefreedictionary.com/Supremacy+Clause

5. Main, 124

6. Selected Arguments of Anti-federalists (1780s) http://www.pinzler.com/ushistory/argantfedsupp.html Retrieved 8-26-10

7. Ibid.

8. Ibid.

How Long Did the Limit Last?:

1. The Library of Congress http://www.loc.gov/rr/program/bib/ourdocs/Alien.html Retrieved 8-26-10

2. About.com
http://americanhistory.about.com/od/thomasjefferson/a/tj_lapurchase.htm Retrieved 8-26-10

3. History of the United States
http://www.usgennet.org/usa/ca/state1/ridpath/monroe1911.html Retrieved 8-26-10

Conclusion:

1. PBS
http://www.pbs.org/wgbh/commandingheights/shared/minitext/ess_nixongold.html Retrieved 8-26-10

2. Econospeak
http://econospeak.blogspot.com/2009/02/were-all-keynesians-now.html Retrieved 8-26-10

3. Wolfe, p148.

4. Fox News
http://www.foxnews.com/story/0,2933,509597,00.html Retrieved 8-26-10

5. The American Thinker
http://www.americanthinker.com/2009/04/obama_alinsky_and_scapegoats.html Retrieved 8-26-10

6. The Fox Nation
http://www.thefoxnation.com/chris-matthews/2009/12/29/chris-matthews-saul-alinsky-our-hero Retrieved 8-26-10

7. The Wall Street Journal http://online.wsj.com/article/SB124482152282410185.html Retrieved 8-26-10

8. The Heritage Foundation http://blog.heritage.org/2009/12/04/tarp-will-this-crony-capitalist-slush-fund-ever-die/ Retrieved 8-26-10

9. Seeking Alpha http://seekingalpha.com/article/177022-stimulus-program-not-stimulating-truth-in-reporting Retrieved 8-26-10

10. The Orange County Register http://www.ocregister.com/articles/jobs-222077-job-percent.html Retrieved 8-26-10

11. WorldNetDaily.com "Obama rips U.S. Constitution" http://www.wnd.com/index.php?pageId=79225 Retrieved 8-26-10

12. You Tube http://www.youtube.com/watch?v=APUhVXImUhc Retrieved 8-26-10

13. Oh No You Didn't Say That.com http://www.ohnoyoudidntsaythat.com/house-democrats-astounded-theyre-expected-to-readunderstand-whats-in-bills Retrieved 8-26-10

14. You Tube
http://www.youtube.com/watch?v=gW7mOaPnYYA
Retrieved 8-26-10

15. You Tube
http://www.youtube.com/watch?v=HPESmwBfv4Q
Retrieved 8-26-10

16. Gateway Pundit
http://gatewaypundit.firstthings.com/2009/12/9671/
Retrieved 8-26-10

17. Main, 122.

18. The Fed is Robbing You Blind
http://www.rense.com/general84/consttit.htm
Retrieved 8-27-10

19. Ibid.

Bibliography

Abraham Lincoln Online. "Annual Message to Congress – Concluding Remarks." 12-1-1862.
http://showcase.netins.net/web/creative/lincoln/speeches/congress.htm

_____. "The Gettysburg Address."
http://showcase.netins.net/web/creative/lincoln/speeches/gettysburg.htm

About.Com: Ancient/Classical History. "Economic Reasons for the Fall of Rome."
http://ancienthistory.about.com/od/fallromeeconomic/a/econoffall.htm

About.Com : Economics. "Leviathan."
http://economics.about.com/library/glossary/bldef-leviathan.htm

Absolute Astronomy. "Military History of Ancient Rome."
http://www.absoluteastronomy.com/topics/Military_history_of_ancient_Rome

Alchian, Armen A. Library of Economics and Liberty. "Property Rights."
http://www.econlib.org/library/Enc/PropertyRights.html

All About History. "The Mayflower Compact." http://www.allabouthistory.org/mayflower-compact.htm

Amadeo, Kimberly. About.com. "China Economy." 11-10-08. http://useconomy.about.com/od/worldeconomy/p/China_Economy.htm

Amazon.com. *Arguing with Idiots*. http://www.amazon.com/Arguing-Idiots-Small-Minds-Government/dp/1416595015/ref=sr_1_1?ie=UTF8&s=books&qid=1269515302&sr=1-1

_____, *Liberal Fascism*. http://www.amazon.com/Liberal-Fascism-American-Mussolini-Politics/dp/0385511841/ref=sr_1_1?ie=UTF8&s=books&qid=1269515140&sr=8-1

_____. *New Deal or Raw Deal*. http://www.amazon.com/New-Deal-Raw-Economic-Damaged/dp/1416592377/ref=sr_1_1?ie=UTF8&s=books&qid=1269515193&sr=8-1

America Betrayed. "Supreme Court Revision of The Elastic Clause Paved the Way For Radical Expansion of Federal Power." http://www.america-betrayed-1787.com/elastic-clause.html

An Online Encyclopedia of Roman Rulers and their families. http://www.roman-emperors.org/impindex.htm

Armey, Dick. Freedom Works. "The "War on Poverty" Turns 40." 1-9-04. http://www.freedomworks.org/publications/the-war-on-poverty-turns-40

Aronoff, Alan. The American Thinker. "Representation Without Taxation." 4-10-09. http://www.americanthinker.com/2009/04/representation_without_taxatio.html

Ayres, Chris. The Times. "Try to stay awake: the President has a healthcare Bill to pass." 2-26-10. http://www.timesonline.co.uk/tol/news/world/us_and_americas/article7041663.ece

BAHOOWAH. "Saul Alinsky: An Interview." 3-9-08. http://bahoowah.blogspot.com/2008/03/saul-alinsky-interview.html

Bailyn, Bernard. *The Ideological Origins of the American Revolution*. Enlarged Ed. The Belknap Press of Harvard University Press. Cambridge. 1992.

Baier, Bret. Fox News. "Terrorism is a 'Man-Caused' Disaster. 3-17-09. http://www.foxnews.com/story/0,2933,509597,00.html

Baker, John S. and Elliot Stonecipher. The Wall Street Journal. "Our Unconstitutional Census." 8-9-09.
http://online.wsj.com/article/SB10001424052970204908604574332950796281832.html

Balik, Rachel. Finding Dulcinea. 8-21-08. "U. S. Fertility rate Falling, Census Data Shows."
http://www.findingdulcinea.com/news/Americas/August-08/U-S--Fertility-Rate-Falling--Census-Data-Shows.html

Barlett, Bruce. The Cato Journal, Volume 14, Number 2, Fall 1994. "How Excessive Government Killed Ancient Rome.
http://www.cato.org/pubs/journal/cjv14n2-7.html

Barone, Michael. Real Clear Politics. "The Blame-America-First Crowd." 3-19-07.
http://www.realclearpolitics.com/articles/2007/03/the_blameamericafirst_crowd.html

Bigg, Matthew and Nick Carey. Reuters. "Angry Americans disrupt town-hall healthcare talks." 8-7-10.
http://www.reuters.com/article/idUSTRE5765QH20090807?feedType=RSS&feedName=topNews&rpc=22&sp=true

Bill of Atta inder.
http://www.techlawjournal.com/glossary/legal/attainder.htm

Blomquist, Cord. The Technology Liberation Front. "Localism is the new fairness Doctrine." 4-23-08. http://techliberation.com/2008/04/23/localism-is-the-new-fairness-doctrine/

Blumen, Robert. The Ludwig von Mises Institute. "More Americans Receive Government Benefits Than Do Not." 5-6-07. http://blog.mises.org/6597/study-more-americans-receive-government-benefits-than-do-not/

Bowen, Catherine Drinker. *Miracle at Philadelphia*. Atlantic Monthly Press, Boston. 1966.

Bowers, Brenda. Helium "A History of American Entitlement Programs." http://www.helium.com/items/316120-a-history-of-american-entitlement-programs

Brainy Quote. "Yogi Berra Quotes." http://www.brainyquote.com/quotes/quotes/y/yogiberra135233.html

Breitbart. "Bush says sacrificed free-market principles to save economy." http://www.breitbart.com/article.php?id=081216215816.8g979810

Breitbart on TV. "FNC Analyst Claims Bush Administration Committed 'Extortion' Against Banks." http://www.breitbart.tv/fnc-analyst-claims-bush-administration-committed-extortion-against-banks/

_____. "Obama 'American Agenda' Flashback: Dems Should Not Pass Healthcare With a 50-Plus-1 Strategy." http://www.breitbart.tv/obama-american-agenda-flashback-dems-should-not-pass-healthcare-with-a-50-plus-1-strategy/

_____. "Obama: 'Don't Want the Folks Who Created the Mess to Do a Lot of Talking.'" 8-7-09. http://www.breitbart.tv/obama-dont-want-the-folks-who-created-the-mess-to-do-a-lot-of-talking/

_____. "Obama's Budget Director: Powerful Rationing Panel (Not Doctors) Will Control Health Care Levels." http://www.breitbart.tv/obamas-budget-director-powerful-rationing-panel-not-doctors-will-control-health-care-levels/

_____. "Nancy Pelosi: We Need to Pass Health Care Bill to Find Out What's In It." 3-9-10. http://www.breitbart.tv/nancy-pelosi-we-need-to-pass-health-care-bill-to-find-out-whats-in-it/

_____. "Uncovered Video: Obama Leads SEIU Chant After Vowing to 'Paint the Nation Purple.'" http://breitbart.tv/uncovered-video-obama-leads-seiu-chant-after-vowing-to/

Britannia History. "The Magna Carta." http://www.britannia.com/history/docs/magna2.html

Britannia History / Historical Documents. "Petition of Right, 1628." http://www.britannia.com/history/docs/petition.html

Brown, Carrie Budoff. Politico. "Obama Breaks Five-day Pledge." 2-5-09. http://www.politico.com/news/stories/0209/18441.html

_____. Politico. "White House to Democrats: 'Punch back twice as hard.'" 8-6-09. http://www.politico.com/news/stories/0809/25891.html

Burns, Judith. The Wall Street Journal. "BB&T Chair Blasts TARP as 'Huge Rip-Off.'" 6-12-09. http://online.wsj.com/article/SB124482152282410185.html

Caplan, Bryan. Library of Economics and Liberty. "Inflation: Why We Should Probably Count Food and Fuel After All." 6-2-08. http://econlog.econlib.org/archives/2008/06/inflation_why_w.html

Carney, Timothy P. The Washington Examiner. "Obama, Durbin, Blagojevich, and K Street get biggest earmark in history." http://www.washingtonexaminer.com/opinion/columns/TimothyCarney/Obama-Durbin-Blagojevich-and-K-Street-get-biggest-earmark-in-history-39548692.html#ixzz0xQnU8zJE

Cass R. Sunstein Quotes. http://stopsunstein.com/media/pdf/Sunstein%20quote%20file.pdf

CBS News. "Obama Cautious on Job Creation." 3-26-09. http://www.cbsnews.com/stories/2009/03/26/politics/100days/economy/main4894616.shtml

Cha, Aiana Eunjung. The Washington Post. "Weak Dollar Fuels China's Buying Spree Of U.S. Firms" 1-28-08. http://www.washingtonpost.com/wp-dyn/content/article/2008/01/27/AR2008012702380.html

Center for American Progress. "The Structural Imbalance of Political Talk Radio." 6-20-07. http://www.americanprogress.org/issues/2007/06/talk_radio.html

Chamberlain, Andrew. Tax Foundation. "The Cost of All Those Tax Forms." 4-20-05. http://www.taxfoundation.org/blog/show/348.html

Checks and Balances. http://www.mcwdn.org/GOVERNMENT/ChecksBalances.html

Cho, David, Jai Lyn Yang and Brady Dennis. The Washington Post. "Lawmakers guide Dodd-Frank bill for Wall Street reform into homestretch." 6-26-10. http://www.washingtonpost.com/wp-dyn/content/article/2010/06/25/AR2010062500675.html

Cho, David, Jia Lynn Yang and Brady Dennis. The Washington Post. 6-26-10. "Lawmakers guide Dodd-Frank bill for Wall Street reform into homestretch."

Cho, David, Zachary Goldfarb and Tomoeh Murakami Tse. The Washington Post. "U. S. Targets Excessive Pay for Top Executives." 6-11-09. http://www.washingtonpost.com/wp-dyn/content/article/2009/06/10/AR2009061001416.html

Cillizza, Chris. The Washington Post: The Fix. "Senate: Deflating Democrats' Dream of 60 Seats." http://voices.washingtonpost.com/thefix/senate/senate-talk-of-60-fades.html

Citizens For Immigration Law Enforcement. "Who Says." http://www.citizensforlaws.org/index.php?option=com_content&view=category&layout=blog&id=37&Itemid=80

Climate Progress. "Waxman's speed-reading clerk — hired to thwart GOP stalling tactics — gets 2 minutes of fame." 3-21-09. http://climateprogress.org/2009/05/21/the-speed-reading-clerk-waxman-marke/

Cline, Edward. Capitalism Magazine. "No Friend of Freedom: Obama's Supreme Court Nominee, Elena Kagan." 5-18-10. http://www.capitalismmagazine.com/law/5984-Friend-Freedom-Obamas-Supreme-Court-Nominee-Elena-Kagan.html

Cloward-Piven.com. 6-15-10. http://cloward-piven.com/

CNN Late Edition 2008, with Wolf Blitzer: on Energy & Oil. http://www.issues2000.org/Archive/2008_Late_Edition_Energy_+_Oil.htm

CNS News.com. 10-5-09. "FCC Won't Allow 'Diversity' Chief Mark Lloyd to Be Interviewed about Public Policy Views." http://www.cnsnews.com/news/article/55040

Congress.org. "Czars."
http://www.congress.org/congressorg/bio/userletter/?id=3181&letter_id=4164753236

Cooper, Helene. The New York Times. "Putting Stamp on Afghan War, Obama will send 17,000 troops." 2-17-09.
http://www.nytimes.com/2009/02/18/washington/18web-troops.html?_r=2

Coppock, Nancy. American Thinker. "The Cloward-Piven Strategy of economic Recovery." 2-7-09.
http://www.americanthinker.com/2009/02/the_clowardpiven_strategy_of_e.html

Corbin, Cristina. Fox News. "ACORN to Play Role in 2010 Census." 3-18-09.
http://www.foxnews.com/politics/2009/03/18/acorn-play-role-census/

Cornell University Press. *A New New Deal*.
http://www.cornellpress.cornell.edu/cup_detail.taf?ti_id=5458

Corsi, Jerome R. WorldNetDaily.com. "Federal Obligations Exceed World GDP."
http://www.wnd.com/index.php?fa=PAGE.view&pageId=88851

Corsi, Jerome R. and Kenneth Blackwell. Human Events. "Democrats' War on Poverty Has Failed." 9-6-06.
http://www.humanevents.com/article.php?id=16860

Cover, Matt. CNS News.com. "FCC Won't Allow 'Diversity' Chief Mark Lloyd to Be Interviewed about Public Policy Views." 10-6-09.
http://cnsnews.com/news/article/55040

Craig Space: Historia. "The Roman Senate."
http://pages.interlog.com/~gilgames/senate.htm

Curl, Joseph. The Washington Times. "At Summit Obama Mostly Hears Obama." 2-26-10.
http://www.washingtontimes.com/news/2010/feb/26/obama-listens-at-health-summit-but-mostly-hears-fr/

Daily News. "Census Bureau: Number of Americans without health insurance rises to 46.3 million." 9-10-09.
http://www.nydailynews.com/money/personal_finance/2009/09/10/2009-09-10_number_of_americans_without_health_insurance_rises_to_463m.html

Danger - 2 States From Constitutional Convention.
http://www.rense.com/general84/consttit.htm

Dash, Eric and Andrew Martin. The New York Times. "Wells Fargo to Repay U. S., a Coda to The Bailout Era." 12-14-09.
http://www.nytimes.com/2009/12/15/business/economy/15bank.html

Declaration of Independence Online
http://www.ushistory.org/declaration/document/index.htm

Department of Health and Human Services. "Children's Health Insurance Program."
http://www.cms.gov/home/chip.asp

de Rugy, Veronique. Big Government. "Politics: Democratic Stimulus Haul is Almost Double Republicans."
http://biggovernment.com/vderugy/2010/03/26/politics-democratic-stimulus-haul-is-almost-double-republicans/

Desert Invasion USA. http://www.desertinvasion.us/

Discover the Networks.org "MOTOR VOTER LAW (NATIONAL VOTER REGISTRATION ACT)"
http://www.discoverthenetworks.org/viewSubCategory.asp?id=808

_____. "Saul Alinsky." http://www.discoverthenetworks.org/individualProfile.asp?indid=2314

Dowd, Maureen. The New York Times. "A Storyteller Loses the Story Line." 6-1-10. http://www.nytimes.com/2010/06/02/opinion/02dowd.html

Dufour, Jules. Global Research.CA. " The Worldwide Network of US Military Bases The Global Deployment of US Military Personnel." http://www.globalresearch.ca/index.php?context=va&aid=5564

Easton, Terry. Human Events. "Cap and Trade: A new Disaster Waiting to Happen in 2009." 4-14-09. http://www.humanevents.com/article.php?id=31438

EconoSpeak. http://econospeak.blogspot.com/2009/02/were-all-keynesians-now.html

Edwards, James R., Jr. Human Events. "Obama's Homeland Security Hobbles Local Immigration Enforcement." 11-5-09. http://www.humanevents.com/article.php?id=34269

Eddlem, Thomas. The New American. "Obama's HHS Concludes His Health Care Reform Will Increase Costs." 3-23-10.
http://www.thenewamerican.com/index.php/usnews/health-care/3387-obamas-hhs-concludes-his-healthcare-reform-will-increase-costs

Encyclopedia Britannica eb.com. "Social Democracy."
http://www.britannica.com/EBchecked/topic/551073/social-democracy

Famous Quotes. "Alexander Fraser Tyler, Cycle Of Democracy (1770)."
http://www.famousquotessite.com/famous-quotes-6934-alexander-fraser-tyler-cycle-of-democracy-1770.html

FederalRepublic.net. "What is the Purpose of Government?" http://www.federalrepublic.net/?p=8/

FindLaw for Legal Professionals. "U.S. Constitution: Seventeenth Amendment"
http://caselaw.lp.findlaw.com/data/Constitution/amendment17/

FindLaw for Legal Professionals. "U.S. Constitution: Fourteenth Amendment."
http://caselaw.lp.findlaw.com/data/constitution/amendment14/

Fleischer, Ari. The Wall Street Journal. "Everyone Should Pay Income taxes." 4-13-09. http://online.wsj.com/article/SB123958260423012269.html

Fox Nation. "Chris Matthews: "Saul Alinsky 'Our Hero.'" http://www.thefoxnation.com/chris-matthews/2009/12/29/chris-matthews-saul-alinsky-our-hero

_____. "Geithner: 'U. S. Can no longer drive global economy.'" http://www.thefoxnation.com/business/2010/06/25/geithner-us-can-no-longer-drive-global-growth

Fox News.com. " Administration Warns of 'Command-and-Control' Regulation Over Emissions." 12-9-09. http://www.foxnews.com/politics/2009/12/09/administration-warns-command-control-regulation-emissions/

_____. "Al Qaeda Chief Khalid Sheikh Mohammed Confesses to Planning Sept. 11, Gitmo Transcript Shows." http://www.foxnews.com/story/0,2933,258817,00.html

_____. "Chavez Pledges 'Socialism or Death' at Swearing In Ceremony." 1-10-07. http://www.foxnews.com/story/0,2933,242780,00.html

_____. "$250,000 or $150,000? Democratic strategist defends Obama's definition of 'rich.'" 12-22-09. http://video.foxnews.com/v/3916896/250000-or-150000

_____. "Flashback: Carville Wanted Bush to Fail." 3-11-09. http://www.foxnews.com/politics/2009/03/11/flashback-carville-wanted-bush-fail/

_____. "Lyrics: Songs About President Obama." 9-24-09. http://www.foxnews.com/politics/2009/09/24/lyrics-songs-president-obama/

_____. "Michigan Congressman wants 50-cent Tax Hike on Every Gallon of Gas." 3-19-08. http://www.foxnews.com/story/0,2933,339589,00.html

_____. "Napolitano Riles Canadians By Suggesting 9/11 Terrorists Crossed Their Border." 4-22-09. http://www.foxnews.com/politics/2009/04/22/napolitano-riles-canadians-suggesting-terrorists-crossed-border/

Frodal, Michael G. and John M. Manoyan. National Defense. "Cap-N-Trade: The Triumph of Politcs over Economics and Science." 8-09.
https://www.nationaldefensemagazine.org/ARCHIVE/2009/AUGUST/Pages/Cap-and-TradeTheTriumphofPoliticsOverEconomics,Science.aspx

Global Warming Hoax.
http://www.globalwarminghoax.com/news.php

Goodman, John C. National Center for Policy Analysis. "What is Classical Liberalism?"
http://www.ncpa.org/pub/what-is-classical-liberalism

Goodreads. "Margaret Thatcher Quotes."
http://www.goodreads.com/author/quotes/198468.Margaret_Thatcher

_____. "Ronald Reagan Quotes."
http://www.goodreads.com/author/quotes/3543.Ronald_Reagan?page=2

Goodwin, Michael. The New York Daily News. "Obama's search for an enemy: The President keep beating the class warfare drum." 3-7-09.
http://www.nydailynews.com/opinions/2009/03/08/2009-03-08_obamas_search_for_an_enemy_the_president.html

Google. "Constitutional Compromises."
http://www.google.com/search?q=constitutional+compromises&hl=en&client=firefox-a&rls=org.mozilla:en-US:official&hs=FiP&tbs=tl:1&tbo=u&ei=XGD1SoHCFZn48Qaa36ShAQ&sa=X&oi=timeline_result&ct=title&resnum=11&ved=0CB4Q5wIwCg

_____. "History of American Overseas Involvement."
http://www.google.com/search?q=history+of+american+overseas+involvement&hl=en&client=firefox-a&channel=s&rls=org.mozilla:en-US:official&hs=PS&tbs=tl:1&tbo=u&ei=ipFxSo3pBI38tgeclKmNBA&sa=X&oi=timeline_result&ct=title&resnum=11

Google Books. Democracy and the Problem of Free Speech."
http://books.google.com/books?id=1oBUoJFjr8gC&pg=PA92&lpg=PA92&dq=sunstein++A+legislative+effort+to+regulate+broadcasting&source=bl&ots=Yccdt_bkpS&sig=gyEgTMErrIs8ivCBETBEzzEVQtQ&hl=en&ei=cvdyTLvzIuadlQfWpqWWDg&sa=X&oi=book_result&ct=result&resnum=6&ved=0CCoQ6AEwBQ#v=onepage&q&f=false

_____. "The Road to Serfdom."
http://books.google.com/books?id=qg61T_I1mwsC&printsec=frontcover&dq=road+to+serfdom&source=bl&ots=3bgmAhUJVG&sig=hyTL8CEvtV_pNGfFWUrAsYjCdHo&hl=en&ei=h0OtS5GbAoWglAez0aWQAQ&sa=X&oi=book_result&ct=result&resnum=8&ved=0CEgQ6AEwBw#v=onepage&q&f=false

Gourlay, Chris and Georgia Warren. The Times. "Barack Obama: orator in the mould of history's best." 11-9-08.
http://www.timesonline.co.uk/tol/news/world/us_and_americas/us_elections/article5114841.ece

GPO Access. "Constitution of the United States: Main Page."
http://www.gpoaccess.gov/constitution/index.html

Grabianowski, Ed. How Stuff Works. "What Exactly is Inflation?"
http://money.howstuffworks.com/question737.htm

Graham, Tim. News Busters. "Is Obama's New FCC Transition Head Talk Radio's 'Executioner'?" 11-7-08.
http://newsbusters.org/blogs/tim-graham/2008/11/06/obamas-new-fcc-transition-head-talk-radios-executioner

Grant, Tobin. Christianity Today. "Kevin Jennings, 'Safe school Czar.'" 10-23-09.
http://www.congress.org/congressorg/bio/userletter/?id=3181&letter_id=4164753236

Griffing, John. The American Thinker. "Enough is Enough." 7-16-09.
http://www.americanthinker.com/2009/07/enough_is_enough.html

Grim, Ryan. "Obama To Progressives: This Is Just The Foundation" Huffington Post, 3-4-10.
http://www.huffingtonpost.com/2010/03/04/obama-to-progressives-thi_n_486426.html

Gross, Daniel. Econo Speaks. "We're All Keynesians Now." 2-6-09.
http://econospeak.blogspot.com/2009/02/were-all-keynesians-now.html

Gun Owners of America. "Obama Pushing Treaty to Ban Re-Loading. " 4-21-09.
http://gunowners.org/a042109.htm

Hair, Connie. Human Events. "Pelosi's Iron Curtain Surrounds Health Care."
http://www.humanevents.com/article.php?id=35086

Hancock, Ernest. Freedom's Phoenix. "U. S. Two States Away From Constitutional Convention." 12-12-08. http://www.freedomsphoenix.com/Feature-Article.htm?InfoNo=042460

Hannity, Sean. Fox News. "'Terrorism' No Longer Exists for Secretary Napolitano?" 3-18-09. http://www.foxnews.com/story/0,2933,509655,00.html

Henwood, Doug. The Nation. "A Post-Capitalist Future is Possible." 3-30-09. http://www.thenation.com/article/post-capitalist-future-possible

Hart, Kim. The Hill. "Blackburn: Net neutrality is 'Fairness Doctrine for the Internet'" 10-20-09. http://thehill.com/blogs//hillicon-valley/605-technology/63875-blackburn-net-neutrality-is-qfairness-doctrine-for-the-internetq

Herold, Marc. Counter Punch.. "Barack Obama and Afghanistan." 8-6-08. http://www.counterpunch.org/herold08062008.html

Historic Documents. "The Constitution of the United States." http://www.ushistory.org/documents/constitution.htm

History Channel.com. "The Battle of New Orleans." 2000.
http://www.historycentral.com/1812/NewOrleans.html

History of the United States. "Monroe's Administration."
http://www.usgennet.org/usa/ca/state1/ridpath/monroe1911.html

History: Russians Abroad.com. "Russia: Historical Background"
http://www.russiansabroad.com/russian_history_251.html

History Wiz for Lovers of History. "The Enlightenment."
http://www.historywiz.com/enlightenment.htm

History World. "Hitler's revolution: AD 1933-1934."
http://www.historyworld.net/wrldhis/PlainTextHistories.asp?gtrack=pthc&ParagraphID=qhp

Hoft, Jim. First Things. "Harry Reid Says Republicans Are Pro-Slavery For Not Supporting His Crappy Health Care Plan." 12-7-09.
http://gatewaypundit.firstthings.com/2009/12/9671/

Hogue, Heather. The Washington Examiner. "Update: The Obamas' date cost taxpayers $250K?" 6-2-09
http://www.examiner.com/republican-in-phoenix/update-the-obamas-date-cost-taxpayers-250k

Holmes, Stephan and Cass R. Sunstein. Chicago Tribune. "Why We Should Celebrate Paying Taxes." 4-14-99.
http://home.uchicago.edu/~csunstei/celebrate.html

Horswell, Cindy. The Houston Chronicle. "Physicians speak out on health care bill: Many say the costly plan won't fix problems." 8-6-09.
http://www.chron.com/disp/story.mpl/metropolitan/6563705.html

Hudson, Audrey and Eli Lake. The Washington Time. "Napolitano Stands by Controversial Report." 4-19-09.
http://www.washingtontimes.com/news/2009/apr/16/napolitano-stands-rightwing-extremism/

Hurt, Charles. The New York Post. "OBAMA FIRES A 'ROBIN HOOD' WARNING SHOT." 10-15-08.
http://www.nypost.com/p/news/politics/item_iQRtIQHjYPcEoMZ0IJX0hI

I Go Pogo. http://www.igopogo.com/final_authority.htm

InfoPlease.com. Order of Presidential Succession. http://www.infoplease.com/ipa/A0101032.html#axzz0wy0EU24s

Ingold, John. The Denver Post. "Pelosi's visit to Denver a lightning rod." 8-7-10. http://www.denverpost.com/ci_13011617

Investor's Business daily. Real Clear markets. "The Stunning Level of TARP Waste, Fraud, and Abuse." 4-22-09. http://www.realclearmarkets.com/articles/2009/04/the_stunning_level_of_tarp_was.html

Invetopedia. "Crowding Out Effect." http://www.investopedia.com/terms/c/crowdingouteffect.asp

_____. "Hyperinflation." http://www.investopedia.com/terms/h/hyperinflation.asp

Irwin, Neil. The Washington Post. "Fed to Pump $1.2 Trillion Into Markets." 3-19-09.
http://www.washingtonpost.com/wp-dyn/content/article/2009/03/18/AR2009031802283.html

Is Babylon America? "Revelation Chapter 18:1-10.
http://revlu.com/Rev18.html

Jennings, Kevin. The Washington Times. "At the President's Pleasure." 9-28-09.
http://www.washingtontimes.com/news/2009/sep/28/at-the-presidents-pleasure/?source=newsletter_opinion_headlines

Jensen, Kristin and Catherine Dodge. Bloomberg Businessweek. "Obama Tells McCain 'Election's Over' at Health Summit (Update1)." 2-25-10.
http://www.businessweek.com/news/2010-02-25/obama-tells-mccain-election-s-over-as-he-presses-health-plan.html

Johnson, Jeff. GOPUSA. "Gonzales: 'Constitution Is What the Supreme Court Says.'"
http://www.gopusa.com/news/2005/july/0707_gonzales_court1.shtml

Johnson, Simon. The New York Times. "The G-20's China Bet." 7-1-10.
http://economix.blogs.nytimes.com/2010/07/01/the-g20s-china-bet/

Kamen, Al. The Washington Post. "The End of the Global War on Terror." 3-24-09.
http://voices.washingtonpost.com/44/2009/03/23/the_end_of_the_global_war_on_t.html

Karl, Jonathan. ABC News. "The $100 Million Health Care Vote?"
http://blogs.abcnews.com/thenote/2009/11/the-100-million-health-care-vote.html

Kellmeyer, Steve. Renew America. "The Children We Never Had." 4-6-06.
http://www.renewamerica.com/columns/kellmeyer/060406

Kelly, Martin. About.com: American History. " Jefferson and the Louisiana Purchase Jefferson Compromises His Beliefs for a Huge Achievement."
http://americanhistory.about.com/od/thomasjefferson/a/tj_lapurchase.htm

"Separation of Powers."
http://americanhistory.about.com/od/usconstitution/g/sep_of_powers.htm

_____. About.com. "What is the necessary and proper clause?"
http://americanhistory.about.com/od/usconstitution/f/elastic.htm

King, Marjorie. City. "Queering the Schools." Spring 2003. http://www.city-journal.org/html/13_2_queering_the_schools.html

Klein, Aaron. The Arizona Sentinel. "Obama 'In 5 Days we will fundamentally transform America'" 8-31-09.
http://thearizonasentinel.com/2009/08/31/obama-in-5days-we-will-fundamentaly-transform-america/

Kopel, David. Fifty-nine Deceits in Fahrenheit 9/11
http://www.davekopel.com/terror/fiftysix-deceits-in-fahrenheit-911.htm

Kraushaar, Josh and Patrick O'Connor. "Politico. Republicans launch a listening tour in Democratic-leaning suburbs." 5-4-09.
http://www.politico.com/news/stories/0509/22056.html

Kravitz, Derek. The Washington Post. "Obama's Technology Czar on the Outs." 3-13-09.
http://www.washingtonpost.com/wp-dyn/content/article/2009/06/10/AR2009061001416.html

Kristof, Nicholas D. The New York Times. "Bleeding Heart Tightwads." 12-20-09.
http://www.nytimes.com/2008/12/21/opinion/21kristof.html?_r=1&hp

Krugman, Teh. Corrente. "The Difference Between Liberals and Progressives." 1-5-08.
http://www.correntewire.com/the_difference_between_liberal_and_progressive

Kuhn, David Paul. Real Clear Politics. "Culture Wars Will Endure." 7-2-09.
http://www.realclearpolitics.com/articles/2009/07/20/culture_wars_will_endure_97535.html

Laffer, Arthur. The Heritage Foundation. "The Laffer Curve: Past, Present, and Future." 6-1-04.
http://www.heritage.org/Research/Reports/2004/06/The-Laffer-Curve-Past-Present-and-Future

Lasar, Matthew. ARS. "FCC asked to monitor "hate speech," "misinformation" online."
http://arstechnica.com/web/news/2010/05/should-the-government-keep-tabs-on-hate-speech.ars

Letter from Senator Byrd to President Obama. 2-23-09
http://www.washingtonpost.com/wp-srv/politics/documents/byrd_to_obama.pdf

Lew Rockwell.com. 7-22-02. "Keynes Was Right."
http://www.lewrockwell.com/orig3/hein6.html

Lewis, James. The American Thinker. "Obama, Alinsky, and Scapegoats." 4-24-09.
http://www.americanthinker.com/2009/04/obama_alinsky_and_scapegoats.html

Lewis, Laura Dawn. Government Structures 101.
http://www.couplescompany.com/features/politics/structure1.htm

Liberty-Tree Quotes. "Marcus Tulius Cicero Quotes."
http://quotes.liberty-tree.ca/quotes_by/marcus+tullius+cicero

_____. "Vladimir Lenin Quotes."
http://quotes.liberty-tree.ca/quote/vladimir_lenin_quote_068c

Library of Congress. "James Madison Papers 1723-1836."
http://www.loc.gov/rr/program/bib/presidents/madison/memory.html

Lifton, Jack. Gerson Lehrman Group. "China Is Using Its Horde Of Dollars To Buy Natural Resources." 5-5-09. http://www.glgroup.com/News/China-Is-Using-Its-Horde-Of-Dollars-To-Buy-Natural-Resources.-Is-This-Because-The-Chinese-Believe-That-The-US-Dollars--38786.html

Lone Star Junction. "Antonio Lopez de Santa Anna (1794-1876)." © 1995-96.
http://www.lsjunction.com/people/santanna.htm

Lone Star Internet. "The Mexican War." 3-11-10.
http://www.lone-star.net/mall/texasinfo/mexicow.htm

Long, Hamilton Abert. "An Important Distinction: Democracy versus Republic." 1976.
http://www.lexrex.com/enlightened/AmericanIdeal/aspects/demrep.html

Longstreet, J. D. "The Law of the Sea Treaty is back." 4-12-09.
http://www.smallgovtimes.com/2009/04/the-law-of-the-sea-treaty-is-back/

Lott, John. Fox News. "As Obama Pushes National Health Care, Most Americans Already Happy With Coverage." 6-24-09.
http://www.foxnews.com/politics/2009/06/24/obama-pushes-national-health-care-americans-happy-coverage/

Long, Rob. Richet. "Dodd, Frank, Fannie & Freddie: the Axis of Evil Headed for your Wallet." 7-2-10.
http://www.ricochet.com/conversations/Dodd-Frank-Fannie-Freddie-the-Axis-of-Evil-Headed-for-your-Wallet

Lowery, Rich. NOR. 7-3-09
http://www.nationalreview.com/articles/227823/our-founders-realists/rich-lowry

Lucas, Fred. CNSNEWS.com. "Obama Names Pope-Basher to Faith-Based Initiative Board."
http://cnsnews.com/public/content/article.aspx?RsrcID=46192

Main, Jackson Turner. *The Anti-Federalists*. Quadrangle Books, Chicago. 1961

Maier, Pauline. *American Scripture*. Alfred A. Knopf, New York, New York. 1997..

Malcolm, Andrew. The Los Angeles Times. "A little secret about Obama's transparency." 3-21-10. http://articles.latimes.com/2010/mar/21/nation/la-na-ticket21-2010mar21

Maklin, Michelle. "The ACORN Obama Knows." 6-25-08. http://michellemalkin.com/2008/06/25/the-acorn-obama-knows/

_____. "Waxman clueless about his cap&trade bill: 'You're asking me?!'" 5-21-09. http://michellemalkin.com/2009/05/21/waxman-clueless-about-his-captrade-bill-youre-asking-me/

Merriam-Webster Online. "Presentism." http://www.merriam-webster.com/dictionary/presentism

Martin, Anthony G. Examiner.com. "FCC 'diversity czar' proves Obama gov't has declared war on America." 8-27-09. http://www.examiner.com/conservative-in-columbia/fcc-diversity-czar-proves-obama-gov-t-has-declared-war-on-america

McCullagh, Declan. CBS News. "Obama Aides Take Axe To Chrysler's Budget." http://www.cbsnews.com/8301-503983_162-5012735-503983.html

McDonald, Forrest. *Novus Ordo Seclorum*. University Press of Kansas. 1985

McGirk, Tim. Time. "Can the U.S. Still Work with Afghanistan's Karzai?" http://www.time.com/time/world/article/0,8599,1920954,00.html

McTeer, Bob. Seeking Alpha. "Stimulus Progran Not Stimulating Truth in Reporting." 12-8-09. http://seekingalpha.com/article/177022-stimulus-program-not-stimulating-truth-in-reporting

Midwest Free Press. "Who Was Saul Alinsky?" 5-7-09. http://www.midwestfreepress.com/2009/05/07/who-was-saul-alinsky/

Mitchell, Daniel. The Heritage Foundation. "Russia's Flat tax Miracle." 3-24-03. http://www.heritage.org/Research/Commentary/2003/03/Russias-Flat-Tax-Miracle

Moeft, J. R. Bearing Drift. "Cantor runs afoul of Obama at Healthcare Summit." 2-25-10. http://bearingdrift.com/2010/02/25/cantor-runs-afoul-of-obama-at-healthcare-summit/

Molinski, Dan and John Lyons. The Wall Street Journal. "China's $20 Billion Bolsters Chavez." 4-18-10 http://online.wsj.com/article/SB10001424052748703594404575191671972897694.html

Morison, Samuel Elliot. *American Revolution 1764-1788*. 2nd Ed. Oxford University Press, New York. 1965.

Moreell, Ben. The Future of Freedom Foundation. "Power Corrupts." 8-97.
http://www.fff.org/freedom/0897f.asp

MSNBC.Com. " Obama says stimulus spending must pick up: Doesn't expect public to be satisfied with how quickly recovery is coming." 6-23-09.
http://www.msnbc.msn.com/id/31508658/ns/business-stocks_and_economy/

_____. Rachel Maddow Show. "Interview with Senator Schumer." 4-4-09.
http://www.msnbc.msn.com/id/30110064/

_____. "Why not use the budget reconciliation process?" 4-7-09.
http://www.msnbc.msn.com/id/30110064/

Nasaw, Daniel. Guardian.Co.Uk. "Obama says delay on stimulus 'inexcusable.'" 2-6-10.
http://www.guardian.co.uk/world/2009/feb/06/obama-senate-economic-stimulus-congress

National Alliance. "The NEA's Anti-American Agenda Threatens our Nation." 3-13-93.
http://www.natall.com/american-dissident-voices/adv031393.html

National Center for Constitutional Studies. "Natural Law the Ultimate Source of Constitutional Law."
http://www.nccs.net/articles/ril17.html

NECN A Comcast Network. 6-20-09. "President Obama: 'We're going to level the playing field for consumers.'"
http://www.necn.com/Boston/Politics/2009/06/20/President-Obama-Were-going/1245498900.html

New York. "Mad as Beale." 4-16-10.
http://nymag.com/news/intelligencer/65501/

News Patriot. "The Czars of Obama." 7-18-10.
http://newspatriot.com/?p=2536

Nimmo, Kurt. InfoWars.com. "EPA Threatens "Command-and-Control" Economy to Push Climate Change Agenda." 12-9-09.
http://www.infowars.com/epa-threatens-command-and-control-economy-to-push-climate-change-agenda

NPS.gov. "Independence hall."
http://www.nps.gov/inde/independence-hall-1.htm

Numbers USA. "Comprehensive Amnesty Threat." http://www.numbersusa.com/content/news/june-19-2009/president-obama-committed-comprehensive-immigration-reform.html

O'Brien, Michael. "The Hill. Clyburn: 'We've got to spend our way out of this recession.'" 2-1-10. http://thehill.com/blogs/blog-briefing-room/news/79039-clyburn-weve-got-to-spend-our-way-out-of-this-recession

Oh No You Didn't Say That.com. "House Democrats astounded they're expected to read/understand what's in bills." http://www.ohnoyoudidntsaythat.com/house-democrats-astounded-theyre-expected-to-readunderstand-whats-in-bills

Operation Rescue. "Obama Violates Own Executive Order, Funds Abortions." 7-14-10. http://www.operationrescue.org/archives/obama-violates-own-executive-order-funds-abortions/

Oracle ThinkQuest. "Marbury v. Madison unanimous vote, February 24, 1803." http://library.thinkquest.org/2760/madison.htm

_____. "The Living Constitution." http://library.thinkquest.org/11572/constitution/important/living.html

Orszag, Peter. Why Government Matters. "Cass R. Sunstein. http://www.whorunsgov.com/index.php?title=Profiles/Cass_R._Sunstein

Our Changing Globe. "Announcing An Early Withdrawal Date From Afghanistan Was A Huge Obama Blunder!" http://www.ourchangingglobe.com/announcing-an-early-withdrawal-date-from-afghanistan-was-a-huge-blunder/

Owens, Robert R. America Won the Vietnam War. http://www.americawonthevietnamwar.com/

_____. The History of the Future. http://drrobertowens.com

Palin, Sarah. The Washington Post. "The 'Cap And Tax' Dead End." 7-14-09. http://www.washingtonpost.com/wp-dyn/content/article/2009/07/13/AR2009071302852.html

Paletta, Damian. The Wall Street Journal. 6-25-10. "U.S. Lawmakers Reach Accord on New Finance Rules." http://online.wsj.com/article/SB10001424052748703615104575328020013164184.html?mod=WSJ_hpp_LEADNewsCollection

Payne, James. The American Conservative. "Deconstructing Nation Building." 10-24-05. http://www.amconmag.com/article/2005/oct/24/00013/

PBS-Extra. "Taliban retreat from Afghan capital." http://www.pbs.org/newshour/extra/features/july-dec01/kabul_11-14.html

Pleuger, Gilbert. "Totalitarianism." http://www.history-ontheweb.co.uk/concepts/totalitarianism.htm

Politico. "GM CEO resigns at Obama's behest." http://www.politico.com/news/stories/0309/20625.html

Polijam. The Polijam Times. "Krauthammer: ObamaCare Doesn't Help the Uninsured, But Un-Insures the Insured By Making the System Broke." 3-2-10. http://polijamblog.polijam.com/?p=15560

Political Culture of the United States. http://academic.regis.edu/jriley/421elazar.htm

Poston, Dudley L., Jr., Steven A. Camarota, and Amanda K. Baumle. FrontPageMag.com. "Illegal Immigrants Reshape the Political Landscape." 10-28-03 http://97.74.65.51/readArticle.aspx?ARTID=15733

Preston, Julia. The New York Times. "Obama to Push Immigration Bill as One Priority." 4-8-09. http://www.nytimes.com/2009/04/09/us/politics/09immig.html?_r=2

Principles of Progressive Politics. http://principles-of-progressive-politics.blogspot.com/

Progressive America Rising, http://www.progressivesforobama.net/

Publius. Big Government. "Rep. Phil Hare (D-IL): "I don't worry about the Constitution." http://biggovernment.com/publius/2010/04/01/rep-phil-hare-d-il-i-dont-worry-about-the-constitution/

Quotes Daddy. "Mark Twain Quotes." http://www.quotesdaddy.com/quote/1040548/Mark+Twain/the-past-may-not-repeat-itself-but-it-sure-does-rhyme

Quote BD. Thomas Jefferson Quotes.
http://www.quotedb.com/quotes/2283

Rand, Ayn. *Atlas Shrugged*.
http://atlasshrugged.com/

Real Clear Politics. "Pelosi: Town Hall Protestors are carrying swastikas.'" 8-5-09.
http://www.realclearpolitics.com/video/2009/08/05/pelosi_town_hall_protesters_are_carrying_swastikas.html

_____. "Obama At Health Care Summit: 'I Don't Count My Time Because I'm The President'" 2-25-10.
http://www.realclearpolitics.com/video/2010/02/25/obama_at_health_care_summit_i_dont_count_my_time_because_im_the_president.html

Regan, Lori. The American Thinker. "Liberalism and the Dumbing Down of America." 8-1-09.
http://www.americanthinker.com/2009/08/liberalism_and_the_dumbing_dow.html

Reich, Robert B. The American Prospect. "It's the Economy, Stupid -- But Not Just the Current Slowdown." 12-5-07
http://www.prospect.org/cs/articles?article=its_the_economy_stupid_but_not_just_the_current_slowdown

Religion and Ethics. "Barack Obama: 'I am my brother's keeper.'" 1-2-08.
http://www.pbs.org/wnet/religionandethics/blog/2008/01/barack-obama-i-am-my-brothers.html

Respectfully Quoted: A Dictionary of Quotations. 1989. NUMBER: 75, 3 Henry David Thoreau
http://www.bartleby.com/73/753.html

Reston, Maeve. The Los Angeles Times. "Obama tells veterans Afghanistan is 'war of necessity.'" 8-18-09.
http://articles.latimes.com/2009/aug/18/nation/na-obama-vfw18

Reuters. "Bernanke: No Inflation Threat."
http://www.reuters.com/news/video?videoId=98951

_____."FACTBOX-China, the U.S. Treasury's top foreign creditor." 2-10-10.
http://www.reuters.com/article/idUSN1017254120100210

_____. "Obama: U. S. in worst crisis since Depression. " 10-7-08.
http://www.reuters.com/article/idUSN0749084220081008

Reynolds, Maura and Peter Nicholas. The Los Angeles Times. "Job Losses Highest Since 1945." 1-10-09.
http://articles.latimes.com/2009/jan/10/business/fi-jobs10

Richman, Sheldon. Library of Economics and Liberty. "Fascism."
http://www.econlib.org/library/Enc/Fascism.html

Rohde, David and Barbara Crossette. New Your Times. "A NATION CHALLENGED: IDENTITY; Loyalty in Rural Afghanistan Places Tribe Before Country." 12-17-01.
http://www.nytimes.com/2001/12/17/world/nation-challenged-identity-loyalty-rural-afghanistan-places-tribe-before-country.html

Rome.Info. "The Fall of Rome."
http://www.rome.info/history/empire/fall/

Rousseau, Jean Jacques. The Social Contract or Principles of Political Right. Translated by G. D. H. Cole, public domain. Rendered into HTML and text by Jon Roland of the Constitution Society. 1792.
http://www.constitution.org/jjr/socon.htm

Rove, Karl. The Wall Street Journal. "The President's Apology Tour." 4-23-09.
http://online.wsj.com/article/SB124044156269345357.html

Russia, Past and Present. "Banned Dissident Literature of the Soviet Era Now on Display." 7-25-09. http://russiapastandpresent.blogspot.com/2009/07/banned-dissident-literature-of-soviet.html

Ryan, Jason. ABC News. "Obama to Seek New Assault Weapon Ban." 2-25-09.
http://abcnews.go.com/Politics/story?id=6960824

Sahadi, Jeanne. CNN Money.com. "47% Will Pay No Federal Income Tax." 10-3-09.
http://money.cnn.com/2009/09/30/pf/taxes/who_pays_taxes/index.htm

Said What. Winston Churchill Quotes."
http://www.saidwhat.co.uk/quotes/political/winston_churchill/those_that_fail_to_learn_from_2804

Samuelson, Robert J. The Orange County Register. "Rhetoric, Uncertainty Stifles Jobs." 12-2-09.
http://www.ocregister.com/articles/jobs-222077-job-percent.html

Savage, Michael. "Liberalism is a Mental Disorder."
http://www.amazon.com/Liberalism-Mental-Disorder-Savage-Solutions/dp/1595550062

Sean. Discover. "Post-Christian America." http://blogs.discovermagazine.com/cosmicvariance/2009/04/05/post-christian-america/

Schoen, John W. MSNBC.com. "No End in Sight to Fannie, Freddie Bailout." 7-15-10. http://www.msnbc.msn.com/id/38250967/ns/business-eye_on_the_economy/

Schorr, Daniel. NPR. "A New 'Post-Racial' Era in America." 1-28-08. http://www.npr.org/templates/story/story.php?storyId=18489466

Sciabarra, Chris Matthew. History news Network. "George Washington and the Perils of Foreign Entanglements." http://hnn.us/blogs/entries/3572.html

Selected Arguments of Antifederalists. http://www.pinzler.com/ushistory/argantfedsupp.html

Shaw, Jonathan. Harvard Magazine. "Debtor Nation: The rising risks of the American Dream, on a borrowed dime." http://harvardmagazine.com/2007/07/debtor-nation.html

Smith, Ben. Politico. "Most Transparent White House Ever…." 4-20-10. http://www.politico.com/blogs/bensmith/0410/Most_transparent_White_House_ever.html

Spartacus Educational. "Black Shirts." http://www.spartacus.schoolnet.co.uk/SPblack.htm

St. Petersburg Times. Politifact.com. "Barack Obama Campaign Promise No. 234." 5-26-09. http://www.politifact.com/truth-o-meter/promises/promise/234/allow-five-days-of-public-comment-before-signing-b/

Stan, Adele. The Huffington Post. "Collapse of the GOP? Tea Party Beats Grand Old Party in Poll." 12-8-09 http://www.huffingtonpost.com/adele-stan/collapse-of-the-gop-tea-p_b_384618.html

Stanford Encyclopedia of Philosophy. "Equality of Opportunity." http://plato.stanford.edu/entries/equal-opportunity/

Suderman, Peter. Reason. "Ben Nelson Gets a Basket of Goodies, Senate Democrats Get 60 Votes For Health Care Reform." 12-19-10. http://reason.com/blog/2009/12/19/ben-nelson-gets-a-basket-of-go

Sunstein, Cass R. and Richard H. Thaler. Social Science Research Network. "Libertarian Paternalism Is Not An Oxymoron." http://papers.ssrn.com/sol3/papers.cfm?abstract_id=405940&rec=1&srcabs=957369

Sun Tzu Quotes. http://www.military-quotes.com/Sun-Tzu.htm

Sweetness and Light, "Obama: Constitution Is Living Document." http://sweetness-light.com/archive/obama-constitution-is-living-document

Tapscott, Mark. The Washington Examiner. "Obama Appointee Lauded NAMBLA Figure." 10-1-09. http://www.washingtonexaminer.com/opinion/blogs/beltway-confidential/Obama-appointee-lauded-NAMBLA-figure-63115112.html

Tax Incentive. http://www.businessdictionary.com/definition/tax-incentive.html

Tea Party Patriots. http://teapartypatriots.org/

Tenth Amendment Center. "Who's Supreme? The Supremacy Clause Smackdown." 3-20-10. http://florida.tenthamendmentcenter.com/2010/03/who%E2%80%99s-supreme-the-supremacy-clause-smackdown/

The American Resistance. "Anchor Babies." http://www.theamericanresistance.com/issues/anchor_babies.html

The Apocalypse Project. "Revelation 18." http://www.apocalypseproject.com/index.php/revelation-18/

The Charters of Freedom. "The Delegates to the Constitutional Convention." http://www.archives.gov/exhibits/charters/constitution_founding_fathers.html

_____."The Bill of Rights." http://www.archives.gov/exhibits/charters/bill_of_rights_transcript.html

The Cicero Homepage. http://www.utexas.edu/depts/classics/documents/Cic.html

The Economist. "When too much Democracy Threatens Freedom." 12-17-09. http://www.economist.com/blogs/democracyinamerica/2009/12/when_too_much_democracy_threat

The Federalist. http://www.constitution.org/fed/federa00.htm 9-15-10

The Federalist 51 http://www.constitution.org/fed/federa51.htm 9-21-10

The Founder's Constitution. "Article 1, Section 9, Clause 8." http://press-pubs.uchicago.edu/founders/tocs/a1_9_8.html

The Frankfurt School. http://filer.case.edu/ngb2/Pages/Intro.html 9-1-10

The Free Dictionary by Farlex. "Balance of Powers." http://legal-dictionary.thefreedictionary.com/Balance+of+powers 9-10-10

_____. "Egalitarianism" http://www.thefreedictionary.com/egalitarianism

_____. "Federal." http://www.thefreedictionary.com/federal

_____. "How immigration destroyed Rome. Oxford historian Peter Heather has reexamined the fall of Rome. His new book, The Fall of the Roman Empire, holds many lessons for today." http://www.thefreelibrary.com/How+immigration+destroyed+Rome.+Oxford+historian+Peter+Heather+has...-a0141907543

_____. "Lumpenproletariat." http://www.thefreedictionary.com/lumpenproletariat

_____. "Statist" http://www.thefreedictionary.com/Statists

_____. "Supremacy Clause." http://legal-dictionary.thefreedictionary.com/Supremacy+Clause

The Fundamental Orders. http://www.constitution.org/bcp/fo_1639.htm

The Heitage Foundation. "EPA Admits Cap-N-Trade Won't Work." 7-8-09. http://blog.heritage.org/2009/07/08/epa-admits-cap-and-trade-won%E2%80%99t-work/

_____. "Side Effects: Obamacare Fueling Higher Insurance Costs." 4-5-10.
http://blog.heritage.org/2010/04/05/side-effects-obamacare-fueling-higher-insurance-costs/

_____. "TARP: Will This Crony Capitalism Slush Fund Ever Die?" 12-4-09.
http://blog.heritage.org/2009/12/04/tarp-will-this-crony-capitalist-slush-fund-ever-die/

The History Place. "Pearl Harbor, Hawaii, Sunday, December 7, 1941."
http://www.historyplace.com/worldwar2/timeline/pearl.htm

The Laws of Nature and Nature's God. "The First Charter of Virginia April 10, 1606."
http://www.lonang.com/exlibris/organic/1606-fcv.htm

THE LEGAL SIGNIFICANCE OF PRESIDENTIAL SIGNING STATEMENTS. 11-3-93.
http://www.justice.gov/olc/signing.htm

The Lid. "Ten Obama Promises About Health Care That Expired This Morning." 3-15-10.
http://yidwithlid.blogspot.com/2010/03/ten-obama-promises-about-health-care.html

The Literature Network. George Orwell / Animal Farm. http://www.online-literature.com/orwell/animalfarm/10/

The National Archives.gov / The Federal Register. "The Amendment Process." http://www.archives.gov/federal-register/constitution/

"The Zimmermann Telegram." http://www.archives.gov/education/lessons/zimmermann

"The Constitution of the United States: Article V." http://www.archives.gov/federal-register/constitution/article-v.html

The New King James Bible, 1982. Thomas Nelson, Inc. Nashville, TN.

The Powers that Be. "Obama Names New GM Board of Directors." http://dougpowers.com/2009/04/01/obama-names-new-gm-board-of-directors/

The Quotation Page. "Jean Francois Revel Quotes." http://www.quotationspage.com/quote/34469.html

The Realignment Project. "FDR's Second Bill of Rights and the Progressive Mission." 7-4-09. http://realignmentproject.wordpress.com/2009/07/04/fdrs-second-bill-of-rights-and-the-progressive-mission/

The Social Contract and Constitutional Republics © 1994, 2007 Constitution Society. http://www.constitution.org/soclcont.htm

THE SOCIAL CONTRACT OR PRINCIPLES OF POLITICAL RIGHT by Jean Jacques Rousseau 1762 Translated by G. D. H. Cole, public domain Rendered into HTML and text by Jon Roland of the Constitution Society. http://www.constitution.org/jjr/socon.htm

The Stanford Encyclopedia of Philosophy. "Karl Marx." 6-14-10. http://plato.stanford.edu/entries/marx/

The Wall Street Journal. "Obama Wants to Control the Banks." 4-4-09. http://online.wsj.com/article/SB123879833094588163.html

The Washington Post. "Washington Post-ABC News Poll." http://www.washingtonpost.com/wp-srv/politics/polls/postpoll_042609.html

Theodore Roosevelt. http://www.theodore-roosevelt.com/trpresident.html

Thierer, Adam. The Heritage Foundation. "Why The Fairness Doctrine Is Anything But Fair." 10-29-93. http://www.heritage.org/Research/Reports/1993/10/EM368-Why-The-Fairness-Doctrine-Is-Anything-But-Fair

Thinkexist.com. Thomas Jefferson Quotes http://thinkexist.com/quotation/i_would_rather_be_exposed_to_the_inconveniences/144520.html

_____. Will Durant Quote. http://tabacco.blog-city.com/thinkexistcom_quotations_re_fooling_people_includes_quote_f.htm

ThinkExist.com. Ruth Bader Ginsburg Quotes. http://thinkexist.com/quotes/ruth_bader_ginsburg/

This Nation.com. "What is an Executive Order." http://www.thisnation.com/question/040.html

Thomas, Andrew. The American Thinker. "Beware the Counter-Revolution." 8-16-09. http://www.americanthinker.com/2009/08/beware_the_counterrevolution.html

Thomas Jefferson on Politics & Government. "Thomas Jefferson to James Madison, 1789. ME 7:455, Papers 15:393."
http://etext.virginia.edu/jefferson/quotations/jeff1340.htm

_____. "Thomas Jefferson to James Madison, 1789. ME 7:457, Papers 15:398n The National Debt."
http://etext.virginia.edu/jefferson/quotations/jeff1340.htm

Topix. "Charitable Giving: McCain Vs. Obama." 9-12-08. http://www.topix.com/forum/city/jacksonville-fl/TOC2ERP9CMGVA1PKV

Treasury Direct. "Historical Debt Outstanding."
http://www.treasurydirect.gov/govt/reports/pd/histdebt/histdebt_histo1.htm

Underwood, Mike. The Boston Herald. "At Last Michelle Obama is Proud of America." 2-19-08.
http://news.bostonherald.com/news/national/politics/2008/view.bg?articleid=1074519&srvc=home&position=0

United States Department of Labor: Bureau of Labor Statistics. "Federal Government." 2010-2011 edition.
http://www.bls.gov/oco/cg/cgs041.htm

_. "State and Local Governments."

United States History. "Taxation Without Representation." http://www.u-s-history.com/pages/h640.html

Urban Dictionary. "Wannabe" http://www.urbandictionary.com/define.php?term=wannabee

U. S. Census Bureau. "Congressional Apportionment." http://www.census.gov/population/www/censusdata/apportionment/history.html

U. S. Constitution Online. "Amendment 10." http://www.usconstitution.net/xconst_Am10.html

_____. "Article One." http://www.usconstitution.net/const.html#Article1

_____. "Article Two, Section One." http://www.usconstitution.net/const.html#A2Sec1

_____. "Article Three, Section 3, Clause 2." http://www.usconstitution.net/xconst_A3Sec2.html

_____. "Article Six."
http://www.usconstitution.net/xconst_A6.html

_____. "Constitutional Amendments."
http://www.usconstitution.net/constam.html

_____. "Constitutional Topic: Checks and Balances."
http://www.usconstitution.net/consttop_cnb.html

_____. "The Articles of Confederation."
http://www.usconstitution.net/articles.html

_____. "U. S. Constitution – 25th Amendment."
http://www.usconstitution.net/xconst_Am25.html

U. S. Environmental Protection Agency.
http://www.epa.gov/

U. S. History.org. " French & Indian War 1754-1763 (The Seven Years War)."
http://www.ushistory.org/declaration/related/frin.htm

_____. "Independence Hall."
http://www.ushistory.org/tour/independence-hall.htm

U. S. House of Representatives Committee on Rules. "THE BUDGET RECONCILIATION PROCESS."
http://www.rules.house.gov/archives/bud_rec_proc.htm

U. S. Immigration and Customs Enforcement.
http://www.ice.gov/

Vadum, Matthew. The American Spectator. "ACORN's Stimulus." 1-27-09.
http://spectator.org/archives/2009/01/27/acorns-stimulus

Walker, Bruce. The American Thinker. "The Biggest Missing Story in Politics." 8-25-08.
http://www.americanthinker.com/2008/08/the_biggest_missing_story_in_p.html

War of 1812.
http://www.galafilm.com/1812/e/intro/index.html

Web Guides. Primary Documents in American History. "The Alien and sedition Acts."
http://www.loc.gov/rr/program/bib/ourdocs/Alien.html

Weisenthal, Joe. Clusterstock. "Senate Says Senator Dodd's Sweetheart Loans Were Okay." 8-7-09.
http://www.businessinsider.com/senate-says-senator-dodds-sweetheart-loans-were-okay-2009-8

Whittington, Mark. News. "James Carville 'I Certainly Hope He Doesn't Succeed.'" 3-11-09.
http://www.associatedcontent.com/article/1555110/james_carville_i_certainly_hope_he.html

Who Runs Government. "Christopher J. Dodd (D-Conn.) Current Position: U.S. Senator (since January 1981)"
http://www.whorunsgov.com/Profiles/Christopher_J._Dodd

Will, George. Real Clear Politics. "Conservatives More Liberal Givers." 3-27-09.
http://www.realclearpolitics.com/articles/2008/03/conservatives_more_liberal_giv.html

Wilson, Peter. The American Thinker. "Does Anybody Really Understand ObamaCare?" 4-6-10.
http://www.americanthinker.com/2010/04/does_anybody_really_understand.html

Windish, Joe. The Moderate Voice. "Sunstein's Nudge, 'Choice Archetecture,' and Obama." 6-25-08.
http://themoderatevoice.com/20616/sunsteins-nudge-choice-architecture-and-obama/

Wolfe, Tom. *Radical Chic & Mau-Mauing the Flak Catchers*. Bantam Books. 1971.

Woolley, John T. and Gerhard Peters. The American Presidency Project. "Presidential Signing Statements."
http://www.presidency.ucsb.edu/signingstatements.php

WordiQ.com. "Corporatism."
http://www.wordiq.com/definition/Corporatism

_____. "Statism."
http://www.wordiq.com/definition/Statism

Working Minds. "John Galt's Speech."
http://www.working-minds.com/galtmini.htm

WorldNetDaily.com. "Obama Rips U. S. Constitution." 10-27-08.
http://www.wnd.com/index.php?pageId=79225

Yale Law School: The Avalon Project. "Washington's farewell Address, 1796."
http://avalon.law.yale.edu/18th_century/washing.asp

Yergin, Daniel and Joseph Stanislaw. "Commanding Heights." 1997.
http://www.pbs.org/wgbh/commandingheights/shared/minitext/ess_nixongold.html

York, Byron. The Washington Examiner. "Dems undermine free speech in hate crimes ploy." 10-13-09.
http://www.washingtonexaminer.com/politics/Dems-undermine-free-speech-in-hate-crimes-ploy-8371517-64046162.html

Youngman, Sam and Ian Swanson. The Hill. "White House defends stimulus despite rising unemployment." 9-4-09.
http://thehill.com/homenews/administration/57335-white-house-defends-stimulus-despite-job-figures

Yount, Blake. Exmainer.com. "Cap and trade allows strangers to enter your home; do you meet the national building code standards?" 6-30-09.
http://www.examiner.com/sarpy-county-conservative-in-omaha/cap-and-trade-allows-strangers-to-enter-your-home-do-you-meet-the-national-building-code-standards

Your Dictionary Online.com. "Equality Before the Law."
http://www.yourdictionary.com/law/equality-before-the-law

_____. "Republic."
http://www.yourdictionary.com/republic

You Tube. "Barack Hussein Obama - MMM, MMM, MMM - We Honor You - MMM, MMM, MMM - Indoctrination - MMM !!!"
http://www.youtube.com/watch?v=yaWRXIdRcpI

_____ "Congressman John Conyers: 'Why Read The Bill?'"
http://www.youtube.com/watch?v=gW7mOaPnYYA

_____. "Michele Obama: First Time Proud of USA."
http://www.youtube.com/watch?v=LYY73RO_egw

_____. "OBAMA CAUGHT SAYING ACORN AND FRIENDS WILL SHAPE HIS PRESIDENTIAL AGENDA." 10-11-08.
http://www.youtube.com/watch?v=8vJcVgJhNaU

_____. "Obama: families making $97,000 are "upper class" and should pay more taxes."
http://www.youtube.com/watch?v=z-SavgJIBLA

Zalman, Amy. About.com. "Mujahideen."
http://terrorism.about.com/od/m/g/Mujahideen.htm

_____. "Obama: My Plan Makes Electricity Rates Skyrocket."
http://www.youtube.com/watch?v=HlTxGHn4sH4

_____. "Pelosi Scoffs When Asked Where Constitution Authorizes Ordering Americans To Buy Health Insurance." 10-25-09.
http://www.youtube.com/watch?v=APUhVXImUhc

_____. "Rahm Emanuel: Never Let a Good Crisis Go To Waste."
http://www.youtube.com/watch?v=QrrRWDclbYA

_____. "SHOCK UNCOVERED: Obama IN HIS OWN WORDS saying His Health Care Plan will ELIMINATE private insurance."
http://www.youtube.com/watch?v=p-bY92mcOdk

_____. "Pelosi: we have to pass the health care bill so that you can find out what is in it."
http://www.youtube.com/watch?v=gsV7tWCnlxg&feature=related

_____. "Pink Floyd: Another Brick in the wall."
http://www.youtube.com/watch?v=M_bvT-DGcWw

_____. "Tax Cut, JFK Hopes To Spur Economy 1962/8/13."
http://www.youtube.com/watch?v=aEdXrfIMdiU

_____. "Waxman's Speed Reader." 5-3-09. http://www.youtube.com/watch?v=HPESmwBfv4Q

Zieve, Sher. Canada Free Press. "Van Jones—Just one of Many Obama-Marxists." 9-6-09 http://www.canadafreepress.com/index.php/article/14452

Zimmermann, Eric and Michael O'Brien. The Hill. "Pelosi tells C-SPAN: 'There has never been a more open process.'" 1-5-10. http://thehill.com/blogs/blog-briefing-room/news/74389-pelosi-responds-to-c-span-there-has-never-been-a-more-open-process

Made in the USA
Middletown, DE
24 July 2022

69909256R00225